# TRELAWNY'S WORLD

## OTHER BOOKS BY NOEL B. GERSON

*Fiction*

THE SMUGGLERS

LINER

SPECIAL AGENT

NEPTUNE

ALL THAT GLITTERS

STATE TROOPER

SUNDAY HEROES

DOUBLE VISION

TEMPTATION TO STEAL

ISLAND IN THE WIND

TALK SHOW

CLEAR FOR ACTION

WARHEAD

THE CRUSADER

MIRROR, MIRROR

TR

THE GOLDEN GHETTO

SAM HOUSTON

JEFFERSON SQUARE

I'LL STORM HELL

THE ANTHEM

THE SWAMP FOX

GIVE ME LIBERTY

YANKEE DOODLE DANDY

THE SLENDER REED

OLD HICKORY

THE LAND IS BRIGHT

THE HITTITE

THE YANKEE FROM TENNESSEE

THE EMPEROR'S LADIES

THE GOLDEN LYRE

THE TROJAN

DAUGHTER OF EVE

THE SILVER LION

THE CONQUEROR'S WIFE

THAT EGYPTIAN WOMAN

THE HIGHWAYMAN

THE FOREST LORD

THE IMPOSTOR

THE GOLDEN EAGLE

THE CUMBERLAND RIFLES

THE MOHAWK LADDER

SAVAGE GENTLEMAN

*Nonfiction*

THE GLORIOUS SCOUNDREL

THE VELVET GLOVE

STATUE IN SEARCH OF A PEDESTAL

HARRIET BEECHER STOWE

DAUGHTER OF EARTH AND WATER

THE PRODIGAL GENIUS

BECAUSE I LOVED HIM

FREE AND INDEPENDENT

THE EDICT OF NANTES

P.J., MY FRIEND

FRANKLIN: AMERICA'S LOST STATE

PASSAGE TO THE WEST

SURVIVAL JAMESTOWN

LIGHT-HORSE HARRY

MR. MADISON'S WAR

KIT CARSON

NATHAN HALE

SEX AND THE ADULT WOMAN
 (WITH ELLEN F. BIRCHALL,
 M.D.)

BELGIUM: FUTURE, PRESENT,
 PAST

ROCK OF FREEDOM

SEX AND THE MATURE MAN
 (WITH LOUIS P. SAXE, M.D.)

FOOD

VALLEY FORGE

THE LEGEND OF POCAHONTAS

# NOEL B. GERSON

# Trelawny's World

## A Biography of
## Edward John Trelawny

1977

DOUBLEDAY & COMPANY, INC., GARDEN CITY, NEW YORK

Library of Congress Cataloging in Publication Data

Gerson, Noel Bertram, 1914–
Trelawny's world.

Bibliography: p. 289.
1. Trelawny, Edward John, 1792–1881—Biography.
2. Authors, English—19th century—Biography.
I. Title.
PR5671.T5G4    828'7'09  [B]
ISBN: 0-385-02678-1
Library of Congress Catalog Card Number 76–56294

For
Dee and Mike

Shelley was an enthusiastic student of the Greek poets and greatly influenced by them, especially in his later years. No one who is ignorant of the classics can thoroughly appreciate him. That is partly the reason why Swinburne understands him so well: he has written better things concerning him than anyone else. But he, too, has some of the divine madness.

—Edward John Trelawny

# FOREWORD

Thanks to Edward John Trelawny's own emphasis on his association with Shelley and Byron, principally in his books about them,
posterity has tended to regard him only in the light of his friendship with the poets and to judge him accordingly. Shelley's biographers have praised Trelawny because of his own admiration
for their subject, while such Byron biographers as John Drink-
water and Harold Nicolson raise an eyebrow when discussing
him, his antipathy to Byron being so obvious. Only Newman
Ivey White, perhaps the best of the Shelley biographers, has
maintained a judiciously balanced approach to Trelawny.

What posterity appears to have forgotten is that less than two
years of Trelawny's life, which spanned almost nine decades,
were spent in the company of the poets, and that his contemporaries saw him as the most celebrated man of his era—in his
own right. There was an ever-present consciousness of Greek
tragedy in Trelawny's nature, so it was inevitable that a man
who achieved such fame—some would say notoriety—in his own
day should be half forgotten by succeeding generations.

For most of his eighty-nine years, Edward John Trelawny was

a larger-than-life figure: that was his fascination in the nineteenth century and the cause of his downfall in the twentieth. He was more than a friend of the romantic poets; in his person, his appearance and, above all, his bravura exploits, he was the living epitomization of the ideal romantic and was hailed accordingly. But the cynics and skeptics who came after him found it difficult to believe that any one man could have had so many remarkable adventures.

These critics are similar to some gentlemen of Trelawny's own acquaintance, who scoffed when they heard he was irresistible to women. But his record speaks for itself. He had four wives and mistresses without number, and even the women with whom he formed Platonic friendships found him fascinating. What makes him all the more astonishing was that he was almost a century ahead of his time and was passionately devoted to the cause of equal rights for women, while never failing to appreciate feminine beauty.

His early-twentieth-century detractors simply could not believe that any man could have spent almost ninety years fighting for the cause of individual liberty and the dignity of man. In this sense, they claimed, Trelawny *was* too good to be true. But the facts bear this out: freedom was his ideal, and he never faltered in his tireless pursuit of justice for all.

Almost everything about the man has made posterity view him with suspicion. He was as strong as Paul Bunyan, as gallant and courageous as D'Artagnan, a great sailor and an even greater fighting man. As a lover he had no peer. He consorted with the leading intellectuals of his age as an equal and, although almost without formal education, wrote three spectacularly successful books, two of which are still regarded as classics.

He, Count d'Orsay and Lord Byron were considered the handsomest men of their time, as his portraits by Seymour Kirkup and Sir John Millais indicate. Mary Shelley did not exaggerate in her description of him, written when he was twenty-nine:

*Trelawny is extravagant—un giovane stravagante—partly natural and partly, perhaps, put on, but it suits him well, and if his abrupt but not unpolished manners be assumed, they are nevertheless in unison with his Moorish face (for he looks Oriental yet*

*not Asiatic), his dark hair, his Herculean form; and then there is
an air of extreme good nature which pervades his whole countenance, especially when he smiles, which assures me that his heart
is good. He tells strange stories of himself, horrific ones, so that
they harrow one up, with his emphatic but unmodulated voice,
his simple yet strong language, he portrays the most frightful sit-
uations . . . all these adventures took place between the ages of
13 and 20. I believe them now I see the man, and, tired with
the everyday sleepiness of human intercourse, I am glad to meet
with one who, among other valuable qualities, has the rare merit
of interesting my imagination.*

Trelawny was the sort of man to whom things were always
happening, who inspired acts of violence, often by his own attitudes and conduct. His youngest daughter, for example, told of
an occasion when they were strolling together along the banks of
the Arno in Florence. Trelawny, who stood over six feet tall in
an age when most men were five or six inches shorter, who had
magnetic blue eyes, a deep tan, and a sailor's swagger, inevitably
attracted attention, which his extravagant dress did not mini-
mize. He was followed by a robber, who crept up behind him
and raised a dagger, intending to stab him. Trelawny caught a
glimpse of the shadow of the arm and the dagger, so he whirled,
caught hold of the man's wrist and threw him into the river.
Then, although the would-be robber could not swim and was
drowning, Trelawny picked up his monologue in midsentence
and strolled away from the scene, apparently unflustered.

Most of Trelawny's activities and accomplishments after the
age of twenty-nine can be verified, in large part because he corresponded and associated with some of the nineteenth century's
most literate people, many of whom were almost compulsive letter writers. It was their custom to examine every deed and
thought of a friend under a social microscope, and Trelawny was
so prominent—and such an inveterate correspondent himself—
that it would have been virtually impossible for him to escape
the close scrutiny of those who would *not* have brooked lying,
cheating, or exaggeration on his part.

It was his misfortune, however, that similar documentation did
not exist for the first twenty-nine years of his life, for much of his

renown rests on his exploits during that time. There is only one authority for those years, and that is Trelawny himself, depicted as he would have us see him in his *Adventures of a Younger Son,* a perfect romantic adventure story and one regarded by some critics as straining credulity. His lot was to have been regarded as an English Baron Munchausen by many.

Saner heads have subsequently prevailed, however. H. J. Massingham, in *The Friend of Shelley,* written a half century ago, defends Trelawny with spirit, insisting that he did not exaggerate and declaring that his extraordinary nature made him incapable of telling an untruth.

I am inclined to agree, provided it is understood that truth is relative and is subject to the interpretation of those who behold it. Certainly there are strong reasons for believing that Trelawny told the truth, as he saw it, in *Younger Son.* Chief among them was his initial desire to publish the book anonymously. He was anxious to conceal his identity, he wrote Mary Shelley, because he had been so candid, revealing himself in such an unflattering light that he would be "ruined" if his identity became known. Only when she notified him that his proud mother was telling everyone she knew—and she was acquainted with many of her fellow aristocrats—that her son was the author of a forthcoming autobiography did he realize his attempt to maintain secrecy was futile. The better part of the book was already in print when he finally consented to the appearance of his name on the title page.

Trelawny's habitual bluntness was a quality that astonished those who knew him, sometimes startling and occasionally amusing his friends, and invariably making him new enemies. Living in an age when a gentleman was expected to hide his thoughts and feelings behind a screen of politely contrived subterfuge, he never failed to speak candidly. This unorthodox approach to life was one of his greatest charms and, at the same time, one of his more obvious handicaps.

In *Younger Son* he repeatedly demonstrated qualities that were considered hideous, even loathsome, to a good many civilized people. Frequently he was coarse, brutal and unfeeling. He was indifferent to the suffering of others and callously detached when he himself inflicted pain. His so-called barbarism was all the more deplorable because, when he wished, he was capable of demonstrating the most delicate sensitivity, and this combination of traits, unattractive in any era, horrified the very members of Victorian society whose approval he so eagerly sought. But honesty was more important to him than applause.

In spite of his desire for recognition as an intellectual and man of culture, Trelawny eventually grew to enjoy the role of outcast and misfit. A story is told to the effect that, when he was nearing the age of eighty, he loaned a copy of *Younger Son* to his banker, George Whitley, who expressed shock after reading it and said he assumed it was a work of fiction.

Trelawny assured him that every word was true.

"Then, sir," the indignant banker exclaimed, "you ought to be hanged."

The old man roared with laughter, accepting the observation as a compliment.

When writing the book, he solicited the help of Mary Shelley, the author of *Frankenstein* and other successful novels, accepting her corrections of his syntax, grammar and spelling without a murmur. But he was moved to protest when she suggested he remove "coarse words" and incidents that presented him in an unflattering light:

*It has been a painful and arduous undertaking narrating my life. I have omitted a great deal, and avoided being a pander to the public taste for the sake of novelty or effect. . . . My life, though I have sent it to you, as the dearest friend I have, is not written for the amusement of women; it is not a novel. If you begin clipping the wings of my true story . . . if you begin erasing words, you must then omit sentences, then chapters; it will be pruning an Indian jungle down to a clipped French garden. And I shall be so appalled at my MS. in its printed form that I shall have no heart to go on with it.*

These sentiments could have been expressed only by a man who, at the very least, had convinced himself he had written nonfiction rather than fiction. And he was consistent in his insistence that *Younger Son* was his true story. In 1875, when he was eighty-three, he swore to William Rossetti that the book was "a faithful record of my early life."

Byron thought him a liar, to be sure, but Trelawny returned the compliment by calling Byron a poseur. In the early stages of his all too brief friendship with Shelley, he expressed himself with his usual candor in the presence of the poet and his wife. "Mary," Shelley said, "Tre has found out Byron already. How stupid we were! How long it took us!"

"That," Mary Shelley replied, "is because he lives with the living and we with the dead."

And so it was this exuberance, which Mary Shelley so readily picked up, that caused Trelawny very often to become careless, thus making him vulnerable to the criticism of those who doubted his veracity. They leaped on him with cries of triumph when he said an epidemic of cholera had swept through Java in 1811 instead of 1812, trying, through their nit-picking, to cast doubt on the authenticity of the entire book.

Still, Trelawny's detractors failed in the last issue, it seems to me, because they did not take note of Trelawny's main thrust in writing: his prodigious romanticism. Trelawny, writing about himself in romantic terms, was wholly without artifice. Had he done otherwise he would not have been true to his nature, which tolerated no discipline except that which he exerted upon himself.

—N. B. G.

Clinton, Connecticut

TRELAWNY'S WORLD

# I

## "My birth was unpropitious."

In *Adventures of a Younger Son*, Edward John Trelawny describes his entry into this world in a way that no other writer has been able either to duplicate or to surpass. Born on November 13, 1792, Trelawny says of this:

> *My birth was unpropitious. I came into the world, branded and denounced as a vagrant; for I was the younger son of a family, so proud of their antiquity, that even gout and mortgaged estates were traced, many generations back, on the genealogical tree, as ancient heirlooms of aristocratic origin, and therefore reverenced. In such a house a younger son was like the cub of a felon-wolf in good King Edgar's days, when a price was set upon his head. There have been laws compelling parents to destroy their puny offspring: and a Spartan mother might have exclaimed with Othello, while extinguishing the life of her yet unconscious infant:*
>
> > *"I that am cruel, am yet merciful,*
> > *I would not have thee linger in thy pain,"*

*which was just and merciful, in comparison with the atrocious law of primogeniture.*

The family tree was indeed as old and distinguished as Trelawny claimed. On his paternal side the lineage could be traced for nine hundred years, to the time of Edward the Confessor, when Eduni de Troelen had established his home in a valley on the eastern coast of Cornwall. Thereafter his descendants habitually distinguished themselves. Sir John Tirlawnee was one of the heroes of Agincourt, and was granted the right, by Henry V, to add three oak leaves to his coat of arms. A later Sir John fought on the wrong side in the Perkin Warbeck rebellion but escaped with a fine, Trelawny men being remarkably adept in avoiding the hangman's rope and the executioner's ax. Yet another Sir John demonstrated the same agility, fighting the good fight at the side of his monarch during the civil wars and then, miraculously, being permitted by Oliver Cromwell to retire unscathed to his estates.

One of the most renowned and notorious of the Trelawnys was the first Sir Jonathan, who became bishop of Bristol, Exeter and Winchester. Endowed with such typical family traits as reckless courage, a fiery temper and a shocking bluntness of speech, he was severely reprimanded for his profanity by a colleague. Refusing to accept chastisement, he replied, "When I swear I do not swear as a bishop. I swear as Sir Jonathan Trelawny, a country gentleman and a baronet."

The bishop was one of the few Trelawnys who did not take up arms as at least a part-time profession, but his acceptance of the cloth in no way made him less pugnacious or tempered his fierce love of freedom. When James II issued his clumsy and ill-timed Declaration for Liberty of Conscience, Sir Jonathan was one of the famous Seven Bishops, who refused to permit the reading of the document in the churches of Great Britain, insisting that the king "does not possess this dispensing power." Carted off to the Tower for their insubordination, the bishops were acquitted by their peers in the House of Lords and became the most popular men in the country. Thereafter Bishop Trelawny was given the Order of the Garter, his nation's most coveted award, and crowned William and Mary at their coronation.

The grandfather of Edward John was a full-time professional

soldier, rising to the rank of major general and serving, with no discernible distinction, under Sir William Howe in the American War of Independence. He was the first member of the family to visit the New World, which made as scant an impression on him as he left upon it. His son, Charles Brereton-Trelawny, was also a soldier but never rose higher than the rank of lieutenant colonel. He left the Army to pursue an all-absorbing avocation, that of acquiring and saving money.

Charles was not only a miser but a mean, foul-tempered man incapable of demonstrating affection for anyone. His social life was severely circumscribed, principally because of his abiding hatred for the human race in general and his acquaintances in particular. His only known friend was his brother-in-law, also a miser, and their neighbors in Cornwall said they often spent their evenings together counting their money.

Edward John Trelawny's maternal lineage was distinguished. His mother was Maria Hawkins, a Cornish heiress whom Charles Trelawny married for her money. The first of her known ancestors was William Hawkins, a sea captain and explorer who became famous and wealthy during the reign of Henry VIII by sailing his ship, the *Paul,* to Brazil. All the Hawkins men were seafarers, and William's son, John, who eventually acquired a fleet of his own and was knighted by Elizabeth I, acquired immortality in 1588 when he, his son Sir Richard Hawkins and his cousin Sir Francis Drake defeated the Spanish Armada in one of the most significant sea battles in history. Father and son also engaged in legalized piracy on behalf of the Crown and multiplied their own wealth as well as that of their town, Plymouth, by being the first Englishmen to engage in the slave trade. Their direct descendant Edward John Trelawny "admired them above all men for their daring on the high seas, and despised them from the bottom of my heart for their despicable traffick in human souls." He not only condemned the practice but conducted a lifelong campaign to abolish slavery everywhere, from the Orient to the Mediterranean to the United States.

Maria Hawkins Trelawny was a rawboned woman, almost as tall as her husband, with dark hair and a long, bony face. Her bearing was regal, but only as an old woman was she regarded as handsome. Her personality matched her husband's, and she was cold, domineering and always ready for a quarrel. The marriage, which more closely resembled a small war, was a disaster from the outset. Maria's temper matched her husband's, and when he struck her she retaliated by going to London on shopping sprees that made him old before his time.

The couple owned a handsome estate in Cheshire as well as a town house in London, and although they usually resided under the same roof they lived apart—except on those occasions when they did their duty for the sake of posterity. The results of this infrequent union were substantial: there were two sons, Harry and Edward John, and three daughters.

Life for the children in the unhappy Trelawny household was grim. Their mother showed them a measure of affection, however, and as long as he lived her younger son never wrote a word criticizing her. But he could not say enough against his father, whose petty restrictions made life miserable for a small boy. On Sundays, when the family dined together, Harry and Edward John were not served meat until their father had consumed his first portion and decided whether he wanted a second. His cast-off clothes were cut down for Harry and eventually were passed along to Edward John. The meals were so frugal that the children were ravenous, but under no circumstances were they permitted to eat the fruit of the garden, which sometimes fell to the ground and rotted. In fact, when the boys went into the garden they were confined to the gravel path so they would not trample the grass.

Even though Edward John was born in London, he appears to have spent the better part of his early boyhood at the estate in Cheshire. He does not specify the location of his home in *Younger Son,* but it is obvious he was living in the country, and he developed a lifelong devotion to rural scenes and a corresponding hatred for city life.

An incident that took place when the boy was five years old left a lasting mark on his character, and he recalled it in full detail when he wrote the autobiography of his youth. The grisly story, best told in his own words, was corroborated by other members of his family:

*My father had a fancy for a raven that, with ragged wings and a grave, antique aspect, used to wander solitarily about the gar-*

den. As he abhorred children and used to chase us out of his way, we had all, from the time we could walk, considered him and my father the two most powerful, awful and tyrannical persons on earth.

The raven was getting into years. He had a gray and grizzly look; he halted on one leg; his joints were stiff, his legs rough as the bark of a cork tree, and he was covered with large warts; his eyes had a bleared and sinister expression and he passed most of his time idling in the sun under a south wall against which grew the delicious plums of the garden. Many were the stratagems we used to lure him from this spot; even the garbage on which he gloated was offered in vain. His moroseness and ferocity, and our difficulty in getting fruit were insupportable. We tried to intimidate him with sticks, but were too weak to make the least impression on his weather-beaten carcass and got the worst of it. I used, when I could do so slyly, to throw stones at him; but this had no effect. I in vain sought for redress from the gardener and servants; they laughed at us and jeered us. Thus things continued.

One day I had a little girl for my companion, a favorite sister whom I had enticed from the nursery to endeavor to get some fruit clandestinely. We slunk out, and entered the garden unobserved. Just as we were congratulating ourselves under a cherry tree, up comes the accursed monster of a raven. He seized hold of the little girl's frock; she was too frightened to scream. I threw myself upon him. He let her go and attacked me with bill and talon. I got hold of him by the neck, lifted him heavily, and struck his body against the tree and ground. Nothing seemed to hurt him. He was as hard as a rock. Thus we struggled, I evidently the weaker party. The little girl wanted to call the gardener. But I forbade her, knowing he would tell my father.

"Give me your sash!" I cried, "and I will hang the old fellow."

She did so and, though dreadfully mauled, I succeeded with great exertion in fastening one end of the ribbon around the old tyrant's neck; then I climbed the cherry tree, suspended my foe from a branch and jumped to the ground.

My brother came running up, shouting for joy when he saw our old enemy swinging in the air, and we commenced stoning him to death. When we tired of this sport, and he was to all ap-

*pearances dead, we let him down. He fell on his side; I laid hold
of a raspberry stake to make sure of him, by belaboring his head.
To our utter amazement and consternation he sprung up with a
hoarse scream and caught hold of me. So I again fell upon him
and calling my brother to keep fast hold of the ribbon, I climbed
the tree. The raven's look was now most terrifying; one eye was
hanging out of his head, the blood coming from his mouth, his
wings flapping in disorder, and with a ragged tail which I had
half plucked by pulling at him during his first execution. He
made a horrible struggle for existence, and I was bleeding all
over. At last we succeeded in gibbeting him again and then with
sticks we cudgelled him to death, beating his head to pieces. Afterwards we tied a stone to him, and sunk him in a duck pond.*

The man who told this gory tale showed no remorse, no sense
of shame, but related the facts without emotion. Certainly he
had little reason to feel proud of what he had done as a boy, but
it was a tribute to his rugged honesty that he had the courage to
reveal the cruelty of a small boy.

The story had a greater significance than appeared on the surface, and the raven was a symbol to the man as it had been—
even if unwittingly—to the boy before him. The bird functioned
as a type of emblem for Edward Trelawny's father and paternal
authority. By destroying it, Edward John won a victory over oppression. It did not matter that he had forgotten the plums that
had been his original goal; he had struck a blow against injustice, and even though he had resorted to questionable means, he
had triumphed.

Certainly the man who wrote *Adventures of a Younger Son* realized this incident contained clues to the development of his
adult character and revealed some of his less attractive traits.
"*This was the first and most awful duel I ever had,*" he wrote. "*I
mention it, childish though it be, not only because it lives vividly
in my memory, but as an event that, as I review my life, seems
evidently to be the first ring on which the links of a long chain
have been formed. It shows that I could long endure annoyance
and oppression, but when, at last, excited I never tried half-
measures but proceeded to extremities without stop or pause.
This has always been my most grievous fault, and grievously
have I repented it.*"

As a man, certainly, Trelawny was not lacking in insight, but a great deal of blood, his own included, would be shed before he acquired it. His treatment of the raven had been brutal, but the children of the English aristocracy were reared in a manner almost guaranteed to make them callous. Little boys were awakened at dawn, forced to bathe in icy water and then perform chores for several hours before being allowed to eat a breakfast of bread pudding. Children were deliberately starved so they would not become gluttons, and neither the rod nor the riding crop was spared.

Those who accepted the system passed on its cruelties to their own children. Those who rebelled—the Byrons, Shelleys and Trelawnys of England—became her poets and champions of liberty. The high-spirited Edward John received more than his share of beatings, later writing, "Punishments and severity of all kinds were the only marks of paternal love that fell to my share, from my earliest remembrance."

Edward John Trelawny's brother, unlike him, was a quiet child who frequently suffered from ill health and consequently was coddled by his mother, but never by his father. Edward John was never jealous of his brother, which was remarkable, but the secret of their amity lay in the fact that the younger child was by far the more aggressive and clever and, hence, became the leader. He remained on friendly terms with Harry throughout his lifetime, as he did with his sisters.

Of his mother, it is acknowledged that her increasing neglect of Edward John as he grew older, stronger and wilder was shocking. But still, he went through the dutiful motions of paying filial tribute to her.

By the time Edward John was eight years old he literally escaped from the attention of his indifferent parents by sneaking out of the house at every opportunity, and if they knew he was out they did not care. He soon became the friend of the boys who lived in the local village, little toughs who respected only those who could fight with bare fists, wrestle, kick and gouge. Edward John quickly learned all they could teach him, and soon became a leader of the group, thanks to his quick native intelligence and physical strength. Although tutors were hired for most aristocrats' sons when the boys were five to seven years of age, no thought had been given to the matter by Charles and Maria

Trelawny, whose younger son could neither read nor write by the time he reached his eighth birthday.

Few boys in the area were more adept poachers, however, and he could steal eggs from a barnyard or even food from a kitchen with the best in the neighborhood. Occasionally he was caught, and when a property owner complained, Edward John was whipped, but at no time did these beatings deter him. In fact, they made him all the more cunning in the pursuit of illegal activities, which he enjoyed for the simple reason that they were forbidden. He did not yet realize it, but he was already in full rebellion against parental authority.

The character traits that would mark the man were already in full evidence. Edward John was courageous, and was so lacking in fear that his sometimes reckless conduct was foolhardy. He hated injustice, despised authoritarianism and almost automatically supported the underdog. At times he displayed a degree of sensitivity that was surprising in a small boy, but at others he was callous, unmoved by the sufferings of others. His parents' indifference and cruelty could have produced a monster, but the heritage of the Trelawny and Hawkins bloodlines was too strong.

A seemingly minor incident that occurred when Edward John was nine and one half changed the course of his life. He and his brother went into the forbidden apple orchard, and he climbed a tree, then began to throw fruit down to his brother. They were caught in the act by their father, who ordered them to follow him, and marched in total silence to the town, about two miles away. There Charles Trelawny halted in front of a "walled and dreary building" and knocked "at a prison-looking gate."

The place was a school, and the headmaster, a Mr. Sayer, was a dapper little man with a precise and pedantic manner that was "most fearful to a boy." Charles immediately enrolled his sons as boarding students, and particularly warned Sayer about the younger, saying he "would come to the gallows if the devil were not scourged out of him." The headmaster promised he would do his best to keep the child out of Satan's reach, and Charles, after paying a deposit, withdrew without speaking a word of farewell to either of his sons. In fact, he left them without a change of clothing or a copper in their pockets.

Edward John lived through a nightmare at the school, although it must be admitted that Mr. Sayer's treatment of his pupils was no worse than that found at other, similar institutions for the sons of the gentry. He was flogged for every infraction of the school's many rules, major and minor, and since he was in constant rebellion he was beaten regularly. More often than not, the food was inedible, but he was so ravenously hungry that he ate it, even though he sometimes gagged. In spite of the child's many difficulties, his loneliness and the terror in which he lived, he managed to acquire the rudiments of what would become, in the main, a remarkable self-education. He learned to read and write, even though his spelling would be abominable for the whole of his long life; he gained some idea of the basics of mathematics, and through the classics he found an escape into the world of gods and heroes.

At no time did he excel in his studies, however, and the punishments inflicted on him neither discouraged him nor broke his spirit. His own description of his situation is graphic:

*I was flogged seldom more than once a day, or caned more than once an hour. I became callous and was considered by the master the most obdurate and violent rascal that had ever come into his hands. Every kind and gentle feeling of my naturally affectionate nature seemed subdued by this savage treatment, and I became sullen and vindictive. I vented my rage on the boys and, as I grew in bodily strength, I gained respect by fear, and became the ringleader in all sports and mischief. I thus learned my first lesson as to the necessity of depending on myself, and the spirit in me was gaining strength, in despite of every effort to destroy it, like a young pine flourishing in the cleft of a bed of granite.*

The boys having become his followers, Edward John turned his attention to his natural enemies, the instructors. The most hated of the masters took a group of students on an early-nineteenth-century version of a field trip, and when he stretched out under a tree to rest after a hike of several miles, Edward John saw a long-awaited opportunity. He rallied the other boys, and the entire group seized the master, then beat him unmercifully with sticks. He begged them to release him, but his pleas fell on

young, deaf ears, and they continued to belabor him until he lost
consciousness.

Naturally Mr. Sayer regarded the matter in the most serious
light, and Edward John was confined to a small room and placed
on a diet of bread and water. When Mr. Sayer came into the
room to inquire whether he was repentant, the boy tripped him
and would have jumped on him had other masters, waiting in
the corridor outside, not intervened. By the second night of his
incarceration, the boy became so bored that he set fire to the
curtains with the stub of a candle that provided his only light.

By this time, Mr. Sayer had had enough of the young animal.
Edward John was discharged from the school and was sent home
under guard. The other boys cheered him, but he was not permitted to speak to any of them, and could only wave farewell to
his brother.

Charles Trelawny happened to be away from home at the
time, and when he returned he was so preoccupied with the details of a new inheritance he had just received that he was
scarcely aware of his younger son's presence in the house. Assuming that the boy had come home for a holiday, the elder
Trelawny casually quizzed him regarding his studies and was
horrified to discover that he was inefficient in mathematics,
sloppy in his reading and writing, and totally ignorant of Latin.

Until that time, it had been assumed that Edward John would
follow the family tradition and be sent to Oxford, probably as a
preliminary to a career as a clergyman. But the boy showed no
signs whatever of a predilection for the cloth, and his education
to date was so inadequate that it was obvious Oxford would
never accept him.

While his father pondered the problem, the boy became involved in yet another incident. An old beggar woman came to
the door, and Edward John handed her a plate filled with food.
She was so honest that she returned the dish after eating her
meal, and the parsimonious Charles immediately accused her of
stealing the food, threatening to send her to prison. Edward John
could not permit her to be punished for a "crime" she had not
committed, and admitted that he had given her the food.

This was the last straw. Charles decided his younger son was
incorrigible, and immediately sought some way to get rid of him
for all time.

## II

*"I took to my new life with great joy."*

England's running wars with the genius who had seized control of the destinies of France, Napoleon Bonaparte, placed a tremendous burden on her resources. Late in 1804, when Edward John Trelawny was twelve years of age, Napoleon crowned himself emperor, and it was apparent to his foes across the Channel that his appetite for territory was unappeased. Britain lacked the manpower to match his legions on land, but thanks to the development of her own empire she still reigned supreme at sea, and most of her efforts were designed to expand the powerful Royal Navy.

The demands of the admiralty for ships and men were insatiable. Thousands of skilled workers labored in the shipyards to produce more than one hundred men-of-war, frigates, sloops and bomb ketches each year, an astonishing total in a nation that was just beginning to understand the techniques that would make her the leader in the Industrial Revolution. Life at sea was so brutal that few adult men volunteered for duty in the Navy, so press gangs roamed the streets, kidnaping young toughs from the slums and even middle-class drunks who made the mistake of roaming the streets alone after dark.

Ever-increasing needs for officers were met in two ways. Young gentlemen were sent to the royal academy at the Portsmouth shipyards, but a boy would not be made a midshipman and sent to sea until he was seventeen, and Charles Trelawny believed his younger son would get into far too much trouble to spend five full years at the academy. The second method of officer procurement seemed preferable to him: boys were accepted as "first-class volunteers" at the age of twelve, and after spending two to three years at sea were made midshipmen. Then, after an additional apprenticeship that usually lasted until they were twenty or twenty-one, they were granted commissions as lieutenants.

The idea of sending Edward John into the Navy as a first-class volunteer appealed to Charles Trelawny for several reasons. The Navy's discipline was precisely what the boy needed, and all youths accepted for duty were given a compulsory education. There was yet another, unexpressed reason for the elder Trelawny's preference: there was a long waiting list at the academy, but the Navy would accept a boy as a first-class volunteer immediately, provided his family made its own arrangements in finding him a berth.

So Charles Trelawny immediately sent off letters to various friends and acquaintances, and after a delay of about four and one half months he heard from an old friend, a Captain Morris, to the effect that he would make a place for Edward John on his ship of the line, the *Colossus,* a vessel armed with seventy-four cannon. Morris explained, however, that there was one difficulty: he had no intention of returning to England in the near future, so the boy would have to be sent off to join him. The *Colossus* was cruising somewhere in the Atlantic or the Mediterranean, and Morris made no mention of his precise whereabouts.

But Charles had no intention of allowing such a minor inconvenience to deprive him of the opportunity to rid himself of an unwanted son. So he took Edward John to London, where they outfitted the boy, and then traveled to Portsmouth. Other friends of the elder Trelawny were stationed there, and since all of them knew that the volunteer—who was given no real choice in the matter—was the direct descendant of the fabled Sir John Hawkins, it proved to be a simple matter to make the necessary arrangements.

Captain Edward Keats, commander of the *Superb*, also a seventy-four, was sailing south to join the same squadron to which the *Colossus* was attached, and agreed to take Edward John with him as a passenger. The parting of father and son was as abrupt as that at the school had been, and they never again met.

If Charles Trelawny hoped his son would regard his enlistment as a punishment, he was mistaken. From the moment Edward John first set foot on board the huge man-of-war he knew he was destined to love the sea. He was in uniform, but as a passenger he had no duties to perform, so he was free to explore every part of the ship as he pleased. The sailing of the *Superb* was delayed for several months, and although the boy ate his meals and slept on the ship, he went ashore daily, sometimes venturing into the town of Portsmouth, sometimes making friends with other boys, who invited him to visit their ships. He received no formal schooling during his sojourn in Portsmouth, but he managed to learn a great deal about every kind of ship in the Royal Navy. For the first time in his young life, his interest had been aroused, and his curiosity was so insatiable that amused lieutenants who had nothing better to occupy them while on watch often answered his questions.

By the time the *Superb* finally put to sea, in the early autumn of 1805, Edward John Trelawny was "almost a veteran seaman." Vice-Admiral Sir John Thomas Duckworth came on board the man-of-war at Plymouth, making it his flagship, and the great man summoned the descendant of Hawkins to his cabin and shook his hand. Being a Trelawny, Edward John was discovering, had its advantages, as did standing on his own feet.

The boy ate his meals in the midshipmen's mess, and although others complained about the quality of the food, he did not. He had been starved at home and had been given slops at school, so he actually enjoyed the pickled beef and mutton, the salt fish and the hardtack, from which it was necessary to tap out weevils. The quantity was sufficient, and so for the first time in his life he wasn't hungry.

Edward John's curiosity led him to climb high in the rigging of the great vessel, and as she sailed southward through the Atlantic toward Cadiz, he made himself familiar with every phase of the *Superb*'s operation. By the time he joined the *Colossus*, he would know precisely what was expected of him and how to perform his duties.

One day late in October, the squadron headed by the *Superb* exchanged messages with a schooner, the *Pickle,* which belonged to Admiral Lord Horatio Nelson's fleet, and the entire company was shocked. On October 21, Nelson had won his greatest victory, at Trafalgar, and had died of wounds before the battle had ended. More than two decades later, Trelawny remembered the "deathlike stillness" on board the *Superb* after the news was received.

A day or two later, a number of ships partly disabled in the battle, many of them carrying wounded, were encountered at sea. Among them was the *Colossus,* which carried letters for Admiral Duckworth, and First Class Volunteer Trelawny was transferred to his official ship, beginning his active life in the Royal Navy a few days prior to his thirteenth birthday. His freedom was curtailed now, and for the first time he was subjected to discipline, but he enjoyed a life at sea too much to care, writing in *Younger Son:*

> *I found cockpit life more tolerable than my school and little worse than my home. Besides, I was treated with exceeding kindness, and I began to be delighted with my profession.*

How anyone could have found a cause for pleasure on board the *Colossus* is difficult to imagine. She had taken the worst beating suffered by any Royal Navy ship at Trafalgar: she had lost forty men killed, one hundred sixty had been wounded, among them Captain Morris, and she had been so severely damaged there was a serious doubt that she would be able to ride out a series of severe gales. She carried enough provisions for her officers and men, although her supplies of fresh fruit and vegetables had been exhausted, and only the death of a number of the wounded made it possible to give the survivors the opiates their pain made necessary.

A crisis atmosphere pervaded the ship, and the weather was so bad that Captain Morris had himself carried to the quarter-deck and lashed to the mast so he could supervise operations. Edward John Trelawny responded to the first emergency of his life and worked day and night with such zeal that, when the ship finally reached Portsmouth, on December 29, he was presented with a certificate stating that he had "behaved with diligence and sobriety." It was the first time in his life he had ever been commended by a superior.

A message from Charles Trelawny awaited Captain Morris: under no circumstances was Edward John to be permitted to return home. Instead he was to be sent to Dr. Burney's School for Navigation, at Gosport, a semiofficial academy for pre-midshipmen, and was to remain there until a berth could be found for him on another ship. The elder Trelawny's lack of hospitality neither surprised nor dismayed his son, who had no desire to go home.

Five first-class volunteers were being sent to the School for Navigation under the escort of a young lieutenant who was celebrating his first extended shore leave in more than two and one half years. He was not only eager to taste the delights that awaited him on land but thought it only fair that his young companions be permitted their share of fun and adventure before being locked behind Dr. Burney's high gates.

So the group started its day in Gosport by eating a hearty breakfast of beefsteak washed down with rum at the Crown and Anchor, an inn frequented by officers. Then they went out into the streets, which were filled with townspeople, officers, sailors and "the many scarlet sinners for which Gosport had long enjoyed a dubious reputation." Everywhere, the lieutenant found friends from other ships, and these reunions were celebrated in the local bars, the young first-class volunteers being expected to drink their fair share.

By evening, a party large enough to fill three boxes attended the theater, and thereafter everyone went on to supper, a number of ladies of tarnished reputation having joined the men along the way. Edward John's description of the evening speaks for itself:

*The viands miraculously vanished. Bottles flew about. The empty dishes were cleared away, dried fruit, and wines of all kinds, with sundry cut-glass bottles of brandy, hollands, shrub and rum, garnished the board. The memory of Nelson was*

*pledged. Toasts, songs and unclerical jests wended away the
hours until it was time for the late performance at the theatre
and we sallied out into the high street. I remember nothing of
the play, except that the audience was exclusively composed of
sailors and their female companions. About midnight we supped,
and again turned out. Watchmen, dockyard men and redcoats
were assaulted wherever we fell in with them—by this time the
houses about me appeared to roll and pitch like ships. We were
taken back to the tavern and entrusted to a fiery, red-faced old
harridan who swore she would care for us as if we were her own
children. The lieutenant ordered a bed, a warming pan, a red
herring and a bowl of punch to be ready for him on his return,
and departed.*

The five little boys were so drunk they had to be helped to
bed. But the next morning the celebration began again, and the
festivities of the first day were repeated. That evening, the lieutenant finally delivered his charges to Dr. Burney, who had lived
too long in a Royal Navy town to be upset by the tardiness of
the five volunteers or their obviously intoxicated state.

Life at the School for Navigation was far different from that at
Dr. Sayer's school. The boys attended classes, studying a number
of subjects required by the Navy, but were subjected to virtually
no discipline and did as they pleased at the end of each school
day. Even in this lenient atmosphere, however, Edward John
could not stay out of trouble.

His problems arose when Captain Morris, who knew he had
no pocket money, sent him a gift of two guineas. The money was
stolen by an older, bigger boy, who offered him a pistol in return
and suggested they go into the woods together to hunt birds. Edward John didn't want the gun and had no desire to go hunting,
but he had learned how to deal with superior force, so he pretended to agree. He waited until he and his companion reached
the isolated woods and then demanded the return of his money.
The older boy tried to bluster, but Edward John held his ground,
finally threatening to shoot the other boy unless he received his
two guineas. Finally realizing he was in earnest, his companion
started to run away, and Edward John calmly shot him in the
hip, retrieved his two guineas and reported the incident to Dr.
Burney.

Even in a Royal Navy town the shooting of one volunteer by another might have had serious consequences under ordinary circumstances. But during Edward John's brief absence from the school he had received orders instructing him to report for duty to a new ship. Dr. Burney, who wanted no complications in his already hectic life, held the boy for twenty-four hours, then sent him to Portsmouth.

His new ship, a frigate of forty guns, was fitting for sea when Trelawny joined her. Since he made it his practice in *Younger Son* never to mention the names of captains he disliked or those of the ships they commanded, the frigate was not identified. All that is known about her is that she was one of the Navy's newest and had gone to sea previously only for her trials.

It was on the frigate that Trelawny first learned and followed regular shipboard routines, spending a portion of each day in the classroom, then standing a regular duty watch on deck. He and his fellow volunteers ate their meals in the midshipmen's mess, where their classes also were held. Truly the descendant of Hawkins, he enjoyed the bad food, was undisturbed by the dirt or cramped quarters where he and the other boys slung their hammocks, and not even in the worst of weather did he suffer from seasickness. Having known only harsh treatment since earliest childhood, he accepted the Navy's brutality as a matter of course.

He more than held his own in the midshipmen's mess, where, at the age of fourteen, he was already taller and huskier than most youths of nineteen. He was always ready to use his fists to win an argument with other volunteers or midshipmen, but he was no bully and became aggressive only when attacked. His official relations with the enlisted men were few, volunteers and midshipmen being forbidden to give or receive orders. Unlike some of the other young aristocrats, however, he adopted no airs, and his unofficial relations with most crew members were friendly.

Only in his dealings with superior officers did his lifelong hatred of authority manifest itself. When he liked and respected an officer, he cheerfully accepted any order given him, but when he thought an officer was unfair or tyrannical, he used every stratagem he could command to evade, ignore or forget to do what he had been told.

At no time in his life was he a true commoner, however, and never forgot his Trelawny and Hawkins ancestry. The men he most despised were those who tried to climb higher than the station to which they had been born, and both Captain A. and his first lieutenant were of that breed. Trelawny wrote:

*The captain was a red-gilled, sycophantic Scotsman, the son of an attorney, who had bowed and smirked himself into the notice of royalty. His first lieutenant was a Guernsey man, a low-bred, mean-spirited, malicious scoundrel. . . . I soon realized that the Navy was not suited to me, and although my passion for the sea remained undiminished, I longed for freedom. From that time forward, I brooded over the possibility of breaking my indentures, and seeking my own fortune, as tales and histories tell us people did in the olden times.*

It was typical of the young Trelawny to seek an immediate escape from the authority of a man he disliked, but his excitement over book-found tales and histories indicates a new influence in his life. He makes no mention, as such, of the reasons behind his newly acquired interest in reading, but from the age of fourteen he was an omnivorous reader, devouring every book in the midshipmen's library, badgering every truly literate officer for books and buying still others out of his wages when the frigate put into port. One of the seeming mysteries of Trelawny's life is his sound, broad education—one attained only through self-discipline, through reading scores of books on his own every year. Remarkable as it may sound, Trelawny—with, again, only his own resources to help him—went on to become one of the more literate observers of his age.

Unquestionably, Trelawny had a superior intellect. Not every man is capable of becoming fluent in Latin and Greek and six or seven modern languages as well.

We look for a key to Trelawny's self-provoked and self-maintained drive to learn. And we strike upon Trelawny's unrelenting urge to excel in all things. Until he met his masters in Shelley and Byron, Trelawny could permit no man to become his better.

And so it cannot surprise us that Trelawny had thrust himself into a reading campaign with the same zeal as he had always exhibited in making mischief. Young Trelawny's obsession with obtaining a good education is best explained in his own words:

*At this period of my life an involuntary passion was awakened in my bosom for reading; so that I seized on every occasion for borrowing and collecting books, and every leisure moment for reading them. Old plays, voyages and travels were my principal studies, and I almost learned by heart Captain Bligh's narrative of his voyage to the South Sea Islands and the mutiny of his crew. His partial account did not deceive me. I detested him for his tyranny, and Fletcher Christian was my hero. I wished his fate had been mine and longed to emulate him. The story had a marked influence on my life.*

The youngster made the miraculous discovery that others before him, brave and courageous men, had rebelled against tyranny, succeeded beyond their most optimistic dreams and, prodigiously enough, won both happiness and respectability. It is in no way astounding that Lieutenant Christian, who found serenity in an island paradise, became Trelawny's ideal. However, it was his misfortune that, just at this time, Edward John Trelawny's path crossed that of the captain's clerk.

Ordinarily, a volunteer would have had little do with a captain's civilian secretary, but the clerk noticed that Trelawny owned a number of handsome books and was fond of reading, so he offered the boy a quiet and safe place to store and study his books. Trelawny accepted with pleasure, but one day decided to take a book with him to his hammock and was startled when the clerk ordered him to halt, saying he could read in the cabin but could remove none of the books.

The boy paid no attention and started to leave the cabin with the book, but the clerk seized a ruler, beat him to his knees and tried to take the book from him. Trelawny became so enraged that he fought like a demon and was cheered by the midshipmen and volunteers who crowded in the open doorway.

A table was knocked over, spilling ink, paper and a number of official documents on the deck. Trelawny caught sight of something very valuable to him at this moment, a penknife that the clerk had used to sharpen his quills. It was lying on the deck within reach, and the boy did not hesitate. Seizing it, he stabbed the clerk repeatedly until the man fell back and called for help.

Trelawny picked up all his books and stalked out with them, his face and clothes smeared with the clerk's blood. The other boys cheered him even more loudly, but they—and he—must have realized that he had placed his life in jeopardy. The stabbing of the clerk was a grave offense, and the captain could have ordered the offender hanged or, at the very least, severely flogged.

But Captain A. proved to be less of a tyrant than the boy had supposed. A full-scale inquiry was held, with the captain questioning everyone who had witnessed the fight, and when a midshipman named Murray testified under oath that the books belonged to Trelawny, that the clerk had forbidden him to take possession of his own property and had been the aggressor in the fight, the whole nature of the matter changed. It was as serious an offense for a clerk to strike a midshipman as it was for a midshipman to attack a clerk, so the secretary was placed in irons, Trelawny suffering no worse a form of punishment than forty-eight hours of confinement to his quarters. For two delightful days he was required to perform no sea duties and could spend his time reading, the other boys regarding him as a bona fide hero.

Obviously Captain A. considered Trelawny in the right, and when the frigate returned to England from its blockade duty off France he promoted the boy to full-scale midshipman. This was indeed a special honor, because Trelawny was not yet fifteen, and fifteen was supposedly the youngest age that a volunteer could become a genuine apprentice officer.

The boy's next assignment was dull and short. He was posted to a guard ship, a prison vessel that remained anchored in Portsmouth. And it was at this time that Trelawny first came face to face with the bitter reality that love is not always a result of being someone's son. He wrote to his parents, informing them that he was in England, but he received no reply, no invitation to visit them and no pocket money. To make matters worse, his sea chest was rifled by a fellow midshipman.

Trelawny's financial situation was serious. Midshipmen were

expected to live like gentlemen, and their pay was so small they ordinarily received financial help from their families. The custom had been observed for more than one hundred years, and the Navy expected the boys to receive parental help.

But Edward John Trelawny was brutally, callously cut off by his silent father, and he went off to sea for a long cruise on a sloop of war under the worst of personal circumstances. He could buy none of the delicacies that other boys purchased to supplement the miserable food, and he even lacked the funds to buy replacements for the uniforms that had become threadbare or, worse, had been stolen. The sloop was a small ship, carrying fewer than one hundred fifty officers and men, and the boy's plight quickly became known to everyone on board.

His brother midshipmen came to his rescue. He was so popular with them, enjoying the favor of those who were three or four years his senior as well as the approval of the younger boys, that they gave him new uniforms and equipment from their own supplies and even shared their special food with him.

Their attitude made the long, dreary voyage bearable to the homesick boy. The sloop sailed down the coast of Spain, searched for French merchantmen off the coast of Africa and then crossed the Atlantic to continue the hunt off the coast of South America. When she put into port after weeks of sea duty and her crew was given shore leave by a captain whom Trelawny classified as a tyrant, the boy was too poor to buy a meal, enjoy a drink or seek the company of females. Instead he wandered alone through the streets of alien cities, usually buying an inexpensive book or two, out of his infinitesimal wages, as a memento.

He spent his fifteenth birthday at sea, in November 1807, and when the sloop returned to Plymouth in the Spring of 1808 he was determined to find out where he stood with his parents. No longer displaying the bravado he habitually used as a screen, he wrote a letter to his father, saying he had again returned to England and wanted to come home. He also explained his financial situation in candid detail, making it clear that he was desperate and indicating he would resign from the Navy, as he now had a right to do after two and one half years of service, unless his situation improved.

The possibility that he would return to Cornwall as a civilian alarmed Charles Trelawny, who also realized that his own name would be ridiculed if his son was reduced to virtual bankruptcy. So he took action accordingly, but did not write to his son, instead sending instructions via the captain:

Edward Trelawny was ordered to proceed without delay from Plymouth to Portsmouth, where arrangements had been made for him to join the staff of a frigate that was being readied for a long cruise to the Orient. Although the boy would travel within ten miles of his parents' home, he was directed not to pause there or make any attempt to see his mother or sisters. In return for his complete obedience to these instructions he would, thenceforth, receive a "generous" annual allowance.

The boy was crushed, and more than two decades later he still felt the full impact of the paternal rebuff when he wrote in *Younger Son:*

*Who can paint in words what I felt? Torn from my native country, transported like a felon—at that period few ships returned from the East in under seven years, and cut off from every tie. I was torn away; not seeing my mother, or brother, or sisters, or one familiar face. No voice to speak a word of comfort, or to inspire me with the smallest hope that any human being took an interest in me. Had a servant of my house, or even the old mastiff, companion of my childhood, come to me for one hour, I could have hugged him for joy. But I was even to be separated from my messmates, whom I had learned to love—these are things, which some may feel but none can delineate. . . .*

*I knew now that I was an outcast, thrust from my father's threshold in the hope that I should not cross it again. From that time, my father left me to my fate with as little remorse as he would have ordered a litter of blind puppies to be drowned.*

The boy thought of rebelling, sneaking home and seeing his mother on the sly, but his pride as well as his common sense intervened and caused him to change his mind. No member of his family cared enough about him to have written him a private note wishing him well on his voyage to the far ends of the earth. And he would be foolish to jeopardize the allowance that had been promised to him, the one tangible evidence that Charles Trelawny cared enough about the family name not to let his son become a beggar.

Trying to hide his grief, Edward John Trelawny put his boyhood behind him as he set out across the land of his ancestors in search of a new identity.

# III

## *"My future became my present."*

The captain of the thirty-six-gun frigate held himself aloof from his four hundred officers and men, which was his prerogative, and leaving the operations of his ship in the hands of his first lieutenant, busied himself with the care of the dogs and cats he had brought with him as pets, as well as with the pigs, sheep and chickens that would put fresh meat on his table during the long voyage. But Trelawny's hopes that the captain would remain unaware of his presence were rudely blasted only forty-eight hours after the ship sailed from Portsmouth. Seeing him on deck, the captain paused to issue a solemn warning: he was aware of the midshipman's record, and would tolerate no stabbings, no acts of insubordination. He expected instant obedience to all orders, and any failure on the apprentice officer's part would result in immediate dismissal from the Royal Navy.

Trelawny took the threat to heart, but not in the way his superior meant it. If life on board became unbearable, he would need only to commit a breach of regulations in order to win his freedom. The prospect made life on board more tolerable for him.

Meanwhile he assumed his natural place as a leader of the

midshipmen and spent at least a portion of his spare time dreaming up ways to torment and tease the captain. A favorite trick, and one that amply illustrates the boy's ingenuity, also served a practical purpose that was of benefit to him and his colleagues. One of the boys would sneak up to that portion of the deck where the livestock were kept and run a needle through the brain of a chicken. The captain, unable to find anything wrong with the bird, assumed it had died of an illness and would order a midshipman to throw it overboard. Instead the boy would take it to his mess, where he and his fellows enjoyed a welcome change from the steady diet of bully beef and salt fish.

The exuberance of young Trelawny was as limitless as his imagination, and he conceived scores of tricks and stunts to keep the mind of the unhappy captain occupied. The game was dangerous, which gave it added zest, and he might have found himself in serious trouble had he not found a protector who turned his mind to worthier pursuits. A junior lieutenant named Aston saw a potential in the boy that no one else had ever perceived, and making himself Trelawny's confidant, gave him lessons in seamanship and encouraged his reading, often loaning him books from his own large library.

The boy was ecstatic. He had found a real friend at last, someone who cared whether he lived or died, someone who could help and advise him. Two decades later, he recalled Aston as a man of "stability of character, heroic courage, gentle and affectionate manners and open, manly bearing." Not even the passage of many years dimmed Trelawny's romantic memory of his first real friend, one whose personality Trelawny thought of as nearly flawless. Trelawny wrote:

*I had been in his watch and through the tedious nights he had dived into my real character so as to discover that I was not what I seemed to be. His kindness drew me out of the shell in which I had shrunk. He awakened those feelings which had become torpid and called others forth that I had never felt.*

The boy needed a friend, because he had made a new enemy, another lieutenant to whom he referred only as the Scotchman. Just as there was no evil, for Trelawny's view of it, in Aston, there was nothing good in his colleague. Trelawny described him as "keen, sharp, cunning and villainous . . . his sole delight was in torturing his subordinates." The high-spirited boy was a natural target, and the Scotchman hazed him at every opportunity.

An inevitable incident disturbed the calm of life on board the frigate. The Scottish lieutenant informed the midshipman that his salute was improper; when saluting a superior he was required to remove his hat entirely from his head.

Trelawny promptly retorted that no man on earth was his superior. If the lieutenant referred to a superior officer, Navy regulations merely required that he raise his hand to the brim of his hat.

The Scotchman tried to force him to remove his hat. Trelawny refused.

The impasse might have caused a fight that could have had serious consequences for the boy, but Lieutenant Aston quietly referred the matter to the captain, who ruled in Trelawny's favor. The Scotchman had been humiliated, and awaited an opportunity to obtain revenge.

Stormy weather always brought out the best in Trelawny, and when the ship was battered by gales he demonstrated a wild, raw courage that frequently astonished the officers. He climbed into the highest rigging; he performed any act required of him on the open decks, and in his own words, he became "a son of God shouting for joy." When the seas were tranquil, however, not even the influence of Lieutenant Aston prevented him from becoming indolent, neglecting his duties and sneaking off to a hidden corner where he could read a book.

The Scottish lieutenant, keeping an eye on him, punished him for every infraction of the rules, and Trelawny hated the man more each time he was reprimanded. The boy accepted rebukes and punishments from others when he deserved it but revealed his immaturity by convincing himself that the Scotchman was persecuting him only for the sake of his own pleasure. The two began to play a vicious game.

Most of the midshipmen hated being sent to the masthead for four or five hours, always afraid they would slip and fall into the sea. Trelawny was indifferent to the danger, however, and found a way to torment his oppressor: he stretched out along the cross-trees and pretended to take a nap; sometimes, on a hot day, he really did fall asleep. This caused the Scotchman great anxiety, since he would be held responsible if Midshipman Trelawny fell into the sea and drowned.

The Scotchman was wily, and, at one point, punished the boy for an infraction of the regulations by sending him to the far end of the topsail yard for four hours. It was impossible for anyone to fall asleep there, the angry lieutenant reasoned.

Trelawny accepted the order with a smile and climbed to the yard, high above the sea. Then, with complete composure, he took hold of the topsail lift, found a place for himself between the yard and the studding-sail boom, and stretched out for his customary nap. The fearful officer called out to him repeatedly, urging him to stop behaving like a madman, but the happy midshipman made no reply.

Then Trelawny had yet another idea. On a previous occasion, he had seen a sailor leap from the lower yardarm into the sea without injury when the roll of the ship was in his favor. So, he reasoned, there was every chance he could repeat the feat from the higher yardarm. He stood, waited until a particularly heavy roll of the ship brought him close—or what appeared to be close—to the crest of a huge wave, and then dropped into the ocean.

The insane stunt almost ended his life. He felt himself dropping straight down, and although he tried his utmost to swim, the momentum continued to carry him downward, and every movement of his arms and legs caused him untold agony. He felt certain he would drown, but his pain was so intense it blocked all else from his mind. He scarcely realized what was happening when he was hauled from the sea.

The surgeon was summoned to provide resuscitation, which was another torture, and for the next forty-eight hours Trelawny was a very sick boy. No one even suspected that his jump into the sea had been deliberate, that his intention had been that of balancing the score with his tormentor. The officers and the other midshipmen came to the private cabin in which the invalid had been placed, many of them bearing gifts, and the captain himself loosened the reins enough to contribute a fowl for broth and a bottle of wine.

Trelawny had not changed in the least, in spite of his physical condition. He demanded that the chicken be broiled and the wine be served to him mulled, because, he said, he didn't "hold with anything insipid."

The Scotchman received a severe reprimand for having placed the life of a midshipman in danger, so Trelawny rejoiced, believing he had won a great victory. The fact that his antics had nearly cost him his life did not occur to him.

Soon thereafter, a series of unplanned events enabled him to score yet another triumph over the man he hated with such unrelenting passion. The frigate was cruising between Madras and Bombay, searching for pirates that were preying on British merchant shipping, and one day, off Goa, a too-sleek Malay vessel appeared on the horizon. The captain's suspicions increased when his ship drew closer to the stranger and the stranger tried to escape—might have, in fact, if the wind hadn't died away and the sea become glassy.

Two of the frigate's longboats were lowered, and approached the stranger with considerable caution. Trelawny, who had been the first to volunteer for the enterprise, related the affair in detail:

*I was in the bow of one boat, on fire to realize my ardent love of fighting. The instant we touched the bow of the Malay, I seized a rope and swung myself on board, and before my foot was on the deck I had cut a fellow across the head. Followed by two or three sailors, we cut and slashed away without mercy. The Malays jumped overboard. Furious at the thought of their escaping, I seized a musket and was about to fire on them in the water when Lieutenant Aston laid hold of me.*

*"Don't you hear?" he exclaimed. "I have been roaring to you till I'm hoarse. Are you mad? Put down that musket. You have no right to touch these people. For all we know, she is a harmless merchantman—"*

He almost choked on his words. At that moment, a strong band of Malays appeared on shore and opened fire on the Englishmen with their matchlocks. Badly outnumbered, but realizing beyond doubt that the vessel was indeed a pirate, Lieuten-

ant Aston ordered his men to scuttle the ship and return to the
frigate.

The incident taught Trelawny one of the most valuable lessons
he had yet learned. As an irate Lieutenant Aston made clear to
him, heroism for its own sake was meaningless; courage was an
asset only when directed by intelligence, and "running amok"
was the essence of stupidity. The sheepish boy was forced to
agree.

Others, less critical than Aston, praised him, however, and
their plaudits were sweeter because the behavior of the Scotchman during the incident had been perilously close to cowardice.
The second-in-command of the boarding party, he had shown a
distinct reluctance to leave the safety of his longboat and had
been the last to climb onto the deck of the Malay pirate. The entire ship's company was aware of his hesitation, and although the
circumstances had not warranted a reprimand, it would have
been awkward for him had he continued to make the gallant
midshipman the butt of his bad temper.

A few days thereafter, a dangerous fire in the powder magazine won Trelawny the unqualified approval of the officers and,
more importantly, the captain. Trelawny volunteered instantly
when the first alarm was given, slid down a line into the magazine and quickly extinguished the smoldering blaze. This selfless
act gained him an official commendation, prompted the captain
to give due credit to him in the official dispatches to the admiralty and made him invulnerable to his former tormentor.

The Scotchman found another way to strike at him.
Trelawny's closest friend in the band of midshipmen was a quiet,
rather timid boy named Walter, who shared his love for books.
Walter's background was even more pitiful than his friend's: he
was the illegitimate son of a nobleman, and his mother, a poor
country girl, had reared him in the most abject of poverty, making great sacrifices so he could enter the Navy and win official
standing as a gentleman. Walter had no talent as a sailor and
hated his life at sea but was hanging on grimly so he could jus-
tify his mother's faith in him.

It is significant that Trelawny befriended him. Thereafter, for
the rest of his long, illustrious life, he utilized every opportunity
to act as the champion of the weak. Loathing tyranny of every

kind, he made it his business to come to the aid of tyranny's victims. And seen in this light, his hatred of the Scotchman and his friendship with Walter become symbolic.

In the early stages of the frigate's voyage, Walter had been the butt of his fellow midshipmen's jokes, and they had teased him unmercifully. That situation changed drastically once Trelawny made it known that he would regard any attack upon Walter as an attack upon himself. From that time on, the apprentice officers accepted Walter.

The Scotch lieutenant was also aware of the boys' friendship, and had lost so many rounds in his battle with Trelawny that, in all probability, he would have left Walter strictly alone had circumstances not forced him to act. The two literary-minded midshipmen composed two songs in "honor" of the lieutenant, both of these epics celebrating in doggerel the questionable courage the officer had displayed during the brief encounter with the Malay pirate. This pseudo poetry first saw the light of day when it was dropped, mysteriously, down the hatchway while the officers were eating dinner. It landed in the center of the table, and one of the officers read it aloud. The Scotchman grew scarlet but went through the motions of accepting the insults as a joke.

Everyone on the ship knew that Trelawny was the author of the verses. In fact, he went out of his way to advertise his identification with them, singing them at the top of a loud but none-too-melodious voice as he went about his duties. Not until a week later did the news slip out that Walter had been the co-author of the doggerel.

The Scotchman had been reluctant to cross swords with Trelawny again, but Walter was an opponent for whom he had no fear. He was heard to swear, "By God, I'll make that sickly boy drown himself before he's a week older." The threat was duly reported to Trelawny by a half dozen well-wishers, and the issue was joined.

Walter was punished unmercifully for every real and imagined infraction of regulations, and such abuse was heaped on him that he became desperate, lost his temper and launched a verbal attack on the sadistic officer. That was all the excuse the Scotchman needed. With the captain's permission he degraded Walter by forcing him to dress as a common sailor, sleep with the seamen and eat with them. He was assigned to duty with the mizzentopmen, work for which he was obviously unsuited. The other midshipmen were forbidden to speak to him, and he was treated like a criminal.

Everyone on the ship sympathized with the boy. The seamen, usually the first to join in humiliating a fellow human whose luck was exhausted, treated Walter with great kindness. The bos'ns and mates, who were in direct charge of work details, saw to it that Walter was given the least hazardous assignments. Commissioned officers went out of their way to urge him not to buckle. And the midshipmen separately and together paid no attention to the Scotchman's order to ignore him.

Trelawny made every effort to encourage his friend, but Walter had lost his spirit; apathetic, withdrawn and silent, he seemed unaware that anyone was even speaking to him. In fact, Walter appeared to be a victim of the "strange sickness," a malady with which every sailor was familiar. Those who were stricken by it lost their appetites, could no longer sleep and, in severe cases, sometimes wasted away and died.

Something had to be done to arouse Walter from his torpor, and the desperate Trelawny concocted a new, daring scheme. At the first opportunity, he intended to jump ship and desert the Navy.

At last Walter stirred, and gazed at him with new interest.

Of course, Trelawny said, he assumed that Walter would desert with him.

The weaker boy hesitated.

Naturally, Trelawny declared, they would obtain revenge first, repaying the Scotchman for every unjust deed he had perpetrated. Letting his imagination run freely, he painted a lurid picture, subsequently writing in *Younger Son:*

*I pointed out the exquisite treat we have, in buffeting his enemy to death. The hope of this wild justice did what no other hope could do—it made him calm.*

Continuing the therapy, Trelawny sneaked out of his quarters every night and joined his friend in the mizzentop. Far from home, fanned by hot monsoon winds and occasionally catching glimpses of the dark bulk of the Indian subcontinent on the horizon, the two English boys daydreamed and plotted. Gradually, as Trelawny talked, he convinced himself that his scheme was practical, and what had started as therapeutic assistance to Walter became real to him.

His arguments were powerful. They were men now, not mere boys, and their future was in their own hands. The frigate was not the world, nor were they galley slaves destined to spend the rest of their days chained to an oar. England seemed omnipotent to her loyal sons, but when she abused them, and when those who were hurt finally opened their eyes, they, or at least a discerning few, were able to take note of England's weaknesses. She was a tyrant, but only of the sea. The mythical India, land of a thousand kings, wealthy and mysterious, was beckoning. There were risks, to be sure, but boys who would otherwise be rendered helpless, unable to protect themselves from the whims of the cruel oppressor, had little to lose.

Adolescents of every era have been endowed with an infinite capacity for self-pity, and Walter and Trelawny were no exceptions. Walter began to indulge in his own dreams of a land where Europeans did not dare follow. He longed to cast off country and caste and find a home amid the children of nature. "The leprous pariah lived in bliss compared to what a sailor had to endure," Trelawny later wrote.

But despite this knowledge, Walter's dreams ran away with themselves, becoming more and more unreal. He would not live near salt water, having already filled his bloodstream with it. Instead he would go far inland and would make his home with a gentle, primitive people. He would find a sheltered ravine protected by the shadow of graceful trees, with a quiet stream flowing through the property. There he would build a simple hut, marry and sire children; above all, he would live in brotherhood with the savages.

"*What? Be tattooed and naked?*" Trelawny's barbs always brought his friend back to earth again.

Such comments were typical of Edward John Trelawny's rapidly developing attitude toward life. He would always be a romantic, but there was no hint of the sentimental in his nature.

He might indulge in quixotic behavior, dream of impossible goals and strive to achieve them, but his romanticism would always be tempered by a pragmatic streak of realism. He would lament that the world was not better, but unless the millennium could come in his own time, he would prepare himself to live in an imperfect world and cope with it.

The twelve to eighteen months that had passed since he had last visited England brought with them much maturity. The life at sea and his conflict with the Scotchman, his friendship with Lieutenant Aston and his never-ending reading program were bestowing insights upon him that had, hitherto, been lacking in his nature. Few precise dates are mentioned in the *Adventures of a Younger Son,* but, as nearly as the reader can tell, Trelawny was approximately seventeen years of age at this time when his friendship with Walter was at its height. With four to five years of Navy life already behind him, he was still a boy, to be sure, but in many ways Edward John Trelawny had acquired the dignity of a man.

Walter, probably because of the unruliness of his fantasies, might have regarded their escape scheme as little more than an emotional release from their hard life, but Trelawny was fooling neither himself nor his friend. He meant to make that dream come true, and in order to do so, he developed a number of practical approaches to it. Desertion from the Navy did not have to signal abandonment of the sea, which he loved, so he applied himself to studies of navigation and seamanship with increased diligence. Knowing, however, that he would spend a number of years in the East, he also read whatever he could find on Oriental theology and philosophy in order to prepare for the future he intended to make for himself. To say that Trelawny planned ahead logically and competently is an understatement.

A surprised and pleased Lieutenant Aston encouraged him. So did the studious Walter, who returned to the midshipmen's mess and life when his punishment had ended. It might have been far more pleasant for Trelawny to nap under the stars and enjoy the balmy night air on deck, but he could no longer permit such self-indulgence. Weeks became months, and he still maintained his new, rigid self-discipline. He could not put his plan into operation until he was ready—and he would not be ready until he had learned enough about the sea and the thought patterns of the Eastern people to insure the success of his scheme.

He deliberately bypassed opportunities for desertion when the frigate put into various ports for repairs and supplies. When the right time finally came, he would not only desert from the Navy with Walter, but together they would kill the hated Scotch lieutenant.

# IV

## *"As bold a rover as the sands have seen."*

Bombay, the principal seaport of western India, was the Royal
Navy's principal stronghold on the subcontinent in the early-
nineteenth century, and a large base was situated there, as were
extensive shipyards. The East India Company's hegemony
there having been long established, the maharajahs of Gujarat
and Maharashtra had become subservient to the representatives
of King George III. No one had bothered to take a census of the
native population, which stood at approximately one half million, and few Royal Navy visitors ventured beyond the confines
of their own world. Senior officers dined at the homes of high-
ranking Indians and in clubs as exclusive as London's finest. Junior officers dined in taverns that served English food prepared in
the English way and frequented brothels reserved for their exclusive use. Common seamen roamed the waterfront, drank and
made love where they pleased, became embroiled in innumerable, senseless fights.

Edward John Trelawny made a valiant attempt to convey the
impression, in *Younger Son,* that he was nothing but a reckless

apprentice officer on shore leave in Bombay. Having abandoned
his resolve to avoid the favors of native women, he boasted of his
adventures:

*What time I could spare from women and wine I devoted to
playing at the billiard table, galloping about the country and
rioting in the bazaars. My horse was a vicious-looking brute,
with an ambiguity in his eye that gave him an uncommon sinister expression. But I had a fellow feeling for his independent
spirit, and found the excitement of contention a delight—for I
loved to stem the stream and have never followed the footsteps
of the prudent who keep the high-beaten track of the world.
Thanks to a Turkish bit and saddle which I substituted for the
mockery of English ones, I, drunk or sober, kept my seat, and my
horse and I became a show-lion to the sober natives. I would go
galloping about the narrow streets to the imminent peril of men,
women and brats. Countless were the complaints of stalls upset,
bruises and fractures; notwithstanding a hundred conflicting
castes, all joined in a hearty curse against me.*

This was the self-portrait he seemed determined to paint for
the world, that of a callous young roisterer totally indifferent to
the health, safety, property and personal rights of the people
whose hospitality he was abusing. But he inadvertently gave
himself away, revealing another, infinitely more sensitive side of
his nature.

Unlike virtually all Englishmen of his class and time, he was
totally lacking in racial prejudice, and did not share the feelings
of his fellow countrymen that all Easterners were inferior to Europeans. Only a few pages after describing his alleged mode of
living in Bombay, he wrote:

*In India Europeans lord it over the conquered natives with a
high hand. The greatest kindness from Europeans, for long and
faithful services, never exceeds what is shown to dogs—they are
patted when their masters are in good humour and beaten when
they are vexed—at least it was so when I was there. As long as
you refrained from political interference, and presumed not to
question the omnipotency of the Holy of Holies, the East India*

*Company and their servants, as they are pleased to designate the*
*governor and all in office, you could do no wrong.*

*I hated this officialdom, not only for the tyranny it represented*
*—which alone would cause any honourable man to despise them*
*—but even more so because of their indifference to the suffering*
*of the natives, poor wretches who were half-starved, dressed in*
*rags, who performed their natural functions in the streets be-*
*cause they had no homes of their own, and all the while the*
*mighty of the East India Company were draining out the natural*
*wealth of the land, wealth that rightly belonged to those whose*
*heritage was there. Were I an Indian, of any caste, I would feel*
*impelled to lead a rebellion and drive the usurper from the land*
*of my ancestors. No man can walk with dignity when a foreign*
*tyrant places a yoke on his shoulders.*

It is probably true that the seventeen-year-old Trelawny drank
too much, visited the officers' brothels and played billiards by
the hour; it may be true, too, that he rode recklessly through the
streets. But what is far more important is that the youth no
longer thought of liberty exclusively in personal terms. He was
expanding his horizons, and having known the yoke himself, was
yearning for the freedom of all men, everywhere.

Trelawny, in his late teens, was ripe to become a nineteenth-
century inheritor of the principles of the American and French
revolutions. He was already proving himself the spiritual son of
John Locke, the brother of Thomas Jefferson. And so it is not
surprising that Trelawny soon became the kinsman of Shelley
and Byron, espousing all of their worthier theories and beliefs.

Trelawny's plan for escape from a constricting and very often
cruel navy duty had been nurtured during a seemingly endless
series of long days and ink-black nights at sea, far from the
newspaper events of everyday life on land. The feel of solid
earth beneath his feet, the sound of the hustle and bustle about
him, however, brought home to Trelawny, even in faraway
India, the fact that desertion could, under no circumstances, be
regarded lightly. And yet he knew he had to get out of the Navy,
knew he would.

His family had rejected him, to be sure, but now he was intending to reject his country, to become an outcast from it. If

captured he would face a possible death penalty and, without doubt, be contemptuously regarded by his peers. Knowing all this, but nonetheless motivated by high and demanding principles, Trelawny decided that the only way he could make his way in life as a thinking, righteous person was by unfettering those chains that bound him to things he could not believe in, could not countenance. Escape he would.

Trelawny had to make his desertion plans alone, since Walter had not been granted shore leave, but he sent his friend frequent messages in a complicated code that they had devised together. Walter was to remain on board the frigate, showing no sign of his intentions, and he was to wait until the last possible moment before the ship put out to sea again before acting. Trelawny had learned that the frigate would sail after dark in three days' time, and that was all to the good. He had engaged a canoe, and it was to approach the ship after dark. At the appointed hour Walter would drop quietly into the sea from the port bow. He would then swim to the canoe. The friends manning it would take Walter ashore and convey him to that secret place where Trelawny would await his arrival. Then the reunited friends, free of the Navy's shackles, would make their way in the world together.

Trelawny's messages made no mention of the plotted revenge against the Scotchman other than to indicate that Trelawny would take care of the matter himself. Circumstances made it impossible for Walter to help him. Actually, Trelawny was very much concerned about his pledge to even the score with the lieutenant. He realized that violence might spark counter violence and that the entire escape plan could be placed in jeopardy, but that risk had to be taken. What troubled Trelawny was the question as to when and how to launch his attack against the hateful Scot.

His path and that of the Scotchman had crossed frequently in Bombay, but Trelawny refrained from inciting a brawl that could have jeopardized the more important portion of his overall scheme: rescuing his close friend Walter. Nonetheless, Trelawny felt he could not desert and begin a new life until he had struck a satisfying blow at the man who had tormented him and Walter. He would be guilty of cowardice if he did not lash

back at the Scot, and for the rest of his life he would regret that
he had left the business unfinished.

As the days passed, his mounting anxiety as to the success of
the total plan—escape coupled with revenge—gave way to a
feeling bordering on panic. Only a developing association with a
new acquaintance prevented him from giving in to sudden impulse and assaulting the Scotchman prematurely. Trelawny met
a gentleman in his thirties who was known locally as the
Stranger. From the outset—from the initial game of billiards
played together in an officers' tavern—Trelawny was intrigued
by his new companion. The Stranger spoke English fluently, although his accent was unlike any the boy had ever heard; the
mysterious gentleman, who was well dressed and had impecca-
ble manners, was equally at home in Malay, Hindi and Persian.

Little by little, Trelawny gleaned that the man's name was De
Ruyter. He was a native American and a citizen of the United
States. He earned a living as a merchant. Nevertheless, this gentleman remained, for the most part, uncommunicative about
himself and, in fact, was so vague about his activities as a merchant that the boy suspected he was not telling the truth. At no
time did Trelawny learn that his real name was De Witt, that he
had been born and reared in New York and that he had commanded a privateer in 1798, during America's undeclared naval
war with France.

Inasmuch as the boy had no way of knowing the utter truth
about this man who called himself De Ruyter—and never would
—still Trelawny would have admitted that, next to Percy Bysshe
Shelley, De Ruyter had a greater influence on his life and character than anyone else he would ever know. Trelawny's comments on the man in *Younger Son* bear this out. Twenty years
after their first meeting, he still regarded De Ruyter through the
eyes of a hero-worshiping adolescent. He was a man of "invincible determination," who "drank little, slept less and ate sparingly." Long residence in the tropics had not affected his energies, and his enthusiasms were so infectious that Trelawny
admitted he *"became my model. The height of my ambition was
to imitate him, even in his defects. For the first time I was
impressed by the superiority of a human being."*

The pair dined together and soon became inseparable. De

Ruyter showed his young companion neighborhoods and places
in Bombay that outsiders never visited, and, everywhere, the natives knew him and treated him with the greatest of respect. He
seemed interested in everything he saw, from an unusual face to
a rock formation to the shape of a flower.

He also displayed a great curiosity about Trelawny, and particularly about the Royal Navy ships being readied for sea duty
at the naval base. At his instigation they visited a number of
ships together, although they did not go on board the frigate,
and the boy began to wonder whether his new friend might be a
spy. In spite of his growing uneasiness, however, the man's
strength made an increasingly great impression on him:

> There was a self-possession and decision about de Ruyter's or-
> dinary acts, with a general information, that made me feel what,
> I suppose, I should not have thanked any one for remarking, as,
> at that age, we are loth to allow any to be our superior. Perhaps
> I might not have felt this so strongly, had he not been as much
> my superior in physical as in mental endowments. In stature he
> was majestic, the length and fine proportion of his limbs, and the
> shortness and roundness of his body, gave to his appearance a
> lightness and elasticity seldom seen but in the natives of the
> East. It was only on close examination that you discovered, that
> under the slim form of the date tree was disguised the solid
> strength of the oak.

Trelawny was more successful than he realized in his desire to
model himself after De Ruyter, for nature had done its part to
help him along. Trelawny's physical description of the man, in
fact, paralleled numerous portraits of his own appearance and
character that were written by the literary friends of Trelawny's
mature life. Yet he saw himself as similar to De Ruyter only
when he called himself "half-Arab."

At the age of seventeen Trelawny stood about six feet tall,
towering above most of his contemporaries. He was beginning to
fill out at this time, too, even though he remained slim until the
end of his days. His hair and eyebrows were a deep black, and
the tropical sun had made his skin as dark as that of the Indian

or Malay; only his eyes, which were an intense shade of blue, revealed that he was an Occidental.

The young Trelawny—maybe because De Ruyter seemed so similar to him but, more importantly here, possibly because he admired the subtle differences between them—began to feel De Ruyter's influence almost immediately. While the boy and the other midshipmen drank to excess in the officers' tavern, the American sat quietly, sipping black coffee and observing them with an air of amused tolerance. Not realizing what was happening to him, the boy began to curb his own drinking.

Nonetheless, for a considerable amount of time nothing could dispel Trelawny's uneasy feeling that his new friend was a spy. But De Ruyter spoke more openly as they came to know each other better, and his sympathy for the poverty-stricken Indians who were allowed to wallow in their own misery by their English conquerors was so great that Trelawny eventually concluded that he could not be an espionage agent. No spy could have been filled with such noble sentiments.

At last the boy confided his own secret to his new friend, telling De Ruyter that he and Walter intended to desert. The man did not appear shocked or surprised and offered a bungalow he owned in the countryside near Bombay as a refuge. Trelawny accepted with gratitude and so decided that his escape plans were complete now—even though he had not yet obtained vengeance in respect to his long-term feud with the Scottish lieutenant.

On the last day of his shore leave he sat in the tavern with De Ruyter and told his friend of his experiences in the Navy. Midshipmen suffered the fate of the damned, he said. But apparently De Ruyter did not agree. He came back at him by making light of the miseries suffered by apprentice officers. Trelawny's reaction was one of anger and disappointment at failing to win the agreement of his model gentleman. Trelawny began to cite chapter and verse to back his views. Indeed Trelawny was in the midst of his diatribe when the tavern door opened and the Scotchman came in. The mysterious forces of destiny had delivered him into the hands of his adversary.

The lieutenant, who had no idea of what was in store for him, bowed to De Ruyter and reminded Trelawny that the frigate was sailing the following morning and that all the officers were required to report for duty before sunrise. The harmless comment enraged the boy, who was seeking any excuse for a fight:

*I dashed my hat into the rascal's face with a cry of rage: "You told me once never to stand in your presence with my hat on. For the last time I obey!"*

*I stripped off my coat and drew my sword. He attempted to pass me. I caught him by the collar and swung him into the middle of the room. "Draw!" I cried. "This gentleman and the billiard maker shall see fair play."*

*He appealed to De Ruyter, calmly smoking. De Ruyter advised him to "draw and fight it out," adding, "He is but a boy and you should be a man by your beard."*

*The fellow began wimpering, begging to be let off. He humbled himself, protesting he had never intended any wrong; asked my pardon, entreating me to put up my sword and go on board with him, promising he would never take advantage of what had passed. Disgusted at his meanness, I struck him from me.*

*"Remember Walter!" I cried. "You cowardly and malignant ruffian. You white-livered scoundrel! Can no words move you? Then blows shall!"*

*And I hit him with the hilt of my sword in his mouth, and kicked him, and trampled on him, I tore his coat off and rent it to fragments. His screams added fuel to my anger, I was furious that such a pitiful wretch should have lorded it over me so long. I roared out, "For the wrongs you have done me I am satisfied. But nothing but your currish blood can atone for Walter!"*

*Having broken my own sword at the onset, I drew his from beneath his prostrate carcass and should have despatched him on the spot, had not a stronger hand gripped hold of my arm. It was De Ruyter's.*

*He said in a low, calm voice, "Come. No killing." He took my sword and handed me a billiard cue. "A stick is a fitter weapon to chastise a coward. Don't rust good steel."*

*I belabored the rascal, his yells were dreadful, he was wild with terror. I never ceased till I had broken the butt end of the cue over him and he lay motionless.*

De Ruyter, who had been standing guard duty at the door, now moved forward to assess the damage, and a crowd of natives, attracted by the commotion, rushed into the tavern. With them was a Caucasian: Walter!

Trelawny stared at his friend in bewilderment. Walter should have been waiting on board the frigate, prepared to jump overboard at sundown.

Walter did not hear his friend's questions and looked down at the Scotchman, then asked a pressing question of his own. Was their enemy dead?

Trelawny didn't know, and turned to De Ruyter, who shrugged, bent down to take the unconscious man's pulse and then ordered the servants to take him without delay to a physician.

There was a silence in the tavern as the Scottish lieutenant was carried out.

Trelawny began to laugh, but De Ruyter cut him short. De Ruyter realized what the boy did not: that the fight could result in imprisonment and disgrace at the very least. It was imperative, he declared, that Trelawny leave at once and escape from Bombay before an alarm was given and the town gates were closed. Walter, he said, was in less danger because he had "changed his uniform."

Trelawny looked hard at his friend for the first time and realized he was wearing the scarlet tunic and white trousers of an army officer, with the insignia of an ensign, the lowest commissioned rank, on his shoulders.

A smiling Walter indicated that he was not in disguise, was entitled to wear the uniform. Thanks to God and the activities of his mother on his behalf, a commission had been procured for him from the East India Company, in whose service he had now entered after receiving his discharge from the Navy that same morning. He had come at once to tell Trelawny his news, and to discuss their revenge, which his friend had already obtained.

De Ruyter halted the babble of the excited boys. Trelawny was in danger, and it would be impossible to predict the consequences if he did not flee at once. Ordering him to go to the bungalow and telling him how to proceed there, De Ruyter promised that he and Walter would join him as soon as the frigate sailed and the affair blew over.

The man's tone was so urgent the boy obeyed without further discussion. He called for his horse, borrowed a white civilian coat from De Ruyter to wear as a disguise, and also had the good sense to borrow a saber. Then, in a gesture typical of Edward John Trelawny, he poured a glass of claret for himself and downed it in a toast to Walter before hurrying off.

The streets were crowded, perhaps even more than usual, and he made his way with difficulty toward the gate that led to the interior. His heart pounding, he saw a guard of sepoys drawn up under the archway that led to the gate, and surmised the word had already been passed. Although he couldn't be certain, it was likely that the sepoys had been sent to apprehend him. Half standing in his saddle, the boy spurred his mount, galloped past the troops and thundered through the open gate.

# V

## *"Free at last!"*

Beyond the gates of Bombay lay a sandy wasteland, and Trelawny changed his position in the saddle, crouching low to make a smaller target of himself if the sepoys opened fire on him. But there were no shots and no one followed him. He was taking no chances, however, and galloped on:

> *I spurred my willing horse to the centre of the sandy waste, hallooing and screaming myself hoarse with rapture. I drew the sabre de Ruyter had given me, and flourished it about, regardless of my horse's head and ears. As I lost sight of the town gate I pulled in my foaming steed, then looking around and seeing nothing human, I dismounted, when patting the horse's reeking neck, I exclaimed, "Here we are, thou only honest creature, free at last! The spell of my bondage is broken!"*

Resuming his journey, Trelawny came to the aid of a dismounted soldier being attacked by his maddened horse, and after killing the beast he happily accepted a pistol from the man as a gift. Carrying two weapons now, he went on to a village he had previously visited with De Ruyter, and happily spent the evening there, eating, listening to native music and drinking the strong liquor that was provided for English visitors.

A new arrival created something of a stir, and Trelawny was horrified when he saw the captain of the frigate. It would be the supreme irony, after the drama of his escape, to be returned to bondage. The man who wielded the power of life or death over him apparently had not yet learned, however, of the incident involving the Scottish lieutenant. Obviously at home in the village, the captain showed a slight annoyance when he recognized his midshipman, but soon relaxed over a drink.

Trelawny lost no time taking his departure, murmuring something to suggest that he was heading back to town and ship. Then, for the last time in his life, he saluted an officer of the Royal Navy. As soon as he left the village, he headed his mount toward the remote hinterlands. It finally dawned on him that he had been foolish to tarry in search of pleasure, and he rode toward the sanctuary of De Ruyter's bungalow, which lay in the direction of the Deccan frontier.

After what seemed like a long time, he became fearful that he was lost, and hired a peasant to guide him. The man led him through fields of cereals, across a ford and up a trail cut in a jungle. At last they came to the cottage.

It was set in a grove of coconut palms and had a blue mountain for its background. The garden was filled with pomegranate, banana, guava, mangrove and lemon trees. Behind the garden stood a bathing pool, which was hidden by bushes laden with roses, jasmine and geranium. The place looked like heaven on earth.

Trelawny was admitted by an elderly caretaker, who had received orders from De Ruyter to admit him, and found that the interior, resting on bamboo uprights, was as attractive as the exterior. Food and rest were far more important than an examination of the décor, however, and after eating a huge meal provided by the caretaker's wife, Trelawny went to bed.

For the next forty-eight hours he did little but eat, sleep, and swim in the pool. He even developed a friend in a small, wiry-haired yak owned by the caretaker's children. But hiding out was a new experience for him, and he became increasingly restless.

At last a messenger arrived with a letter bringing good tidings from De Ruyter.

The frigate had sailed, leaving Bombay twenty-four hours late because of a search that had been conducted for the missing midshipman. Walter had been suspected of aiding his escape and had been placed under arrest for a short time. He had been released, though, when De Ruyter appeared on his behalf and testified that he had acted as Walter's escort from the time the newly commissioned army officer had come ashore. Neither had seen Midshipman Trelawny.

De Ruyter's report on the Scottish lieutenant's condition gave Trelawny a great deal of pleasure. The semiconscious officer had been carried on board the frigate suffering from two broken ribs and a dislocated jaw. He had also lost several teeth and, not yet being able to speak coherently, hadn't been able to reveal that his injuries were caused by the missing midshipman.

For the next few days, Trelawny lounged around the property, wearing nothing but an Indian loincloth of striped cotton. He swam, climbed coconut trees, worked in the garden and sun-bathed his already dark skin. In the evenings he smoked a hookah and read books he found in De Ruyter's extensive library —the most enjoyable of which was a life of John Paul Jones.

Neither then nor at any later time did Trelawny suffer a twinge of remorse or guilt over his desertion from the Royal Navy. Having found the life of an apprentice officer confining and lacking in dignity, he abandoned it. Not once did he look back over his shoulder. The Navy had deprived him of his free-dom, and that was sufficient justification for his act, even if it was in time of war. To a boy who had been forced to make his own way in the world since childhood, what mattered was the achieve-ment of his goal: liberty. He had succeeded, and the Navy could do without him as easily as he could do without it.

Never before had he known entire days of full happiness. In his ecstasy he imagined that his joy would never end. He learned to make "toddy," a mixture of fresh and fermented coconut milk, and he prepared a large quantity of it for the celebration he would make for his friends when they joined him. After he had spent a week at the bungalow he finally received a message say-ing they had left Bombay and were on the road.

So he went to meet them, wearing only the loincloth, riding the small yak and balancing a bamboo pole—pots of toddy at either end—across his shoulders. His disguise was so effective that, when they finally met, De Ruyter recognized his yak before he was able to place the man atop it.

The party went on to the bungalow, and for several days Trelawny and Walter lived the dream that had sustained them high in the rigging of the frigate. They ate when they were hungry, slept when they were tired and swam when they were hot. They climbed hills, chased jackals and visited several villages, where they were fascinated by the native customs.

But Walter, it soon developed, no longer had intentions of leading a primitive life. When his leave of absence ended, he planned to return to Bombay and resume those activities he had first mentioned to Trelawny in the Bombay tavern: army duties.

Walter tried in vain to persuade his friend to join him, but the mere idea caused Trelawny to erupt. When one served the King and the East India Company, one was bribed with gold, with hollow charms. The honors bought nothing, and the gold could buy only bread. There was bread of a higher sort to be found in India's soft mountains, Trelawny was convinced.

Walter's experiences had made him a more shrewd observer of human nature, and he commented that his friend could not survive without glory and fighting. It was true, Trelawny admitted, that he enjoyed a good fight, but he found no pleasure in taking part in a battle at another's command, and at another's expense. When he fought hereafter it would be to help others attain freedom from the tyranny of oppressors.

Walter was impressed by his rhetoric but was insistent that his friend look into the possibilities of army life. Trelawny finally agreed to go back to Bombay with him for the purpose of conducting an investigation. Neither boy seemed to be afraid that Trelawny would be arrested as a deserter, and De Ruyter made no objection either, for he realized that the Royal Navy and the Army took care not to know too much about each other's affairs. Each frequently found it convenient to grant a commission to the other's deserter.

Barracks life seemed pleasant enough on the surface. The food was far superior to navy fare, the officers were convivial, hard-drinking gentlemen who didn't work too hard and spent a great deal of time participating in sports, and the atmosphere was congenial. But Trelawny did not allow himself to be fooled by these surface manifestations of military existence. An army officer's life, like that of a navy officer, was regimented; there were regulations to be obeyed, and the transgressor was punished. No man who wore the King's uniform could be truly free, the boy decided, and after bidding Walter good-by he returned to the bungalow.

De Ruyter, who awaited him, allowed him to resume his holiday, and for several days more Trelawny ate, drank, swam and played in the open. Then, one afternoon, De Ruyter brought him up short with a question: what did he intend to do for the rest of his life?

Trelawny was startled; he had been enjoying himself so much that he had been a complete hedonist and had not thought in terms of tomorrow.

He was welcome to stay at the bungalow as long as he pleased, De Ruyter told him. The children of the caretaker lived there, and he could make his home there, too. The man paused, then added quietly that he gathered his young friend had abandoned his idea of living a life of adventure.

The prospect of staying on at the bungalow was irresistible, driving every other consideration out of Trelawny's mind.

De Ruyter, who was leaving at once, shook hands with him, strolled to the door and turned.

*"Remember," he said, "if you should weary of your pastoral life, I have a lovely little craft, well armed and formed for peace or war, as occasion serves; she lacks an enterprising young officer, and I had thought you might fill the vacancy."*

*"You never told me," I cried. "Where is she? Let me have a look at her! How is she rigged? Where does she lie? How many tons? How many men?"*

De Ruyter's laugh cut through the torrent of questions, and after raising one hand in a mocking salute he vanished.

Trelawny returned to earth—the bathing pool, coconut trees and other manifestations of paradise losing their savor. He would have followed De Ruyter but did not know where his friend had gone, and the servants were unable to help him, knowing nothing of their master's activities. A full week passed, and by the time De Ruyter had returned the boy's restlessness had driven him almost mad. He was ready to abandon his "pastoral" life without delay and eagerly agreed to accompany De Ruyter into Bombay the following morning.

They rode together into the city, with Trelawny wearing the appropriate civilian attire his friend had purchased for him. They went down to the familiar waterfront, where they saw De Ruyter's two vessels. The hands were hustling about, unloading a cargo of cotton and spices that the East India Company had already purchased. But Trelawny's eyes fixed only on the vessels themselves. One was a dhow, a clumsy cargo vessel with a raking of bamboo. But the other, an "Arab grab brig," which was a slender version of a sleek English schooner, was a real beauty. Trelawny particularly admired her long bow—as lean as a thin wedge—and the ease with which she rode in the water.

They were welcomed on board by her captain, an English-speaking Arab, and Trelawny noted that the sailors working on deck were also Arabs, savage-looking men in turbans and gold-embroidered red tunics. Below, keeping carefully out of the sight of the port authorities, were a number of other Caucasian seamen: most of them Danes, Swedes and Americans.

Without exception they were all good men, De Ruyter remarked, "ready to fly aloft in a squall or board an enemy in battle."

The statement was provocative, and Trelawny tried to question him.

The grab had a gross weight of three hundred fifty tons, De Ruyter said, and was fitted for war as well as peace. So was the dhow, he added, and changed the subject by asking his young friend's opinion of the cargo ship.

Trelawny sputtered. The grab was a sailor's dream, but the dhow was a seagoing elephant, little better than a garbage scow fit to haul potato peelings and scrap down the Thames from London.

De Ruyter laughed. His opinion of the dhow wasn't important, because he would sail in the grab. How would he like to sail her down the coast to Goa, as her captain?

Trelawny could only gape at him, certain he was joking. A promotion from midshipman to captain was beyond even his own vivid imagination.

But De Ruyter was serious. He had kept his young friend under observation for weeks and was certain he was a leader of men; they had never sailed together, to be sure, but anyone who had been a student officer in the Royal Navy for five years obviously knew ships and the sea.

Trelawny was still too stunned to speak.

Would he accept?

The boy nodded.

Very well. De Ruyter issued crisp orders. Trelawny would command the grab, with the Arab captain, known as the rais, acting as his first lieutenant and translating his orders for the benefit of the non-English-speaking members of the crew. Trelawny would go on board during the evening and would sail promptly at midnight. In the meantime he would tell no one of his assignment, would avoid Walter and, if he went to the navy officers' tavern, would not drink. De Ruyter hurried off down the wharf and disappeared into the crowd on shore.

Trelawny followed more slowly, afraid he was dreaming. Without thinking, he started in the direction of the tavern, then realized where he was going and turned away in time. Throughout the long day, he followed De Ruyter's instructions to the letter, and at noon, when he ate a light meal at a bazaar stall, he drank nothing stronger than tea. It occurred to him that he had no gear for a new seafaring expedition, so he bought a chest, then made purchases of various items to fill it. Ordinarily he would have had these new belongings sent to the ship, but he preferred to take no chances whatever, and in spite of the heat he carried the cumbersome chest all afternoon. He could not resist buying several books and, late in the day, found a pistol he liked, as well as an Arab scimitar.

Heavily laden, he went on board shortly before sundown, and the rais, who had received a detailed letter from De Ruyter, greeted him with a salute. What were his orders?

Modeling his behavior on Lieutenant Aston's, Trelawny was friendly—but not too friendly. The boats were to be hauled in, he directed, giving his first orders; all equipment was to be inspected, and the ship was to be made ready to sail at midnight. Nodding to the crew, again imitating Aston, he went below to inspect his realm.

Her waist was deep, and her portholes were battened, except for two forward and four aft, where 9-pounder cannon were situated. Her forecastle was raised, and under the low poop was the cabin he would occupy. It was large, with good light, and was cooled through the stern ports. The forward bulkhead was lined with weapons: muskets, bayonets, pistols, metal-tipped spears with weighted bamboo shafts and the most wicked of swords, the wavy-bladed Malay *kris*. The young captain could not resist the urge to slip one into his belt.

The after bulkhead was filled with books, many of them on navigation and seamanship. There were shelves piled with writing materials, drawing materials, telescopes and nautical instruments. Charts were suspended from the deck above, and the transposed compass was hanging from the center beam. There were two berths in the cabin, each of them as comfortable as the best of beds on shore; there were a writing table and three chairs as well. The boy who had been forced to hang his hammock in the midshipmen's quarters just a few months before was slightly dizzy when he realized that all this luxury was his.

Night had fallen by the time he came on deck again; the lights of Bombay were burning beyond the wharf, and the members of the crew were eating their evening meal. The Westerners were gathered in one group and ate a stew of meat, potatoes and vegetables. The Indians and Arabs, divided by caste, squatted on their heels and consumed various dishes, among them rice, ghee, fresh fruit, dried chilies, curry and bummalo.

It occurred to Trelawny that he, too, was famished, and at the same instant he realized that the etiquette of the sea required him to dine alone. He returned to his cabin, passing the quarters of the rais and second officer, who were eating there, and when he pulled a bell rope for the steward after reaching his cabin, his own meal was produced with alacrity. He ate it at the writing desk, discovering that the food was first-rate, the best he had ever consumed on a ship. He was served neither wine nor beer; the only beverage was tea. He did not regret the absence of alcoholic beverages, though: not only did he remember De Ruyter's instructions, but his sense of responsibility was so acute he wanted nothing to interfere with his judgment.

It is of great significance that, for the first time in *Younger Son,* Trelawny mentions his awareness of personal responsibility; it had been born the moment De Ruyter gave him command of the grab. The man's gamble was paying dividends; he had judged the character of his young friend correctly. He suspected that Trelawny would not shirk his duty, and he was right. In fact, this former midshipman who had detested any form of discipline suddenly saw the matter in a new light. Reasonable discipline was necessary at sea, he realized, and it was essential that a captain's orders be obeyed without delay or question.

A half hour before midnight, the master of the grab went for the first trip up to his quarter-deck and was pleased to see that the crew was hustling about the main deck below him under the able supervision of the rais and the second officer. There was no need for him to give any commands; every man knew his business, and the new captain could enjoy the sensation of watching an efficient crew at work.

Only he could give the final orders, however, and at one minute before midnight he once again imitated Lieutenant Aston as he spoke quietly to the rais. "Be good enough to raise your foresails, mister."

"Aye aye, sir."

Sixty seconds later, Captain Trelawny spoke again. "If you please, mister, cast off!"

The grab began to inch her way out of the crowded Bombay harbor, and Trelawny truly embarked on the life of adventure and discovery that had controlled his dreams for the past five years.

## VI

## *"The sea was my true and only home."*

Trelawny was on his quarter-deck at daybreak, and when the early-morning mist began to clear away, he saw another ship heading toward him under full sail. He recognized the dhow, changed course in order to meet her, and a short time later welcomed De Ruyter on board. The man and his young protégé went to the cabin together for breakfast, and Trelawny finally learned the story of his mentor's life, which so impressed him that he retold it in detail twenty years later, in *Younger Son*.

It was De Ruyter's idealism that had left an indelible mark on him, permanently coloring his own thinking. The man was a passionate advocate of democracy and believed that his native United States guaranteed greater liberty for all men than any other nation. But America was a weak, struggling little country, completely lacking influence in a world of cynical, self-aggrandizing giants. The worst offender, in De Ruyter's opinion, was Great Britain, which paid lip service to freedom while accumulating vast wealth at the expense of the people whom it conquered and then quickly exploited. The East India Company in particular was a cruel octopus that was strangling tens of millions of persons. It held a vast subcontinent in a state of semislavery and permitted only a few men, its own of course, to enjoy wealth and power.

De Ruyter had achieved a modest success as a legitimate merchant, but when it had become obvious to him that the principles in which he believed were being stifled by Britain, he declared a personal war on her and also on her semiofficial subsidiary the East India Company. He called himself a privateer, although a more accurate word would have been pirate. Within the past month, he told Trelawny, he had captured a merchantman belonging to the East India Company, had sold the captured vessel to the French and had disposed of her cargo in Bombay. He had thereby forced the company to pay him a handsome profit for its own merchandise. As a rule he sailed under the French flag, and as the war between Europe's major powers was still raging, Napoleon's colonial governors in the East were delighted to co-operate with their ally.

Trelawny's enthusiasm for his friend's approach to life was so overwhelming that it is impossible to determine whether De Ruyter was sincere, whether he rationalized, or whether he put an attractive coating on his piracy for his young friend's sake. Whatever his motives, the young Englishman accepted his statements at face value. Apparently, it did not occur to Trelawny that De Ruyter, who was supposedly striking blow after blow for freedom, was accumulating a massive fortune of his own. Everything that the man said confirmed the youth's own views, and Trelawny was convinced that by joining De Ruyter he, too, would be an active participant in the fight for universal liberty. Neither in *Younger Son* nor in any of his other writings did Trelawny indicate that he might be guilty of faulty reasoning, that he leaped at the excuse to become a fighter for human rights because the life De Ruyter offered him would be one filled with the adventure he craved.

Certainly Trelawny was not greedy, and the possibility that he could amass a fortune of his own by disreputable methods did not occur to him. He enjoyed personal comforts, but his life had been a Spartan one since early childhood. He did not crave the luxuries that made other men turn to piracy. Romantic adventure for its own sake mattered more to him than all else. And if he could be convinced that he was pursuing his goal of attaining liberty and dignity for men of all nations, races and creeds, why then he could not ask for more.

He thought of himself as blessed by fate, and so, although he listened with care to the instructions De Ruyter gave him, he did not flinch. The British authorities in India might very well take a dim enough view of piracy that they would simply ignore English common law and hang buccaneers without bothering to place them on trial first. Nevertheless, the youth Trelawny believed that by exercising caution he could get along dashingly. He would keep his new vocation to himself and adopt a disguise. He was so dark that De Ruyter ordered him to assume the disguise of an Arab. The rais would attend to the details; De Ruyter urged him only to learn the Arab tongue as rapidly as possible.

De Ruyter returned to the dhow, and Trelawny put himself in the hands of the rais, who gave him an Arab costume to wear and taught him the fundamentals of Mohammedan behavior. He learned to go through the motions of facing Mecca and praying, how to squat or sit on a low cushion at meals and eat only with one hand. When he appeared on deck the entire crew applauded him, and he was assured that he could pass as an Arab anywhere.

The voyage down the coast was virtually uneventful. The dhow rejoined the grab as Trelawny approached Goa.

Situated about two hundred fifty miles south of Bombay, on the south western coast of India, the town of Goa was the capital of Portuguese India. It had been conquered in 1510. Once one of the most important settlements in the East, Goa had declined over the centuries and was, when Trelawny knew it, a sleepy little community built on the land adjacent to the ruins of a very ancient city. There was hardly any real shipping activity in Goa, for trade had declined enormously since Portugal's halcyon days as a sea power. Goa was used principally as a port where contraband merchandise could be sold or bought with no questions asked.

Surprisingly enough, however, during the months before Trelawny's stopping there, the governor and his aides had been displaying a stern attitude. Portugal was Britain's close ally, and the strain of the war with France was being felt all over the world. So the officials of Goa had been instructed by Lisbon to display greater vigilance in apprehending and prosecuting all privateers working against Britain's best interests.

De Ruyter had business of his own to attend to—with a maharajah living inland. Thus, he left the disposal of the cargo of rice and coffee to Trelawny and the rais. Trelawny's anxiety mounted with each passing day, as did that of the rais and the crew. If the grab and the dhow were recognized, the authorities would place their officers and men under arrest. They would be compelled to execute the adventurers even though, in past days, Portuguese colonial authorities had been lenient in their treatment of men such as these.

Still, the cargo was able to be sold within a few days, and so Trelawny had nothing to occupy him while he awaited instructions from De Ruyter. There were waterfront taverns in the town, but he was afraid to drink when he might be urged to put out to sea on short notice. From the deck of the grab, which rode at anchor in the harbor, he could see attractive young women on shore, but caution, nevertheless, was stronger than desire. One of these women could turn out to be a government informer, and certainly his Arab pose was a bit too new and his knowledge of Arabic too limited for him to be able to trust himself to maintain his fiction to the point of not arousing suspicion with those whom he might make love to. Hence, he remained on board and fretted.

After a long week of waiting, however, he received a message from De Ruyter, who promised to arrive at sundown and wrote, too, that they would sail as soon as he arrived. When night came, everything was set for an immediate departure. But Trelawny was nonetheless relieved when he saw his mentor signaling to him in the flesh as he started toward Trelawny's ship in a boat rented from the docks. Trelawny gave the order for the dhow to sail without further delay.

As De Ruyter was being rowed to the ship, a Portuguese government cutter was sighted. It was filled with armed customs agents and was approaching from the other direction. De Ruyter seized the oars from the Goan with him in the boat and rowed himself. As he leaped on board, Trelawny, who had been standing with an ax in his hands, cut the grab's cable, accidentally "taking a chip" out of the leg of an Arab sailor who was standing too close to him.

The grab's sails were hoisted. And she began to move out of range of the cutter, customs men being unable to fire at her because the harbor was crowded with small merchantmen. Trelawny hurried to the quarter-deck. Yet, even in this emergency, De Ruyter did not assume the command himself; he allowed his young friend to take the ship out to sea himself.

Two small warships were stationed at Goa, either of them capable of overtaking the grab. But Portuguese lethargy reasserted itself, and at dawn the following day, Trelawny was able to reassure himself that they had not been followed. De Ruyter, Trelawny and the rais were joined for a celebratory breakfast by two other crew members: Louis, the purser, whom Trelawny liked for his amiable manner and competence in cooking, and Van Scolpvelt, the surgeon, whom Trelawny disliked for what he believed was a sadistic streak and an overly clinical mind.

Louis, as custom and duty would have it, prepared breakfast for the group in the main cabin, and while they ate his exquisite food, everyone alike praised the conduct of the young captain. He was indeed earning the right to call the quarter-deck of the grab his own.

At the conclusion of the breakfast, De Ruyter revealed his plans. Instead of making a cruise in search of British merchant shipping, they would sail to the island of Mauritius, known to the French occupation authorities as the Île de France. De Ruyter would be carrying important letters from the maharajah of Mysore and other prominent Indians to the French governor at Port Louis. But this did not mean that he would neglect his primary business: the Laccadive Islands would be the first port of call, and De Ruyter would simply let the French governor wait if he encountered a heavily laden British merchantman.

As fate would settle it, though, a dead calm delayed the voyage, and for days the grab was forced to sit still like "a painted ship upon a painted ocean." De Ruyter, always on the alert, however, ordered Trelawny to change the grab from a ship of peace into a ship of war. The 9-pound cannons were mounted and the gun ports lowered. Two furnaces were stoked so that shot might be heated; the magazine was put in order, and the crew was exercised daily in the use of small arms. Trelawny himself took hours of instruction from the rais in the use of the *kris* and the bamboo-shafted spear.

After sundown, when the rais or the second officer took the watch, things eased down considerably and Trelawny would sit in the main cabin and listen to De Ruyter discuss literature. De Ruyter spoke with equal facility about the works of Shakespeare and the novels of Defoe, Fielding, Sterne and Smollett. He talked intelligently about the poetry of Milton, Pope and Ossian and delved at length into the philosophy of Jeremy Bentham, John Locke and Rousseau. Delivering numerous lectures on the exploits of the great military captains of history, from Alexander and Caesar to the 1st Duke of Marlborough, he found time to bring mathematicians alive for his young disciple.

Trelawny was fascinated, his interest doubly roused when he discovered that most of the books under discussion were within reach on the bulkhead. Had he been in England now, his chronological age would have permitted his attendance at Oxford. De Ruyter, knowing that such a thing would never come to pass, was indeed responsible for doing all that could be done to spark Trelawny's desire for the equivalent of a higher education. Over a period of many months, Trelawny not only read every book in the cabin's library but added many others to it as he made purchases on his travels.

De Ruyter was an educated man. And Trelawny wanted to emulate his mentor. But the youth was motivated, in the main, by a general, almost self-generating desire for knowledge—a thirst that would remain active for as long as he breathed. He enjoyed no more than three years of formal schooling, yet he later associated as an intellectual equal with some of the most brilliant, best-educated men of the age. Trelawny believed he was in De Ruyter's debt, but that is only a part of the story; he acquired an education because of his own curiosity and also because of his rapidly developing, and prodigious, ability to remember all he read. It is no wonder that, many years later, Tom Moore, a fine poet, would comment that Trelawny could have become a renowned bishop or professor had he enjoyed a different background.

Trelawny was listening to one of De Ruyter's lectures on literature when a thunderstorm called him to the quarter-deck. The wind sprang up, and thirty-six hours later the grab found itself approaching the Laccadive Islands. No accurate charts had ever been made, but De Ruyter knew the treacherous coral reefs and negotiated them with ease. Natives appeared in proas, or outrigger canoes, to welcome the ship, and after casting anchor Trelawny led a party ashore to buy bananas, coconuts and fish, and to obtain water from a natural spring—"the most delicious that ever I tasted."

While he was about this errand, three Persian merchantmen dropped anchor nearby, and after Trelawny returned to the grab, De Ruyter sent him to the flagship accompanied by ten heavily armed men. Trelawny was sent to obtain information and brought back exciting news. The Persians had been attacked only a few hours earlier by a Malay pirate, which had made off with their most valuable merchandise. Even the inexperienced Trelawny knew how De Ruyter would react; he was not surprised when he was ordered to sail without delay.

The grab went in search of the Malay, and less than twenty-four hours later found her making her way eastward. De Ruyter took charge, ordering the French flag raised, and the Malay tried to run. When she came within range, a shot was fired across her bow as a warning, but her captain immediately served notice that he had no intention of giving in without a fight. He had eight cannon on board his pirate ship and greeted his enemy with a salvo of grape—or nails, bits of jagged metal and broken glass. Three members of the grab's crew were wounded.

De Ruyter ordered the grab to close in, and then directed a well-aimed fire just above the water line, hoping to incapacitate but not destroy his foe. The Malay continued to fight, however, and when the two vessels drew together Trelawny failed in an attempt to lead a boarding party onto the deck of the enemy ship.

De Ruyter was forced to fall back, making it clear to his disciple that he could not give up the battle without losing face to the Easterners he so often dealt with. He no longer had a choice, he declared, and gave orders to sink the Malay. Scores of shots were fired, and soon after the Malay's superstructure was destroyed, a shot landed in her powder magazine. The explosion rocked the grab, and a plume of smoke rose from the Malay, followed by high, leaping flames.

Members of the grab's crew believed they saw bolts of cloth, treasure chests and boxes of rare spices floating around in the water, but Trelawny, participating in his first major naval engagement, could see only the men jumping into water. More than three hundred Malays abandoned ship; a number of them were wounded, and their blood attracted a vast number of sharks. A few shrill cries of terror and pain reached the quarterdeck of the grab, but within minutes the seething sea grew quiet again. No bodies were visible, and only broken spars, shreds of sail and bits of tackle could be seen floating in the water. A few moments later, the shattered Malay vessel seemed to rear high in the air for a moment and then vanished beneath the surface.

De Ruyter called the spectacle sad, but said the obstinacy of the Malay had given him no choice. Had he allowed the enemy to escape, word would have spread throughout the Indian Ocean that he was a coward, and other privateers would have given him no peace.

The grab returned to her original course and, after again passing the Laccadives, put into Diego Rayes for food and water. The following morning, while Trelawny and De Ruyter were at breakfast, an urgent summons from the rais brought them to the quarter-deck. Two ships were heading toward them, twin dots on the horizon that grew larger by the moment. Trelawny looked at them through his glass and knew at once they were Royal Navy frigates. It was not difficult to figure out their mission, either; they were searching for French privateers en route to Port Louis.

Discretion was the better part of valor, and the grab fled. But the British frigates pursued her, and the chase lasted for days. The race was too swift for one of the warships, and she dropped away, but the other persisted, even though De Ruyter used every trick he knew to shake it. Sometimes, at sundown, he thought he had escaped her, but she reappeared the following morning, still tailing him. After several days of playing hide and seek, he decided to make a run for a small island he knew, a place surrounded by dangerous reefs. His destination was a cove "scarcely larger than an albatross's nest," which could be reached only by a channel so narrow and tortuous that the larger frigate could obviously not follow. She would have to send boats ashore if her captain demanded a reckoning.

The grab reached the island; it was fortunate the sea was calm, as not even De Ruyter would have tried to navigate through the reefs and the channel in rough seas. At last the ship dropped anchor in the cove, gunports were lowered, and cannon crews were ordered to their battle stations. A tense period of waiting followed, broken only when Van Scolpvelt appeared, a surgical instrument in one of his bony hands, and "looking like a carrion kite smelling blood." He wanted to know how soon he could expect wounded in his surgery, and Trelawny, on edge as never before, sent him below again with a curse.

After more than a half hour's wait, a longboat from the frigate began to negotiate the reefs and eventually moved into the channel. The grab was sighted, and the crew of the longboat, thinking the quarry had been cornered, began to cheer. De Ruyter immediately ordered the French flag raised and opened fire on the longboat.

The battle was joined, and moments later other British boats appeared. They closed in on the grab, and a fierce hand-to-hand fight broke out. When Trelawny first saw the Union Jack fluttering from the prow of the lead boat he was momentarily stunned, but his loyalty to De Ruyter overcame every other obstacle; he soon forgot that he was fighting his fellow countrymen.

Trelawny fought like a demon, a cutlass in one hand, a *kris* in the other. He received a flesh wound in his left arm but was unaware of it. A pistol butt smashed into his face, but he felt no pain. He sustained a number of additional injuries but continued to fight until he saw the longboats drawing off. Scarcely able to believe what he was witnessing, he watched the British withdrawing, leaving their wounded behind on the deck of the grab.

Suddenly a tall British officer ran toward the grab's quarterdeck, apparently the only uninjured member of the boarding party who had remained behind. He had a sword in his hand, and a moment later was locked in a duel with De Ruyter. The Englishman was gallant but was no match for the seasoned privateer, who wielded his cutlass with such cold efficiency that the officer's sword flew out of his hand and sailed into the sea.

The exhausted Trelawny, leaning wearily against a mast and trying to wipe the blood from his face with his sash, peered hard at the quarter-deck and thought he was dreaming. The disarmed officer was Lieutenant Aston!

# VII

## *"Aston—don't you know me?"*

The incredulous Trelawny staggered toward the quarter-deck
and screamed. De Ruyter and the man he had just beaten in a
duel looked at the youth, who now, more than ever, resembled
an Arab. There was no recognition in Lieutenant Aston's eyes.

"Aston—don't you know me?" Trelawny asked, and crumpled
unconscious on the deck.

For the next forty-eight hours he hovered between life and
death. Occasionally he awakened for a few moments, sometimes
seeing the face of De Ruyter above him, sometimes that of Lieutenant Aston. The latter convinced him he was dreaming.

After two days and nights, however, he passed the crisis point
and again became conscious of his surroundings. He learned that
the British wounded who were able to be moved had been safely
returned to the frigate. The frigate had then sailed away, leaving
Lieutenant Aston and a midshipman, a marine captain and several enlisted men as prisoners.

Aston, who had moved to another ship soon after Trelawny's
desertion, had a brief reunion with him that morning. The

youth's first friend and teacher did not say in so many words that
he had forgiven him for his abandonment of the Navy but indicated that he was willing to let bygones be bygones. He hinted
that he could not blame Trelawny for feeling as he did.

That night, a gala dinner was held in the main cabin of the
grab. De Ruyter had shot a wild boar on the island that afternoon, so there were ample quantities of fresh grilled meat on the
table. The privateer's best Madeira was, likewise, served. All
three of the captured British officers were in attendance, and
they agreed the frigate captain had been stupid to send his longboats against an enemy whose position had been invulnerable.

Trelawny had the time of his life, even though his face and
head were heavily bandaged, his wounded arm ached and there
was a large, unhealed gash in his side. His comments in *Younger
Son* reveal his euphoria:

> *Everything went by pleasantly and merrily. I was associated
> with the two men I most admired and loved, Aston and De
> Ruyter. Although, to a casual observer, no two men could seem
> so dissimilar, at the core they were the same; they had the same
> stability of character, heroic courage, gentle and affectionate
> manners and open, manly bearing. They soon grew fast friends.
> I now wanted only Walter; and then, if a deluge had swallowed
> up all the world and the grab had been our ark, I should have
> lost nothing to weep for.*

The presence of a dozen and a half prisoners made life on
board the grab too crowded for comfort, and conditions were so
unsanitary that De Ruyter, who knew something about diseases
in the tropics, became concerned. His problem was solved, however, when a French corvette anchored off the coast and her captain proved to be an old and trusted friend. De Ruyter conferred
with him, and thereafter all the Englishmen, with the exception of Lieutenant Aston and four select seamen, were transferred to the larger vessel.

The same evening, the corvette captain invited De Ruyter,
Aston and Trelawny to dine with him. The conversation was ex-
clusively in French, and Trelawny, who was taking lessons in
French from Louis, happily found that he had mastered enough

to understand most of what was said and to make a few contributions of his own to the conversation.

The corvette was on a mission to Madagascar, where Maratti pirates were making life miserable for all European shipping, and its captain wanted De Ruyter to join him. But the American was reluctant, in part because his letters to the governor of the Île de France had not yet been delivered and partly because he disliked making war on natives. All Europeans, he declared, regardless of whether they were English, Dutch, French, Spanish or Portuguese, were alike; they were in the habit of "slaughtering natives whenever they wanted a salad or a fresh egg."

The corvette captain did not give up easily, however, and reminded De Ruyter that the Maratti were notorious slave dealers, which put another light on the matter. He suggested the grab sail with him in the hope of finding another ship that would deliver the letters. De Ruyter agreed, and the two vessels sailed together the next day, having taken on ample supplies of fresh water and wild fruits.

Two days later, they encountered a schooner sailing in the opposite direction, and De Ruyter, standing with Trelawny on the quarter-deck, immediately identified her as American. Ships built in the United States, he declared, could be recognized anywhere in the world. They were sleek, with clean, functional lines, American naval architects being more practical than most of their competitors.

The grab and the corvette raised their French colors; the schooner captain hoisted an American flag, and within minutes he was crossing the water in his gig. He had a long chat with De Ruyter, who was eager to hear news from home. That news was ominous. A new war threatened to erupt between the United States and Great Britain in spite of efforts being made by President James Madison to avert open hostilities. The British were insisting on maintaining the right to halt and search American merchantmen on the high seas, and many innocent men were being impressed into the Royal Navy. But this, the schooner captain declared, was just an excuse. The real cause of the harassment was British jealousy of America's growing foreign trade.

It developed that the American captain was bound for the Île de France with a cargo, but he was disturbed when De Ruyter told him the Royal Navy was maintaining a blockade of Port Louis. De Ruyter eased some of the American's distress, however, when he told him that he could enter via the somewhat difficult harbor of Port Bourbon, on the opposite side of the island. De Ruyter, furthermore, provided a number of charts for the purpose.

The grateful schooner captain readily agreed, in return, to deliver De Ruyter's letters to the governor and, in addition, sent over a hogshead of claret, a pipe of brandy and a supply of various delicacies. De Ruyter, whose home had been Boston, was particularly pleased with a gift of white beans, which he baked himself with strips of wild hog bacon. Louis turned up his Gallic nose at the dish, calling it "swill," and neither Trelawny nor Aston was particularly fond of it. But De Ruyter pronounced it ambrosial.

A messenger having been found to deliver the letters from the Indian potentates to the governor of the Île de France, the grab sailed on to Madagascar with the corvette. And Trelawny learned about the people the expedition intended to conquer.

The Maratti were a predatory tribe who made their strongholds deep in the mountainous interior of Madagascar. Originally natives of the African mainland, they had made their living for centuries by preying on the weaker, agricultural tribes of the island. Then, when Europeans had come to the waters of the East, the Maratti had resumed their seafaring ways and for the better part of three hundred years had been successful as marauders. At one time or another the English, Dutch and Portuguese had sent naval expeditions against them, and each of these ventures had been seemingly successful. The Maratti had abandoned their frail craft and had retreated into their walled towns in the northern part of Madagascar, but they had reappeared as soon as the Europeans had gone.

Since the middle of the seventeenth century, the Maratti had added an even more profitable vocation to their work as pirates. They sent expeditions to the mainland or to other parts of Madagascar, and their raiders returned with large numbers of young captives, who were branded and held in pens, then sold to slave traders of various European countries, who earned vast fortunes in the slave markets of North America and the Caribbean.

So many prominent citizens of every leading European nation were involved in the slave trade that their governments found it convenient to close their eyes to the entire degrading procedure. The Maratti would have been let alone if they had not made one major mistake. They had captured a French merchantman, confiscated its cargo and murdered the entire crew, thereafter scuttling the ship. The Emperor Napoleon, before whom the monarchs of the world's most advanced nations bowed in meek submission, felt his honor had been stained at the hands of savages. So he sent the corvette to teach the Maratti a lesson, even though every warship was needed in the war with Great Britain.

The corvette carried a crew of only two hundred officers and men, and even though she carried heavy armaments, there was relatively little she could do against a tribe as strong and belligerent as the Maratti. That was why her captain had been so anxious to obtain help from De Ruyter; that was also why De Ruyter had shown no great enthusiasm for the project.

Trelawny, always eager for the battle, saw a campaign against slave traders as a holy crusade. Each evening, while the commanders of both ships and their immediate subordinates dined together, he attempted to ignite De Ruyter's spirit to fight. Lieutenant Aston, whose position was that of a non-participating guest, was both amused and impressed by Trelawny's unflagging energy.

As the two ships drew nearer the coast of the huge island of Madagascar, they came upon the remains of a fleet of small Arab vessels straggling homeward after an encounter with the Maratti. They had been attacked, they said, by approximately twenty proas, each one manned by forty Maratti, and the encounter had been catastrophic. Every able-bodied man on board the Arab ships had been taken off into slavery, cargoes had been confiscated and only the elderly and infirm were still on board.

The news finally dispelled the last of De Ruyter's reluctance. It was believed the Maratti could send a total force of about two thousand men into combat, regardless of whether it be a battle on land or on sea. Approximately half of this number made their permanent headquarters in Nossi Ibrahim, on the eastern coast of Madagascar, the town that had gained notoriety throughout the civilized world as a slave market. In all probability hundreds, perhaps thousands of slaves were there, awaiting sale, and there was little doubt in De Ruyter's mind that they would rise up and co-operate with a landing party that offered them the hope of freedom. But neither the grab nor the corvette carried spare firearms—which the slaves had never used in any case—and these nineteenth-century freedom fighters would be mercilessly slaughtered by their captors, before they could revolt.

A careful analysis of the situation indicated that the two ships, with total manpower of perhaps five hundred useful men, could not make a successful assault on Nossi Ibrahim. A far more attractive target was the town of St. Sebastian, on the northern coast of Madagascar. This was the central headquarters and main administrative center of the Maratti, and De Ruyter reasoned that, with eight hundred men having just taken part in the attack on the Arab merchant fleet, a force of no more than two hundred had been left to protect St. Sebastian.

So it was agreed that St. Sebastian would be the operational target, with men from the two ships raiding, burning and killing, then withdrawing once more under cover of their ships' guns. There were three main gates, and it was agreed that De Ruyter, who would be in over-all command of the landing party, would, with the largest single force, attack the main gate. The corvette captain was to stay on board his vessel to direct the cover operation, so it was arranged that his first lieutenant would lead the assault on the second gate.

Command of the third landing party, a tiny force of the best and most seasoned of the grab's Arabs was given to Trelawny. Although his force was small, his assignment was critical. The last of the town gates was on the inland side of St. Sebastian, on high ground, making it necessary for Trelawny and his men to scale a cliff, then circle to the rear of the town wall and storm the gate. If they failed to seal this "port of entry" off, the Maratti would be in a position to utilize their traditional and, up to this point, invincible means of escape to the mountains.

As the two ships drew closer to St. Sebastian, they saw a small Portuguese merchantman coming from the town and halted her so they could question her captain. He was able to give them one piece of valuable information: some of the prisoners who had been captured in the attack on the Arab merchant ships had already reached the town and were being held there under close guard.

This news gave De Ruyter and the corvette captain the perfect excuse for launching their own assault. The Western world might regard a retaliatory attack for its own sake with a somewhat skeptical eye, but the release of helpless prisoners, peaceful and honorable people who would be forced into slavery if not rescued, was a highly commendable motive. So De Ruyter issued firm instructions to the landing parties. Maratti women and children were to be spared, he said, and Maratti warriors were to be killed only when they resisted the invaders. The purpose of the attack was the release of prisoners, and the shedding of blood was to be avoided whenever possible.

Neither the officers nor the men who would take part in the landing accepted these orders at face value, and it is unlikely that De Ruyter put stock in the force of his own words. He knew, as did every man to whom the instructions were given, that a battle with piratical slave traders would be fought without the granting of quarter by either side.

The two ships waited at sea, out of sight of St. Sebastian's watchtowers, until darkness fell, and then made a swift run for the town. The entrance to the harbor was hard for the novice to negotiate, but De Ruyter knew it as well as he did numerous others in the East. The landing was completed by midnight. The assault units were to take their assigned positions, and the attack was to start at dawn, all three legions closing in when De Ruyter fired a rocket as a signal.

Trelawny had the lengthiest and most harrowing march. He and his men had to work their way up a cliff. They soon found themselves on the lip of a ravine from which they could hear the sounds of rushing water below them. It was obvious then that they would have to find another approach, but Trelawny set a pace so rapid that his men could scarcely keep up with him.

Hours passed before he found a narrow sheep path, overgrown with bushes and prickly pears; it seemed to lead toward the town, so he followed it, even though rocks underfoot made the march even more difficult. Gradually the path got wider and

smoother, which encouraged him, and finally, by the light of a
waning half moon, he caught a glimpse of white clay huts ahead.
He made a reconnaissance, accompanied by only two of his men,
and when he reached the crumbling wall he knew he had
reached his goal.

He sent the two aides for the rest of his party, then explored
the length of the wall until he found a hole through which the
men could crawl. The discovery relaxed his task, making it unnecessary to use the scaling ladders and ropes the men had been
carrying all night. Rain began to fall as the men joined him, and
they crouched together outside the wall as the first, dirty gray
streaks of dawn appeared in the sky.

De Ruyter gave no signal, however, and the sullen sky was
growing lighter with each passing moment. There was no sound
except for the steady hiss of the rain and, in the distance, the
pounding of the surf. Trelawny had complete faith in De Ruyter
but couldn't help wondering if an unexpected catastrophe had
incapacitated his friend.

Right then and there, though, a rocket arched high in the air,
and the instant Trelawny saw it he started to crawl through the
hole, his men close behind him. As soon as he stood erect, a sentry hurried toward him, and the young Englishman killed him
with a single stroke of his *kris*. The man's scream of pain and terror as he died alerted other guards, however, so Trelawny and
his Arabs had to fight their way toward the center of St. Sebastian. They used only cutlass and *kris*, refraining from firing their
muskets because they did not want to reveal their location to an
enemy bewildered by simultaneous assaults from three directions.

The tactics De Ruyter had devised were completely effective;
the Maratti had been taken by surprise and were unable to or-
ganize their defenses. They fought with wild courage, and not
one warrior surrendered; but the carnage was frightful, so much
so that for the rest of Trelawny's life he would feel shame and
self-disgust whenever he remembered the battle. It probably
didn't help his conscience very much when, looking back on the
scene, he would recall that he had completely forgotten about
rescuing the Arab prisoners. Not until he was reunited with the

main body and De Ruyter would Trelawny and his men be sent hurrying toward the collection of huts on sand hills that served as prisons for the prospective slaves.

Had the rescue operation been delayed only a few minutes, all the prisoners would have been dead. The Maratti women, as violent as their men, were using short knives to stab helpless captives, who were bound hand and foot on the ground. Only the quick reflexes of the men from the grab had halted the murders; they killed some of the Maratti women and sent others off and running in wild flight.

Trelawny led several of his men into a hut and stopped short for an instant to take in a frightful scene. An elderly Arab was sprawled on the ground, tied to a stake, covered with blood and half dead. He was making feeble efforts to avoid the cuts and slashes of an old Maratti harridan armed with a coconut knife. Crouched at his feet was a young, half-naked girl, who was trying to protect him but who lacked the strength to ward off the ruthless woman.

Trelawny recovered, killed the old woman and threw her body aside. His men unbound the old Arab, and Trelawny threw his own cloak over the girl. There was a "desperate question" in the eyes of the dying man as Trelawny knelt beside him, and the girl screamed when the Englishman raised his *kris*. But Trelawny placed the hilt in the hand of the old man, saying, "We are friends, father. Fear not. We are friends."

The old Arab understood his gesture, if not his words, stared hard at him for a long moment and appeared satisfied. Taking Trelawny's hand, he placed it against his cold lips for an instant. Then, with great difficulty, he drew a ring from his finger, placed it on Trelawny's and managed to reach for the hand of the girl, which he placed in that of the Englishman. He mumbled something under his breath—long afterward, Trelawny learned it was a blessing—and breathed his last. The girl threw herself on his body, weeping and crying aloud.

Trelawny made the belated discovery that he had suffered a severe gash in his leg at some time during the fighting and was losing so much blood he felt dizzy. He went outside for air, and a moment later was joined by De Ruyter and Lieutenant Aston, who had come ashore strictly as an observer. Maratti warriors in

large numbers were regrouping in the hills above St. Sebastian
for a counterattack, De Ruyter said, and he ordered an immediate evacuation of the town.

Trelawny returned to the hut, where the sobbing girl was still
clinging to the body of the old man. There was no time to reason
with her, even if he could make her understand his words, so he
picked her up and handed her to Lieutenant Aston, asking his
friend to carry her while he himself acted as an escort. The
members of the landing parties, having been successful in their
initial operation, were now out of control. They had found the
raw liquor supplies of the Maratti, and many were drunk; they
had set the town on fire, and their arms were filled with Maratti
booty.

An undisciplined mob was making its way down to the beach,
which was strewn with gold and silver, food of all kinds, precious cloth and jewelry. De Ruyter, aided by the groggy
Trelawny and several French officers, managed to restore order,
and the landing party began to embark in the longboats, which
would carry them to the two ships that awaited them outside the
barrier of a coral reef.

The Maratti raced down from the hills, and a hail of bullets,
arrows and spears descended on the invaders from the cliffs that
ringed the beach. It was impossible to drive them off, and the
foreigners suffered more injuries during the evacuation than they
had in any other phase of the operation. But the retreat was successful, and many captives who had been released were taken to
the safety of the corvette. As the last of the longboats began to
pull away from the shore, the Maratti raced down to the beach
from the cliffs and fired wildly at their attackers, some of the
hardier tribesmen actually plunging into the water and trying to
reach the boat. But the escape was completed without the loss of
a single man from either ship.

The Arab girl was dazed but unhurt when Lieutenant Aston
and Trelawny brought her on board the grab; Trelawny instructed Louis to make her comfortable in his own cabin, which
he gave up to her. Trelawny put her in the charge of the rais,
who spoke her language.

Then he went up to the quarter-deck and ordered the anchor
weighed and the sails raised. He ate his dinner on deck as

Madagascar faded on the horizon. It was a meal he never forgot.
Louis served him a rich turtle soup, two Indian turtle dishes
called calipash and calipee, and an egg concoction so delicious
that, Louis said, the wealthy merchants of Amsterdam and Rot-
terdam had offered him vast sums for the recipe which he refused to divulge.

In previous fights Trelawny had been so exhilarated that the
feeling persisted for a long time, but the aftermath of the St.
Sebastian battle was different. He was uncontrollably depressed
and, probably for the first time, was fully cognizant of the
finality of death. As night fell and the sea changed colors, he was
sickened by his memories of the gory battle; he could take no
pride in his achievements. When De Ruyter appeared on the
quarter-deck to relieve him, it finally occurred to him that the
wound in his leg was throbbing and that his whole body ached.

He went below to the tiny cabin that served as his home now
and fell into a berth "without troubling to unrig." He was asleep
as soon as his head touched the pillow.

The two ships sailed for the Îsle de France, planning to go to
the sheltered harbor of Port Bourbon rather than blockaded Port
Louis. It developed that De Ruyter owned a country house on
the island, and he proposed a holiday of several weeks' duration
there; he had taken a fortune in gems from St. Sebastian, was
tired of fighting, and felt that a respite from warfare and tension
was due.

Life at sea gradually restored Trelawny's health and vigor. He
recovered from his exhaustion; his leg wound healed, and he
began to look forward to the sojourn on the Île de France. He,
De Ruyter and Aston would swim and fish together, take long
hikes, laze about in the sun and spend their evenings discussing
the philosophy and literature in which the youth was developing
such a keen interest. He could ask for nothing more in all the
world.

Then, after the grab had traveled five hundred miles from
Madagascar, his thoughts turned—for the first time—to the Arab
maiden he had rescued and, until then, managed to put out of
his mind.

# VIII

## *"Zela was my one, my true love."*

The rais knew much about the orphaned Arab maiden and her family. Her father, the old man who had been killed, had been sheik of the island of Sohar, a small paradise in the Persian Gulf. Their tribe, the Beni-Bedar K'urcish, was one of the most noble in Islam and as ancient as the sands of the sea.

The rais, who felt it was an honor to have the gentle girl under his protection, had found appropriate clothes for her. He had sought out one of her waiting women in the ranks of the refugees and placed the woman in constant attendance on her. The rais suggested that Trelawny make her a gift of one of the rescued Malay girls as a slave.

Trelawny, hating the institution of slavery, became indignant.

But the rais was a practical man and hastened to explain. The Malay women who had been taken into captivity by the Maratti would not be accepted again by their own people and, consequently, could not return to their homes. Without exception they would be sold as slaves on the Île de France, so it would be far better to give one of them a kind and considerate mistress rather than condemn her to an unknown fate.

Trelawny was forced to agree.

The rais was not yet finished. Speaking with delicacy, he said the lady wanted to thank her deliverer in person, but she was still suffering from the shock of her father's cruel death and was not yet strong enough.

Trelawny was content to wait.

Soon thereafter he was present during a conversation between De Ruyter and the rais, listening first with incredulity, then with growing alarm.

"I don't know whether you agree with me, father," De Ruyter said, speaking with great solemnity, "but I am inclined to think this Arab girl is the lawful wife of our young friend here. Was she not affianced to Mr. Trelawny by her father according to the customs of your country and of Muslims everywhere?"

Trelawny thought his mentor was joking but, this time, failed to appreciate his sense of humor.

The rais was solemn too. "You are right, malik," he said. "Who can doubt it? Yet it sounded strange to my ears when the men present at the sheik's death told me of the betrothal. Old as I am, never before have I heard of an Arab sheik, whose generations are as countless as the grains of sand on the desert, giving his daughter to a *giaour* belonging to a country so newly discovered that our ancestors knew not of it, nor could her father have heard of its existence, and an infidel."

"Why do you say that?" De Ruyter demanded. "No doubt the sheik thought the young man was an Arab. Does he look like a Christian? Does he not wear the Arab dress? I know that he has a Koran in his cabin. He can say his *namaz.*"

The rais understood. "Wise you are, malik, and that is the truth. For my part, I feel sure that the father of this boy was an Arab, or at least Arab-descended. I never saw any of your Western people sun-dyed and featured like this boy. He is honest and brave, loves our people, fights with our weapons and uses our customs. Now that he has, by the blessing of Mohammed our holy prophet, married an Arab wife, I hope he will search out the tribe of his ancestors and not, like unto his foolish father, go from his own country to dwell on white rocks in the sea."

Trelawny looked at Lieutenant Aston, who was also present, hoping his friend would smile reassuringly, but he was as grave as the others.

The rais suggested that the marriage should be acknowledged by an exchange of rings. De Ruyter not only agreed but offered his protégé a choice of the jewels in his treasure chest. He added that a marriage arranged by a dying man was more binding than most.

The rais agreed, saying that secrets hidden to others were often clear to dying men. Undoubtedly the sheik had known what he was doing when he gave his daughter, the hopes of his house and the care of his children to a stranger.

"Children?" Lieutenant Aston asked. "Are there other children?"

Trelawny was afraid he would faint. On second thought, he came to think he welcomed unconsciousness; when he awakened, he would perhaps discover that he had been suffering from a bad dream.

By children, the rais explained as he went off to the quarter-deck to relieve the second officer, he had meant all the members of the sheik's tribe.

The panicky Trelawny saw his friends were laughing at him, but they admitted the situation was complex. "According to Mohammedan ritual and Arab custom the marriage was legal," De Ruyter said. "But you are not bound. The Koran means nothing to you, my boy. You are not an Arab. Their law is not yours."

Trelawny wanted to know what would become of the girl if he did not honor the marriage.

"Well, as her father has affianced her to you, she cannot marry anyone else," De Ruyter told him. "So you must provide for her and convey her and her Arabs to their native land. You have feeling as well as honor, so you will do what is right."

Lieutenant Aston asked the bewildered youth what he intended doing.

"Doing?" Trelawny asked. "The thing is done. I am married—without banns, or any fuss and feathers. It's like the first shock in bathing; the timid, who creep in by degrees, suffer more than the bold, who plunge in head foremost. If I must go in, give me deep water and a height to leap from. Then the shock will soon be over."

Aston urged him to reconsider, saying the girl was still a baby and that his friend had scarcely seen her.

"No Arab sees anything of his wife until after he is married," Trelawny replied.

Aston protested that the youth could not take the girl back to England and asked if he intended to spend his entire life in the East.

"Why not?" Trelawny replied, thinking that, for all practical purposes, his silent and indifferent family regarded him as dead. "I have no home. Old Father Rais says that I belong here in the East, and I like it well enough—I like the sun better than snow."

Confused as Trelawny was at this time, he was not utterly without reason. But soon a number of strange events occurred which completely bewildered the young Englishman. He became convinced that he was no longer in command of his own destiny. One of the released Arab prisoners was dying, and Trelawny, summoned to his bedside, heard the man commit his two wives and five children to his care. After the man died he was buried at sea in accordance with Mohammedan ritual, and Trelawny, as the inheritor of the sheik's position, was forced to officiate at the funeral service.

It was impossible for the youth to think clearly. Literally overnight, he had been transformed from an English boy reveling in an adventurous, devil-may-care life into an Arab sea sheik, a— Mussulman—married and the father of a tribe. His panic increased; he had to resist the impulse to throw himself into the sea.

But, fortunately, he was young and resilient, and his curiosity about the girl was greater than his fears. Finally he decided to summon her waiting woman, Kamalia, and demand an interview.

The woman resisted.

Trelawny refused to tolerate a further period of waiting.

The woman said certain proprieties had to be observed. Did he have the rings necessary for an exchange?

In his pocket at that very moment, he declared, were the old sheik's ring and a ruby-studded band that De Ruyter had given him.

The woman consented to a meeting, provided Trelawny swore he would abide by certain rules. Under no circumstances could he touch the lady's veil, gown or person. He could not talk too much, ask any questions or stay more than a short time. Above all, he must remember that the girl was still in deep mourning for her beloved father, and he was required to act accordingly.

When he agreed to the conditions, Kamalia went below to prepare her mistress for the interview. Trelawny waited on the deck, sorry now he had requested the meeting. It would be far better, he told himself, never to meet the girl.

At last the waiting woman reappeared and told him the Lady Zela would receive him.

The door of the main cabin was opened by the Malay slave girl, Adoo.

Trelawny hesitated on the threshold, and saw, facing him on a low couch, a disorganized jumble of yellow draperies, yellow being the Arab mourning color. So many veils and shawls were wrapped around the Lady Zela that even her hands were hidden; her long hair, soft and dark, fell over her face like a cloud, concealing it, too. She sat cross-legged and motionless, making no sound.

The boy felt tongue-tied, rooted to the deck; he was overcome by shyness, an emotion he had never been burdened with before. Unable to cope with the situation, he wanted to race back up to the main deck.

The experienced Kamalia intervened before he could bolt, and made an almost imperceptible sign to the figure on the couch. Zela stood, slipped her bare feet into embroidered slippers and crossed the cabin, her body swaying beneath the layers of shawls. Taking the youth's hand, she pressed it to her forehead and lips, and then released him. Her head was bent low, and he still could not see her face.

The swaggering, roistering Trelawny reacted like a little boy, and stammered so badly he was forced to indicate in pantomime that he wanted her to make herself comfortable again in her seat.

Zela returned to the couch; Kamalia produced a cushion for him, and he sat Buddha-like on it. This was the proper moment to begin a conversation, but Trelawny could not speak. First his mind went blank, then his vocal cords seemed paralyzed; he fidgeted, almost fell off the cushion and perspired heavily.

Again Kamalia came to the rescue, producing cups of coffee,

mangosteen and guava jellies, also "syrups tinct with cinnamon."
The silent Zela insisted on serving her lord and master herself
and brought him his coffee.

Trelawny was fascinated by her hand, which was tiny and
pale, and upset his coffee. The girl saved him from further embarrassment by pretending nothing out of the ordinary had happened, and offered him some of the sweetmeats.

He had no idea what he was eating, and didn't know what to
do next until old Kamalia pointed to the deceased sheik's ring on
his finger. He rose again, went to the couch and offered the ring
to Zela.

The girl took it, held it for an instant and then replaced it on
his right forefinger. He could see she was trembling, and his own
hand was unsteady as he produced the ruby ring and slipped it
onto her forefinger. Then, abruptly departing from Arab custom,
he took her hand and kissed the palm.

Kamalia started to intervene.

But Trelawny straightened, and delivered a brief speech in
halting Arabic. The Lady Zela had no reason to entertain fears
for herself or her tribe. Her father's people on board his ship
were free, and he would take care of them. He begged her not to
be lonely, assuring her that even though he was a stranger, with
alien manners, he was eager to learn the customs of her country
if she would only teach him. He bowed and, almost with confidence, placed his hand over his heart in the approved Arab
manner. Yet he was dismayed, as he withdrew from the cabin, to
discover that the girl was weeping.

A week passed, and Trelawny, unable to concentrate, performed his duties as though in a trance. He could think only of
the delicate creature in the main cabin; she was undoubtedly
crying herself to sleep each day. He felt new sensations mingled
with old, and although his feelings sometimes alarmed him, he
was astonished to discover they were not altogether disagreeable. One of his feelings was pity, which was what he had
felt for Walter. Another was tenderness, which was completely
new to him and caused him untold agonies of embarrassment.
Worst of all—or was it best?—he could not forget the light touch
of her lips on his hand.

Each day, he paid a visit to the main cabin, taking with him

another gift from De Ruyter's treasure chest. One day it was a
rare square of embroidered cloth, the next it was a pair of solid-
gold earrings, "as heavy as lead." But the pile of shawls and veils
on the low couch made no move, failed to recognize his presence
and did not seem to hear him. The Lady Zela was too busy
weeping.

Trelawny had never before been held on a leash by a member
of the opposite sex, and after seven days of such treatment his
patience broke. Sending for Kamalia, he informed the elderly
woman that he wanted the air cleared. If Zela did not like him
he had a right to know it, and he would remove himself from her
life.

Kamalia realized he was as inexperienced as the girl, but was
unsuccessful insofar as assurances that etiquette demanded a
show of maidenly modesty fell on deaf ears. It was necessary to
take a more direct approach with the boy. So Kamalia told him
her mistress liked the sound of his voice. The next day, she told
him Zela thought him kind and gentle; and on the day after that
he was informed that he was "as handsome as a zebra."

Trelawny became more optimistic and vowed not to quit. His
persistence began to pay dividends. One day, Zela permitted him
a glimpse of her smooth, sweetly curved cheek. The next day,
she greeted him in a voice as soft as a singing bird's. Finally he
was permitted to hold her hand for a few moments. And when
he released it she raised her head and let him look into her eyes
—an experience from which he never recovered.

His description of Zela in *Younger Son* was pure, lyrical
romanticism:

*She had just turned her fourteenth year; and though certainly
not considered, even in the East, as matured, yet forced into a
flower fanned by the sultry west wind, into early development,
her form, like its petals bursting through the bud, gave promise
of the rarest beauty and sweetness. Nurtured in the shade, her
hue was pale, but contrasted with the date-colored women about
her, the soft and transparent clearness of her complexion was
striking; and it was heightened by clouds of the darkest hair. She
looked like a solitary star unveiled in the night. The breadth and
depth of her clear and smooth forehead were partly hidden by*

*the even silky line from which the hair rose, fell over in rich profusion, and added to its brightness; as did the glossy, well-defined eyebrow, boldly crossing the forehead, slightly waved at the outer extremities, but not arched. Her eyes were full, even for an Orientalist, but neither sparkling nor prominent, soft as the thrush's. It was only when moved by joy, surprise, or sorrow, that the starlike iris dilated and glistened, and then its effect was most eloquent and magical. The distinct ebony lashes which curtained them were singularly long and beautiful; and when she slept they pressed against her pale cheeks and were arched upwards.*

*That portion of eye, generally of a pearly whiteness, in hers was tinted with a light shade of blue, like the bloom on a purple grape, or the sky seen through the morning mist. Her mouth was harmony and love; her face was small and oval, with a wavy outline of ineffable grace descending to her smooth and unruffled neck, thence swelling at her bosom, which was high, and just developing into form. Her limbs were long, full, and rounded, her motion was quick, but not springy, light as a zephyr.*

Trelawny had absorbed more of the nineteenth-century gentlemen's attitude toward women than he knew. His class divided the opposite sex into two distinct groups: there were the ladies, whom one cherished, respected, married and, under the most fortunate circumstances, loved; set apart from these paragons of virtue were the trollops, whom one bedded out of sheer lust. Young Trelawny had known only the latter since early boyhood, when his association with his mother and sisters had ended so abruptly. From his earliest days in the Navy, when a brothel keeper tucked him into his child's bed, he had known countless women who sold him what he wanted and created no complications in his life.

Zela was different. She qualified as a lady in the Western sense, but at the same time she was a woman as the word was understood in the East. She was wise beyond her years, flirtatious and had been trained from earliest childhood to fascinate, tantalize and please a man.

The lonely youth who had known no affection other than the rough camaraderie of the older men who were his heroes reached out to Zela for the love he craved, and she returned it in full measure.

It was not accidental that he was still under her spell, twenty years later, when he wrote:

*That silent pressure wove the first link of a diamond chain which time nor use could ever break or tear away. Love was ignited in my breast; pure, ardent, deep and imperishable. Zela, from that day, was the star I was destined to worship, at whose altar I was to offer up all the incense of my first affections. I consecrated my heart to Zela. When dull mortality returns to dust, when my spirit wings its way like a dove, it will find no resting place, no olive branch of peace, till reunited to Zela.*

All that was needed was a setting for love, the cramped quarters of a crowded brig being inappropriate. It was fitting that the grab was drawing close to the place that Trelawny believed most nearly resembled the biblical Garden of Eden; Mauritius, the lovely Île de France, was soon beneath Trelawny's and Zela's feet.

## IX

## *"My love for Zela knew no diminution."*

Mauritius, occupied by the French for the better part of a half century, was and is a tropical island of volcanic origin about forty miles long and thirty miles wide. Pear-shaped, it lies in the Indian Ocean five hundred miles from the nearest land other than its smaller, sister island, Rodriguez. Trade winds cool it from April to October, and at night the weather in the highlands is chilly; even during the oppressive hot seasons it is almost always cool in the hills.

Deep rain forests abound, and fruits, vegetables and flowers grow in profusion in the rich, volcanic soil, needing little cultivation. Without exception, the Mauritians have been immigrants, most of them the descendants of Indian sailors. Seemingly every race has been drawn there, and many nationalities. Malays settled on the island, as did Africans and Arabs. A surprisingly large number of Europeans came to Mauritius as well: among them the Dutch, who first made the place their colony, the Portuguese, the English and the French.

Although no one yet knew it at the beginning of the nineteenth century's second decade, French rule was coming to an end. The Île de France was the heart of French privateer operations in the Indian Ocean, and Great Britain, dependent on her merchant fleet for the maintenance of her life lines, could not permit her enemy that luxury. At the very time that De Ruyter's grab reached the island, Great Britain was planning an expedition that would establish British rule on Mauritius, an occupation that would be confirmed in the peace treaty of 1814, following the downfall of Napoleon.

The highest mountain peaks stood less than three thousand feet above the sea but picked up the trade winds, and there was enough rainfall to keep the extensive gardens of De Ruyter's plantation house green for twelve months out of twelve. The English had temporarily abandoned their blockade of Port Louis, so the captain of the corvette decided to sail there as soon as he could take on supplies and make temporary repairs to his ship at Port Bourbon. De Ruyter went to his country house with Lieutenant Aston, taking Zela and her women with him, and Trelawny was left behind to put the grab in shape. For seventy-two hours he worked without sleep, and the brig was restored to the pristine condition that had attracted Trelawny when he had first seen the vessel.

His work completed, he hurried inland, afraid the others would go first to De Ruyter's house, then off for a visit to the governor in Port Louis before he could join them. But they had waited for him, and started out the next day on horseback in a holiday atmosphere. De Ruyter, who had divided his treasure with care in order to give the governor the share necessary under French law, was keeping enough to make himself far wealthier and was in a happy frame of mind. Lieutenant Aston was looking forward to the island sojourn before it would become necessary to find a means of returning him to the British fleet in India; he was in high spirits too.

And Trelawny, escorting a suddenly voluble Zela, was positively ecstatic. The girl dropped all her reserve in his presence, her naturally gay spirit came alive, and the pair chatted incessantly in English and Arabic, each learning the other's language while creating a private tongue of their own.

A seemingly trivial incident that took place on the journey revealed Zela's sensitivity to the bridegroom, who had not yet claimed his marital rights. They were riding on a mountain trail, Zela demonstrating that she was completely at home on horseback, when she suddenly dismounted, broke a flowering branch from a small tree and offered it to Trelawny. The scent of the yellow flowers was disagreeable, so he thought she was teasing him, and throwing the branch onto the ground, began to laugh.

To his bewilderment he saw Zela burst into tears. The tree was the yakoonoo, which the Arabs regarded as sacred, and by rejecting it Trelawny was unwittingly indicating that he wanted no more to do with the girl. He cursed himself for his stupidity and debated how he might make amends. Suddenly inspiration came. Dismounting quickly, he ran to the little tree and, using all his strength, pulled it up by the roots.

He presented it to Zela, making a little speech. The tree was beautiful, the loveliest of all growing things; the scent of its flowers was more exotic and enticing than that of the rarest perfumes. He would plant the tree in the garden of their home for her, and it would flower there forever, thriving as a symbol of his love for her. Zela forgave him, harmony was restored, and they resumed their journey, arriving late in the day at De Ruyter's house.

The place was a large, one-story dwelling, painted a dazzling white, its architecture a blend of Oriental and French, and was even more attractive than the bungalow outside Bombay. The veranda was tiled, the central hall was paved with stones, and Persian blinds shielded every room from the sun. A mountain stream ran through the place, supplying a fountain at one point, a fish pond at another and then a tiled bathing pool. Escaping from the lower end of the pool the stream continued its flow from the mountains, irrigating the garden before descending to the lowlands and the sea. Flowering plants were everywhere; the furniture, most of it fashioned of bamboo, was exceptionally comfortable; and paintings brightened the walls.

This was the first real house in which Trelawny had set foot since leaving the home of his parents. It was also the first dwelling with walls in which Zela had ever lived. Trelawny noted, in *Younger Son,* that she had never before sat in a chair; nor had she eaten with a knife and fork. It was the custom of Arab ladies to dine with their women, but De Ruyter and Aston wanted the girl to join them at the table, so Trelawny sent for her. The meal was hilarious as Trelawny tried to teach her to eat curried chicken with utensils, while she attempted to show him how to eat it with his fingers.

After dinner they explored the property, and found the garden truly an Eden, most of the plants having been imported by De Ruyter. There were pineapple, date, coconut and banana palms, as well as mangoes, melons, eggplant and a number of tropical fruits whose names Trelawny did not know. Asparagus and pumpkins grew in profusion, as did strawberries, raspberries, clingstone peaches and grapes of several hues. Purple passion flowers, yellow morning glories, roses and violets were everywhere, and the guests admired Persian lilac, sweet-scented basil, and a bush with red berries called Bois de Demoiselle.

A white summer house stood at the far end of the garden, surrounded by a bamboo thicket for privacy, and the party was served refreshments there. Trelawny, eating sweetmeats, drinking fresh pomegranate juice and watching Zela wander through the garden, her veils fluttering in the cooling breeze, felt certain he had entered Paradise.

He managed to curb his desire for her, and his courtship was gentle; under no circumstances did he want to frighten her, and he waited for her signal to consummate their marriage. Zela was content to take her time, too, and the young couple came to know each other gradually, without strain. Eden was sufficient for them, and they stayed behind when Aston and De Ruyter went into Port Louis, the former to see the town, the latter to report to the governor. De Ruyter was mildly irritated when Trelawny refused to accompany them, preferring to stay behind with the girl who was the first to win his heart.

During the absence of the older men, Zela finally admitted her bridegroom to her chamber. Trelawny showed the proper reticence of the nineteenth-century gentleman and revealed none of the details of that night to his readers. But he made no secret of the fact that he and Zela were wildly, passionately in love:

*My love for Zela knew no diminution. Every day I discovered some new quality to admire in her. She was my inseparable companion. I could hardly endure her out of my sight an instant; and our bliss was as perfect as it was uninterrupted. My love was too deep to fear satiety; nor did ever my imagination wander from her, to compare her with any other woman. She had wound herself about my heart till she became part of me. Our extreme youth, ardent nature, and solitude, had wrought our feeling of affection towards each other to an intensity that perhaps was never equalled, assuredly never surpassed.*

The honeymoon continued after the return of De Ruyter and Aston from Port Louis, and the bride and groom were scarcely aware of the presence of the men. They found a thousand reasons each day to kiss, to reach out for each other; their little games and jokes, incomprehensible to outsiders, were endless. Lieutenant Aston, who was sympathetic, avoided them when he could and was diplomatically bland when in their presence. De Ruyter was less patient, and reminded Trelawny there was a world beyond the little bamboo bridge at the entrance to the property. But the youth paid no attention: his Arab bride comprised his entire universe.

The influence Zela exerted on Edward John Trelawny cannot be emphasized too strongly. Although he would associate with many women in his later life, loving—or imagining that he loved —a number of them, none measured up to the child-wife to whom he gave his adolescent heart. Zela was his ideal, his concept of perfection, and when he was in his late eighties, looking back on his entire life, he admitted to William Rossetti that no one else had ever meant as much to him, that no other had been as lovely or sweet, that she made every other woman he had ever known fade into insignificance.

Some of Trelawny's late-nineteenth and early-twentieth-century critics wondered whether he exaggerated Zela's beauty and charm, as well as their mutual love, but they missed the true import of this early marriage. For all practical purposes, he was an orphan and had been deprived of the affection of his mother, aunts and sisters at an alarmingly early age. Although he didn't realize it, he was starved for love, and after meeting Zela, under dramatically romantic circumstances, it was inevitable that he would endow her with every feminine asset. His description of her, painted in his early thirties, portrayed her as dazzling, and it does not matter if she may have fallen short of the mark in reality. In his mind she was wife and mother, mistress and companion, sister and playmate.

With the aid of the romantic's imagination, Trelawny placed his first wife on a plane beyond human reach, and in his later loves he tried in vain to capture the bliss he had known with Zela. However colored it may have been by Trelawny's romantic fantasies, though, the love of these two orphans who clung to each other was thoroughly real. Their relationship was both genuine and joyous. Zela healed the wounds Trelawny had suffered from since early childhood; she made him whole. With her he found a happiness beyond his ken, and whether their love could have survived had he taken her to England is irrelevant speculation. Zela was responsible for much of Trelawny's development into manhood, and his memory of her, right or wrong, true or exaggerated, later caused him—no one could possibly deny it—to try to fit other women, time and time again, into the mold cut only for her.

The youth on the Île de France rejoiced in the belief that his dreams had come true. He refused to explore the island with De Ruyter and Aston until Zela had been invited to become a member of the party, and he was elated when she had held her own. She hunted wild boar with a spear; she showed no fear of snakes or poisonous insects when trekking through the rain forests, and she demonstrated surprising physical strength when she caught fish double her own weight.

After the party returned to De Ruyter's house, she ingratiated herself with the host by telling stories that were part of the folklore of her native land, as well as by singing Arabic songs to her own accompaniment on a zither-like instrument. De Ruyter grew fond of her but still found it impossible to concentrate on his reading when the young lovers spoke to each other in their own special language, a blend of English, Arabic and words of their own invention.

One day, an invitation was received from the governor of the Île de France that even the lovesick Trelawny could not resist. A banquet was to be given in Port Louis to celebrate the victory over the Maratti at St. Sebastian, and not only was the young hero asked to attend with De Ruyter, but both would be the

house guests of the governor. No invitation was extended to
Zela, and Lieutenant Aston was omitted, of course, because the
presence of an enemy of France would have embarrassed everyone. But De Ruyter wanted Aston present, and communications
were exchanged with the governor, who sent an invitation to the
English officer, specifying that he wear civilian attire.

Port Louis was a green and white town, the trees and neat
lawns providing a soft background for the white houses and
other buildings. The French showed their usual talent for com-
bining their civilization with that of a colony. Most homes were
of Eastern design, but the hospital, theater and library reflected
the influence of French architecture. An aqueduct provided the
town with fresh water, and the most conspicuous buildings were
the warehouses, where East India Company merchandise captured by French privateers was stored. The church built by the
French was baroque, and the governor's residence, made of
stone, was an imposing office and home.

The governor, gracious and urbane, congratulated Trelawny
on the part he played at St. Sebastian and, finding the youth interesting, suggested a meeting with his wife. He conducted
Trelawny down a long, white corridor, and together they entered
a boudoir, the first the young Englishman had ever seen. The
lady, reclining on a chaise and fanning herself with a palm leaf,
was the first Frenchwoman of her class he had ever met.

He was startled to see that she was dressed in the height of
imperial fashion, "as though ready to attend a great ball." She
wore heavy cosmetics, and her dress of India muslin concealed
nothing of her figure. Her hair was arranged in a fashionable
neo-Greek topknot (the style made popular by Napoleon's sister,
Pauline), and on her feet were silver slippers.

The governor, amusing himself, merely presented Trelawny as
"a young Arab chieftain," then hurried back to his other guests.

The lady, speaking very slowly, invited the supposed Arab to
sit on her chaise. She admired each item of his attire, stroked his
cheeks and commented, sometimes to herself, on his male
beauty. She accepted his disguise so completely that the youth
found it difficult to refrain from laughing aloud.

The lady peppered him with questions. Had he ever been
christened? Had he ever attended mass? Did he believe in the

Virgin Mary? Did he think of himself as a barbarian or a civilized man? Had he ever been in love? Did he understand what Westerners meant by love? Would he like to visit Paris and the other great cities of Europe? Had he ever heard of the great Emperor Napoleon? Were Arab women as handsome as French women?

Trelawny played the game with her, sometimes nodding in answer to her questions, sometimes replying in Arabic monosyllables. But he soon grew tired of the entertainment; the room was suffocating, and he couldn't help yawning. Then the lady, feeling sorry for herself, launched into a long monologue for her own benefit, not realizing he understood a word. She lamented her sad fate. She, a sophisticated Parisienne who had many friends at the imperial court and even enjoyed the attentions of the Emperor himself, was living in virtual exile in a remote, tedious and barbarous land. The heat wore her down and undoubtedly had ruined her health. There was nothing to do here. There was no theater. There were no shops. She alone had an interest in fashions. There were no balls or assemblies to attend. There was nothing on this godforsaken place but scenery. She hated mountains and was afraid of them. She was even more afraid of the sea, which made her sick whenever she traveled by boat.

Trelawny was so bewildered he could only stare at her. Always sensitive to natural beauty, he thought the Île de France was the most beautiful place he had ever seen, and he believed the lady's diatribe was almost a sacrilege.

He felt great relief when De Ruyter arrived to pay his respects to Madame. They were old friends, and she bubbled again, calling him the only civilized man on the island. Then, her attention redirected toward Trelawny, she discussed him as though he were not present. He was such a handsome boy, and she was surprised that any Arab could carry himself with such an air of distinction. Was he De Ruyter's slave? If so, she would gladly buy him—or, at the very least, she would beg De Ruyter to loan him to her. She was returning to Paris in a few weeks and could not help dwelling on the sensation she would create with the young Arab at her side. Think what a sensation *he* would create in Paris, especially if he learned to dance! She herself would happily teach him to waltz.

Trelawny was greatly relieved when they were called to tiffin and the absurd conversation ended. The delicacies served at tiffin gave the youth a new respect for French food; he later observed that even at such an early age he suspected the cuisine of Paris was the best on earth.

The captain of the corvette and his officers were present for the ceremony that was held in the library of the governor's mansion, and all the island's dignitaries gathered for the event. De Ruyter and the corvette captain were presented with swords, while Trelawny and the first lieutenant of the corvette received silver goblets on which their names were engraved. Trelawny's goblet was one of his most cherished possessions, and he kept it until the end of his days.

Most of the assembled guests went off to sleep until the banquet that would be held later in the evening, but the young Englishman preferred to see the town. He instinctively drifted to the waterfront, where the American schooner he had admired was at anchor. Her captain invited him to tour the vessel, and he was filled with admiration for her, confirming De Ruyter's opinion that American naval architects and shipwrights produced the most compact, seaworthy and handsome craft afloat.

Then he wandered aimlessly through Port Louis and soon discovered that Paradise was blighted by the presence of vast numbers of slaves, who constituted the better part of the population. They were so cheap—even cheaper than horses—that they were used for many purposes, carrying the ladies of the town in litters for one. The cruelty of masters and overseers shocked him, particularly at the warehouses, and he seethed with anger when he wrote:

*To every appeal they [the overseers] are deaf as crocodiles. While you are talking of humanity, they will lash the bare and festered back of an overloaded female slave, her tender nature one animated mass of ulcers and cancers, half consumed alive by flies and maggots, death her only hope and coming like a bridegroom. I have seen men with their spines knotted like pine trees, and their skins as scaled and callous, the flesh cracked into chasms from which the blood oozed out like gum. I have seen*

*hundreds of these poor wretches undergoing their daily toil in
the dockyards of Port Louis, and the pity and pain I felt at the
sight of these poor slaves could only be equaled by the deep and
overwhelming damnation I invoked on the heads of their oppressors forever. Surely such monsters are annihilated, they cannot
be immortal. Yet they have an eternity to torment them. What
they have done to others should be done to them, and I defy the
invention of hell's demons to be more cunning in cruelty than
themselves.*

His pleasure spoiled, the indignant Trelawny returned to the
governor's mansion and began to prepare for the evening. He did
not realize it, but the plight of the slaves had so aroused him
that he was spoiling for a fight.

The dinner itself was superb, but due to too much food, too
much wine, he could not do justice to the meal. The French
guests irritated him, and the deserter from the Royal Navy felt a
surge of patriotic sentiment as he compared the handsome,
dignified Lieutenant Aston with the "bilious little monkeys with
their sallow skins, bald heads, yellow eyes, and noses like
squashed figs." *Any* Englishman was superior in *every* way to
*any* Frenchman, or, for that matter, to any Dutchman or Portuguese. He commented softly to Lieutenant Aston in English,
which none of the others understood, calling the others "vain,
gasconading harlequins."

Just at that moment one of the guests began to deliver a little
speech on the marvels of Paris, finally calling it as superior to
London as Calcutta was superior to Port Louis. The insult was
more than the youth could tolerate; he stiffened and, as his
friends later told him, he looked as though he might burst like a
grenade. Aston laid a warning hand on his arm, grinned at him
and winked to indicate that he shared his young friend's opinion.
Trelawny regained his self-control and managed to keep silent.

He had spent enough time in French company, however, and
was so anxious to see Zela that he wanted to return to the country that same night. His friends decided to humor him, and they
set out for the estate immediately after the banquet. Trelawny
was so pleased with his silver trophy—despite his distaste for the

French setting in which it had been given him—that he took it from its wrappings, admired it in the moonlight and could scarcely wait until he showed it to his bride.

They returned to a house in turmoil. Zela was weeping, and the mad Van Scolpvelt was running wildly around a room, shutting windows so several bats on which he was making "medical" experiments could not escape. Trelawny immediately released the tortured creatures and would have become embroiled in a fight with the surgeon if Aston had not intervened.

Aston proposed that they play a practical joke on Van Scolpvelt instead, one that would teach him a lesson. So they prepared a booby trap over an old well in the garden and persuaded Van Scolpvelt to place his bed there. He fell into the well and was almost drowned before they consented to haul him out.

The incident is significant only because it reveals that Trelawny was still more of an Englishman than he knew. The trick was a typical English schoolboy prank, and he enjoyed it thoroughly, feeling no guilt and extending no sympathy to the old man.

Trelawny immediately resumed his honeymoon with Zela; Lieutenant Aston began to think seriously about working out some way to return to his duties in the Royal Navy, and De Ruyter busied himself with the life of a planter. Only one member of his household held aloof: the rais refused to have anything to do with planting and harvesting crops. He was a sailor and would not soil his hands in earth. But he was in no hurry and did not lose his equanimity; he had been associated with De Ruyter for a long time and knew his friend and employer would grow tired of playing farmer, that the day would come when he, too, would be unable to resist the call of the sea. The rais continued to sleep on board the grab and paid only daily visits to the house.

Trelawny soon found himself summoned before De Ruyter and the rais, who were studying charts. A heavily laden English merchantman had been sighted in the Mozambique Channel, and the capture of her cargo would be a rich prize. Trelawny hurried down to Port Louis with the older men, and found work had already started on the seeming transformation of the grab

into a corvette. She was being given a false superstructure, which
would be removed after the act of piracy at sea was completed.

Arrangements were being made to sail that same night, and
Trelawny was astonished when Aston informed him that he was
being left behind. Apparently he was too lovesick to be of much
use if a serious fight at sea developed. The youth was grateful,
but at the same time felt a twinge of disappointment. The grab
was his ship, but she was sailing into adventure without him.

He found consolation with Zela, however, and Lieutenant
Aston was on hand for a chat, a swim or a hike. The days passed
quietly, and the young couple occasionally went into Port Louis
to call on the governor's wife. Madame discovered that Trelawny
was not really an Arab, and was amused by the joke; she met
Zela, and the girl enchanted her. But Zela obviously had a mind
and will of her own and refused Madame's offers to dress and
make her up to resemble a French lady of the imperial court.

Early one morning, Trelawny received a message to the effect
that De Ruyter had been sighted making his way toward Port
Louis escorting a prize ship, so he hurried down to the port.
There, to his astonishment, were the grab and the American
schooner with which he had fallen in love, both flying French
flags.

De Ruyter explained the mystery. The American had been
captured by the armed English merchantman, which he, in turn,
had defeated in battle, making the schooner his own prize.
Under the laws of salvage the American ship would rightfully
belong to him as soon as the legal formalities were completed.
He had a plan that made the youth ecstatic. The rais would command the grab in the future. Trelawny would become captain of
the schooner, and the present master of the dhow would keep his
post. De Ruyter, the commodore of the little fleet, would make
the grab his flagship. That meant Trelawny would be in sole
charge of the finest ship he had ever seen.

He raced back to the country to tell Zela and Lieutenant
Aston the news and felt relieved when De Ruyter sent word
from Port Louis that the governor had validated the transfer of
the schooner to his name. Each morning thereafter, Trelawny
hurried down to the port to put his new ship in order for a long

sea voyage, and he helped De Ruyter in the hiring of a crew of Arabs, Europeans and Americans to sail her. The Americans were particularly important, Trelawny felt, because they "alone had the feel for a vessel built in their own yards."

Lieutenant Aston's long holiday was coming to an end, and he and De Ruyter were busily working out a complicated scheme that would enable him to return to duty with the Royal Navy. Aston could not rid himself of the feeling that his life was coming to an end, and his foreboding was natural. The war between England and France had been raging for many years, and scores of his brother officers had, thus, died. It appeared that the war would not end until the manpower on both sides was exhausted, and Aston was convinced he did not have long to live.

Trelawny and Zela were filled with optimism, however, and were looking forward to their new adventure together. Even though Westerners believed that the presence of a woman on board a ship was bad luck, De Ruyter did not share the superstition and had given permission for Zela, accompanied by Kamalia and Adoo, to sail with Trelawny.

The young Englishman of eighteen could ask for nothing more in the world. The finest ship he had seen on the seven seas was his, and his bride, the most beautiful girl, he was sure, in the world, would sail with him in his quest for glory and treasure.

# X

*"Now I am well and happy. I live in his heart."*

Everything was in readiness for a long voyage. The schooner carried enough water and provisions to last ten weeks; there were ample munitions in her magazine, and she was heavily armed with six 12-pounder cannon and four of the 6-pounders that Americans could fire with such deadly accuracy. The gunners would be American, too, eight members of the merchant crew having volunteered to sail with Trelawny. He enjoyed even better fortune when the first lieutenant, a veteran officer named Strong, agreed to accompany him as his second-in-command. Four English veterans of the grab's crew signed on, giving him a nucleus of Westerners whose native tongue was English. The other twenty-one berths were taken by Arabs, all of them experienced sailors; happily enough, Trelawny could speak to them in their own language, thanks to his association with Zela.

Even the dhow was heavily armed, and De Ruyter went in search of game worthy of his flotilla's strength. Only a week after leaving the Île de France, he encountered a convoy of Indian merchantmen flying the East India Company flag and escorted by a forty-gun frigate.

The schooner sailed toward the powerful Royal Navy vessel, tempting her, while the grab stood off and opened fire with her heavy guns. Then Trelawny's 6-pounders went to work at short range with devastating effect. He and De Ruyter knew they were no match for the frigate in a prolonged battle, so their one aim was to cripple her as quickly as possible. They aimed their shots at her superstructure, succeeded in destroying her mainmast, and then made a shambles of her quarter-deck. Retreating before she could get the range and blow them out of the water, they left the disabled giant helpless, her crew compelled to make emergency repairs at sea while the grab, the schooner and the dhow relieved the Indian merchantmen of their cargo of pepper, silk and foods.

That night, the victorious officers dined on board the schooner. But Lieutenant Aston remained on the grab, believing it would be inappropriate for him to take part in the celebration of a triumph over a major Royal Navy ship.

Ten days later, an even greater prize was captured after a short fight in which not one member of De Ruyter's command was injured. The victim was a Dutch merchantman carrying English papers, and her cargo consisted of a fortune in pearls, marble and coral. De Ruyter went to Bombay in the grab to sell his captured merchandise, and Trelawny, waiting for him at sea, enjoyed the respite because it gave him an opportunity to analyze the voyage to date.

He and De Ruyter worked perfectly in tandem, he realized, because they knew each other so well that each understood instinctively how the other would react to any given situation in battle. Trelawny knew, too, that he could usually anticipate the orders De Ruyter would give him in a tight situation. He was also well pleased with the performance of his own crew. The Americans, Englishmen and Arabs worked together without friction, and there was far less of the antagonism between gun crew and sailing crew than he had ever seen in the Royal Navy.

He was able to take the credit for the harmony on board the schooner, and he calmly admitted—without boasting too much— that he had become an exceptionally competent sea captain. His approach to his crew was informal, but at the same time he expected his orders to be obeyed instantly and without question.

He had won the respect of his men, and with his own memories of captains he had hated still fresh in his mind, he did nothing that would deliberately antagonize his subordinates.

His relations with First Lieutenant Strong were good, even though Strong was almost ten years his senior. The American was laconic and hard-working and minded his own business; he was a native of a whaling town, Marblehead, Massachusetts, and the sea had been in his blood since earliest childhood. De Ruyter told Trelawny that he represented all that was good in an American sailor: he was worthy of trust, conscientious in the discharge of his duties, and thrived on excitement.

Believing that a new war between the United States and Great Britain would be inevitable because of the continuing impressment of American seamen in the Royal Navy, Strong hated the English. He delighted in doing them damage and would be content to sail with Trelawny for many years—provided he received every penny of prize money due him. If anyone tried to cheat him, he would slit the man's throat without hesitation, and his conscience would not bother him. In brief, he was a perfect second-in-command of the schooner.

The rendezvous with De Ruyter was scheduled to take place at a small island about fifty miles from Goa. Trelawny was the first to arrive, and after anchoring in the little harbor he sent a party ashore for water, coconuts, bananas and any other food available. Lieutenant Strong was in charge of the landing party and returned with a gift of figs for Zela. She wanted to go ashore too, but Trelawny felt it would have been inappropriate for her to go without him, and it was the captain's place to remain on board his ship.

He was no longer free to do as he pleased, and at no time could he allow himself to forget, even for a moment, that he bore the entire responsibility for the safety of the schooner as well as for the health and well-being of her crew. Zela understood and was proud of him; she pouted for a short time when he refused to allow her to go ashore and would not accompany her, but she quickly recovered her good humor.

The dhow reached the cove a few hours after the schooner's arrival, and the following morning the lookout in the crow's nest reported that another vessel was approaching. Trelawny took no chances and ordered his gun ports lowered, but when the haze burned away, the lookout recognized the grab.

Trelawny went on board for breakfast with De Ruyter as soon as the grab lowered her anchor, and learned of a major change in plans. French privateers and Malay pirates had been doing so much damage to British merchant shipping in the Indian Ocean that the admiralty had taken firm steps to end the expensive nuisance. A rear admiral had been sent to take charge of the effort and was making a mammoth ship of the line, an eighty-four, his flagship. His reinforced squadron also included two new frigates, four or five swift sloops of war and several schooners equipped with extra sail to give them additional speed. It was common knowledge in Bombay that the admiral intended to sink every privateer he found.

For the present, De Ruyter said, there were healthier seas than the Indian Ocean. But the Royal Navy couldn't be everywhere, and the most lucrative waters lay farther to the East. This would not be the first time he had outwitted the British Admiralty, and he looked forward to the challenge.

The captain of the frigate that had been disabled had brought a full description of his attackers to Bombay, so De Ruyter had decided to adopt tactics that would confuse his enemies. Both the grab and the schooner would be disguised before they left the little cove and would sail separately to the Far East, De Ruyter going by way of the Straits of Sunda and Trelawny via the Straits of Malacca. De Ruyter could have paid his friend and subordinate no greater compliment: the young captain would sail alone through waters where the Royal Navy was conducting a search for the schooner that had humiliated a proud frigate.

De Ruyter conferred with Aston, too, and they agreed the lieutenant could not accompany them to the Far East, where the grab, schooner and dhow would meet at an island off Borneo on a predetermined date. A complex and romantic scheme was developed: according to its scenario, Trelawny would take Aston to Penang, at the lower end of the Straits of Malacca, and would see him ashore near Georgetown, a military and commercial base that enabled Great Britain to dominate the Malay Peninsula. There they would part, and Aston would go on into Georgetown, reporting to the authorities there that he had "escaped" from the French after months of captivity.

De Ruyter presented Aston with several gifts as they said their farewells, among them an ancient miniature *kris* and a Chinese pistol, its butt inlaid with ivory and precious stones. Then the grab left the cove, and Trelawny was on his own.

The schooner encountered a British sloop of war on her voyage to the Malabar coast but succeeded in giving her the slip, and Trelawny was able to anchor safely some miles from Penang. He and Aston hired a proa and began the last lap of their journey to Georgetown. The impending parting made the youth sad, and he found it difficult to speak. Then Lieutenant Aston presented him with a gold medallion that had been in his family for many years, and it was difficult for his young friend to hold back the tears. The medallion became one of his most treasured possessions, and he wore it, suspended from a gold chain around his neck, for the rest of his life.

Trelawny elected to ignore De Ruyter's strict order that he was to land Aston at Georgetown and return without delay to his ship. Anxious to put off their final farewell as long as possible, he arranged a later return to the schooner with the Malays who manned the proa and went to a local inn. Meanwhile Aston reported to the local Royal Navy headquarters, where he said he had been picked up by an American schooner after escaping from the French, and his story was accepted without question.

He joined Trelawny at the inn, and they ate a last meal together, making the occasion memorable by drinking considerable quantities of claret and Madeira and finishing with huge snifters of brandy. If Trelawny was not completely intoxicated by the time they left the table, he was at least so giddy that he forgot he was in an English-controlled town, where he could be jailed as a Royal Navy deserter and hanged as a pirate. Lieutenant Aston must have felt his drinks, too, because he suggested they stop in at a tavern to watch some nautch dancers, and Trelawny agreed.

The dancers were disgusting. Their bodies were smeared with rancid oil, their teeth were stained a deep brown from chewing betel nuts, and the odors of garlic in the tavern were nauseating.

Trelawny slipped outside for some air, and when he saw a jeweler's shop across the road it occurred to him that it was the very place for him to return Aston's favor by purchasing his friend a farewell gift.

He finally selected what he wanted. But the jeweler tried to cheat him, and the youth, made reckless by liquor, became embroiled in an argument that ended abruptly when he knocked the man down. A crowd gathered, but Trelawny managed to escape and hurried back to the inn. Realizing that the jeweler and his friends would be seeking vengeance against an Arab, he changed into a white civilian suit of Aston's, then left a farewell note and the gift for his friend.

Cold sober now and thoroughly disgusted with himself, he could think only of escape from Georgetown. It was imperative that he return to the schooner and fulfill his obligation to De Ruyter; he trembled when he pictured Zela waiting for him on the deck. He caught a glimpse of the jeweler, who was stalking through the streets armed with a long Malay knife, but felt reasonably certain the man failed to recognize him.

His immediate task was that of reaching the waterfront, where the proa awaited him, but what he did not know was that Royal Navy marines were on sentry duty after dark, guarding the wharves and warehouses from thieves and saboteurs. Wishing he had brought his Arab attire with him, he realized he could have worn nothing more conspicuous than the white suit. He waited until a sentry marched past his hiding place, then made a wild dash to the shadows of a warehouse wall. There he discovered, almost too late, that a second sentry passed within three or four feet of him, and he stood for at least two hours, flattening himself against the wall and scarcely daring to breathe. Only his knowledge of Royal Navy routines saved him. He was relying on a changing of the guard detail at midnight, which would give him one to two minutes to flee. The guard was changed on time, and Trelawny darted around the warehouse and headed toward the shore.

Suddenly the jeweler, who had not been fooled by his change of clothes, caught up with him, and they fought a savage battle on a wharf that jutted out into the sea. The jeweler still carried his Malay knife, but Trelawny had left his weapons at the inn in his haste to get away and was unarmed. The jeweler struck the first successful blow, inflicting a deep wound in his enemy's arm.

Trelawny realized he had to react swiftly, before his strength ebbed, and grappled with the man, who was stronger than he appeared. Both almost toppled into the sea, but Trelawny managed to regain his balance and staggered backward just in time. The jeweler could not halt his thrust, however, and fell headlong into the water. He could not swim, and Trelawny was too weak to save him, even if he had wished to do so, and the man drowned.

The young Englishman was exhausted but managed to crawl away from the wharf and made his way a short distance down the beach, where he sprawled on his face. He was only semiconscious, too muddled to think clearly until he heard the voice of a sentry calling, "All's well, sir!"

Even the beach was patrolled by marines! He hauled himself to his feet again, kicked off his boots, and staggered into the water. His left arm was useless, and when he discovered he could not lift it he wondered if the jeweler's knife had been poisoned. But he could not afford to dwell on the question; the water revived him somewhat, and he had to concentrate on the difficult task of swimming with only one arm.

His agony was the worst he had ever known, and only his basically sound health and rugged strength saved him. He swam interminably, again and again on the verge of giving up, but his responsibility to De Ruyter and the realization that Zela would be lost without him gave him the determination to continue. At last he reached the proa, where he lost consciousness again.

Salt spray on his face awakened him, but he was more dead than alive, scarcely able to move. He tried to protest when the Malays put into an uninhabited cove, but was too weak. He wrapped himself in a spare sail, watching in silence as one of the Malays went off to spear some fish; the man soon returned and his companions made a fire, but the thought of food made Trelawny gag.

At daybreak the men resumed their trip, which was far longer than Trelawny had remembered it from the opposite direction. His wounded arm had stiffened, and he knew he was suffering from a fever, because he was cold one moment and perspired heavily the next. The proa moved swiftly across the water, but the journey seemed interminable. He began to wonder whether the Malays intended to hand him over to the Royal Navy and claim a reward. The idea was absurd, as part of his mind tried to tell him, since the men did not know his real identity, but he was so fearful for Zela that his imagination was playing tricks on him.

At last the schooner came in sight, and when the proa drew closer he could see Zela on the deck, watching for him through a glass. He was so weak that it was necessary to lower a line for him and hoist him on board his ship. Zela was horrified but took charge quickly, and First Lieutenant Strong ordered the sails hoisted. Trelawny was so groggy he scarcely realized what was happening above.

He was afraid he would be crippled for life, but forgot his troubles for the moment when Strong came to his cabin to report that the men were on the verge of mutiny. According to an old superstition it was the worst of bad luck to begin a voyage on a Friday; this was Friday, and the American, English and Arab members of the crew spoke as one man in their refusal to leave before midnight.

Trelawny had himself carried to the deck and addressed the men, speaking first in English, then in Arabic. A half dozen Royal Navy vessels were at anchor in the Georgetown harbor, he told them—or had been the previous night. By now it was likely that all of them were at sea, searching for the man who had changed his clothes, killed the jeweler and made a miraculous escape. The schooner was known, and every man on board would be hanged if he was caught. Trelawny roused himself sufficiently to swear that he would personally hang every member of the crew for insubordination if his orders were not obeyed. Rallying the last of his strength, he commanded them to put to sea without a moment's further delay, and he emphasized his words by cocking a pistol and pointing it at the bos'n.

The men hesitated, then went to work, and Trelawny again lost consciousness. He was in his own berth when he awakened, and Zela was bending over him. With Kamalia's assistance she had bathed him, his body had been anointed with oil and camphor, and Zela had applied a dressing to his arm. She used one of the ancient prescriptions of her people to draw out the poisons in the wound, and every hour or two she changed the poultices.

By nightfall Trelawny could move his hand again, then his arm, and soon thereafter he discovered he was ravenously hungry. Zela fed him a meal of roast chicken, guava jelly, claret and coffee. The food was delicious, and he became drowsy. Zela sat beside his bed and was keeping watch when he fell asleep.

She was still there in the morning, when Trelawny awakened, feeling miraculously improved. He had recovered the use of his arm, and although it still felt sore to the touch, his wound was healing. Clear-headed and alert, he ate a huge breakfast, and after putting Zela to bed, he went up to the quarter-deck to resume his duties. Thanks to his wife's medication he was none the worse for the incident and had learned an important lesson. Never again would he drink to excess; never again would he disobey the orders of those who were wiser and more farsighted.

## XI

*"Adventure was my profession, and daily I flirted
with danger."*

The life Edward John Trelawny led until he was in his nineteenth year was extraordinary, and thereafter, if his account in
*Younger Son* is to be trusted, it became even more bizarre. Most
of his contemporaries accepted his stories at face value, but later,
skeptics who studied the autobiography of his early years were
inclined to think his tales stretched credulity to the breaking
point. Most of the criticism was directed at the cruise he made
immediately after his parting with Lieutenant Aston in Penang,
and even his most ardent supporters have admitted he was guilty
of exaggeration.

Some of the matters about which he wrote have been verified,
but he is the sole authority for others, so his word must be either
taken or rejected. Many Englishmen and Continentals were familiar with India, Ceylon and Mauritius, not to mention the
Arabic countries and the eastern coast of Africa, but only the
Dutch were familiar with the island kingdoms that lay east of
Singapore. Since his own day, various Dutch authorities have

vouched for the authenticity of his backgrounds and have said he was conscientious in the presentation of his facts.

But his stories present a problem. Some are so outlandish it is almost impossible to accept them as true, and they should be read and enjoyed as tall tales. But it must not be forgotten that Trelawny *was* a man who did strange things and attracted the unusual. One would be inclined to regard his experience at Niagara Falls, which will be discussed in detail in a later chapter, as imaginary, but eyewitnesses corroborated every major point in his account.

Should his first voyage to the Far East be considered fact or fiction? In all probability it was both. Perhaps it should be assumed that Trelawny used truth as his core and then embroidered it, but it must be remembered that he saw life in vivid, highly colored terms, so the generous reader will give him the benefit of the doubt. It well may be that various experiences were not as intensely dramatic as he made them out to be, but it is unlikely that he told deliberate falsehoods. He saw these incidents in an intensified form, perhaps, but it cannot be proved he was wrong. Hence, the modern reader must decide for himself whether to plant his tongue in his cheek or accept this portion of the autobiography at face value.

Certainly no one adventure that befell Trelawny has raised eyebrows higher than the first incident that took place after his schooner left the Malacca Straits. Only two days after leaving Penang, he sighted one of the strangest vessels he had ever seen. She had purple sails, her lines looked as though they were made of long, plaited weeds, and she sat so high in the water that, when she rolled, he could see the barnacles and green slime on her underside. A single musket shot across her bow halted her, and curiosity impelled Trelawny to go aboard her, accompanied by several of his men, all of them armed.

The crew was composed of wild savages, stark naked except for broad-brimmed palmetto hats. Her captain, who wore only a small loincloth, was tattooed from head to foot with red and green serpents. To Trelawny's astonishment—and that of his readers—the man proved to be English. The story of his life, which Trelawny told in capsule form, was as weird as the most outlandish Arabic fancy, and while the captain was telling the tale a shrill cry sounded from below. One of his four wives was in childbirth and was suffering difficulties. Trelawny immediately sent for Kamalia, who delivered the infant, and Trelawny presented the captain with charts, a compass, a bottle of brandy and some hardtack.

A few days later, he saw another ship, a Chinese junk that had drifted off her course, and again he went on board. She was unlike any ship he had ever seen: her bottom and sides were flat; she had double galleries and an exceptionally high, ornamented prow and stern, and in addition to vast quantities of gilding she was decorated with carved dragons painted green and yellow. Her interior was so odd that the startled Trelawny laughed aloud: the ship was filled with tiny bazaar booths and was crowded with the proprietors and their customers, as well as with workmen who were busy making paper and glass, fashioning artifacts of iron, embroidering muslin, painting scrolls on ivory fans and barbecuing pigs, which they then carved and sold. A score of booths were selling live birds and animals, including parrots, monkeys, parakeets, macaws, ducks and pigs.

In the main cabin two fat, handsomely dressed merchants, one a Tartar and the other Chinese, were eating a dog stuffed with herbs and garlic, as well as bowls of shark's-fin jelly, rice, fresh seaweed and salted gulls' eggs. One of them offered him a slice of dog, but he felt ill, hurried away and searched for the captain. He seemed to have disappeared, but at last Trelawny found him, so deeply under the influence of opium that he was almost unconscious.

At that juncture Trelawny crossed the fine line that separated the privateer from the pirate and, his conscience untroubled, did not seem to realize that he engaged in an act of outright banditry. He sent for more of his crew, intending to collect a ransom from the men on the junk. But the Tartar merchant was courageous, and drawing a pistol, pointed it at the young Englishman's head and pulled the trigger. Had the weapon not misfired, Trelawny would have been dead. But he was fortunate, and in turn killed the merchant with a single shot.

Several other Tartars joined in the combat but were no match for the privateer crew and soon were subdued. The struggle was the excuse Trelawny sought to seize the ship's merchandise, and he committed an overt act of piracy by opening every bale and chest. The bulkier cargo, including dyewood, long metal bars and huge barrels of spices, was too large and heavy to be transferred at sea, but everything that could be carried was stolen, the crew returning to the schooner with silks, diamonds, gold dust, copper ornaments, drugs, ivory and tiger skins.

Trelawny also took the pistol that had been fired at him and discovered it was an antique fowling piece, its butt and barrel inlaid with roses carved out of gold. He decided to keep the weapon as a souvenir, and it remained in his possession for the rest of his life.

The incident is important because it exemplifies the callous side of Trelawny's complex nature. In addition to the Tartar merchant, several Chinese workmen were killed, but their deaths, at his hands and those of his sailors, left him unruffled. Neither sorrow nor penitence was felt by Trelawny or his crew. And so we are not taken aback when we learn that, decades later, Trelawny would write about the incident as if it had been an entertaining afternoon's work.

His indifference to the death of ordinary people by accident or violence, even his own violence, was as fatalistic as that of the Oriental, and he could dismiss the matter with a shrug. He wrote in his autobiography:

*An English earl told me the other day that killing a hare on his property was as bad as killing a man. I have done both—killed many of the earl's hares and a leash or two of Chinamen in my time, and for the same reason: I was instigated by excitement, because the acts were forbidden.*

At least Trelawny was fair in his appraisal of his emotions—be it for the moralistic better or the seemingly amoralistic worse. Still, it is no small wonder that, even in his mature years, he was shunned by a number of contemporaries, who regarded him, if not as a sensational liar, then most assuredly as a brutal barbarian. The real answer probably lies in neither of these assessments; as he was willing to gamble with his own life, so, too, he was willing to gamble with the lives of others.

The schooner reached the islands that would later make up the nation of Indonesia, and there both Trelawny and Zela were fascinated by the majestic palms, the brilliant colors, the superb beaches and the mountains that towered high above the dark green rain forests. Zela was pregnant; the couple sometimes discussed the life they would live after they had settled down with their family, but they passed most of their days in silence on deck, staring, like the wide-eyed children they were, at the wondrously lush foliage.

So far, the schooner had avoided the bad luck that supposedly dogged a ship that began a voyage on a Friday, but the vessel was becalmed off a small island when she was less than a day's journey from the rendezvous with De Ruyter. Several of the men became uneasy, and their forebodings seemed justified when one of the sailors went over the side to fasten a loose sheet of copper to the bow. One of his legs trailed in the water, and a shark snapped at the bait. The man screamed and was hauled back to the deck, but bled to death before Trelawny could stem the flow.

The next day, several members of the crew went ashore to swim and take water from a river that fed into the sea. River swimming in the tropics was dangerous, but the seamen were thinking of sharks in the sea and consequently preferred the river. One of them went under the surface, disappeared and was never seen again. No one knew whether he was the victim of a crocodile, an underwater snake or a cramp. The river bottom was dragged for his body, but without success, and the men were terrified, certain now that the curse of a Friday sailing was on their heads.

That night, the moon was a fiery red, and everyone on board became increasingly upset. Heavy clouds appeared overhead and a drenching rain fell, accompanied by howling winds. Trelawny ordered everything on board battened down, realizing that they were trapped by the dreaded simoon, as he called it, a form of typhoon or hurricane common in the South China Sea.

The masts broke, the rigging tore away, spars and yards were scattered. The guns broke loose, adding to the danger, and suddenly the anchor cable snapped. Trelawny and his men were helpless as the schooner was driven out into the mountainous, churning waves of a violently angry sea.

Two of the men were swept overboard, and it was fortunate both could swim, because they managed to keep afloat while Trelawny supervised the lowering of a boat and went to the rescue accompanied by three other members of the crew. The two victims were hauled into the boat, but as the craft was returning to the schooner it capsized and all six of its occupants were thrown into the boiling sea. They saved themselves for the moment by clinging to the boat.

As they rose on the crest of a wave, Trelawny saw a tiny white figure on the open deck: it was Zela, who threw him a line with such accuracy that he was able to catch it with one hand. He hauled himself onto the deck, organized the rescue of the others, all of whom were saved, and then turned to the cold, wet Zela, who collapsed in his arms.

There was no dry place on the entire ship, but he carried her down to the main cabin, which was awash, and there found that old Kamalia had died of a heart attack induced by fright. There was no time to bury the dead, however; Trelawny's concern was with the living, so he left the still unconscious Zela with Adoo and hurried back to the deck.

The worst of the storm was over, although the rain continued to fall heavily. The damage was chopped away, the ship was jury-rigged, and Trelawny ordered First Lieutenant Strong to muster the entire crew. The second officer, seven seamen and the steward, a Swedish boy only a year or two younger than the captain, failed to answer the call, and it became obvious they had been claimed by the sea.

When Trelawny had time to go below in order to see how Zela was faring, he found her conscious but in the throes of premature childbirth. Her pain was agonizing, but there was little that Trelawny or Adoo could do to help her, and at dawn her infant was stillborn. The Friday curse had claimed its last victim.

Trelawny's problems were not yet ended, and Zela's deep depression after the loss of her baby was only one of them. The once-proud schooner looked like a derelict and was undermanned; a portion of the booty taken from the Chinese junk had been damaged, and the provisions were waterlogged, so there was not enough to eat. To make matters even worse, the rendezvous proved exceptionally difficult to find, and Trelawny spent five days searching for it, the schooner limping from one inter-island channel to another in the blazing sun.

These were the worst days he had ever known. His men were hungry, tired and on the verge of mutiny. The ship was dilapidated, and as Trelawny and Strong had to take alternating watches, both were exhausted. The rendezvous was so elusive they began to wonder if it really existed, and Trelawny envisioned the possibility that all hands would die on board, making the schooner a ghost ship.

On the fifth day, however, they came to a little harbor and saw the familiar grab anchored there, two handsome prizes beside her. De Ruyter, as confident, energetic and optimistic as ever, immediately put everything into perspective. Unlimited quantities of the world's best timber were available on the island, and members of the Bajau tribe, who lived there, were his friends and would help repair the damages, which were not as great as they appeared. So many members of the crews of the ships he had captured had volunteered to join him that there would be more than enough replacements for the crew members the schooner had lost. Less of Trelawny's loot had been damaged than he had thought, and his cargo was very valuable. As for food, there were wild boar and sheep on the island, as well as vegetables, rice, Chinese maize, fruits of every description, and fish which, by the hundreds, seemed to leap into nets. Supplies of salt and other preservatives, including the juice of a fruit that resembled a mango, could be found in unlimited quantities, so Trelawny would leave with more food than he had carried at the beginning of his voyage.

The men went to work with a vengeance, their spirits restored, and the Bajaus built a little house on shore for Zela so she could recuperate from her ordeal on dry land. Trelawny's men made such good progress that he, Zela and several of the men took one of the longboats across the channel to Borneo and explored portions of this strange land.

Van Scolpvelt was a member of the party, gathering shells and rock specimens for his collection, and when he bent down to examine a black, shiny stone it moved, and he was frozen with terror as he stared at the square hood of a cobra. Trelawny was the first to recover, and placed the shots of two pistols in the snake's head. First Lieutenant Strong finished off the serpent with his *kris*.

The party was still recovering from the incident when a bird in a nearby tree called at length. Zela said it was faoo bird, and that its cry meant a tiger was near. She was mistaken, but danger still threatened: a creature that bore an uncanny resemblance to an old man crashed through the forest and approached the group, its long and powerful arms at its sides.

Trelawny habitually reloaded his pistols as soon as they were fired, and this precaution saved the life of one or more members of the party. He brought down the beast, which proved to be an orangutan, that large member of the ape family which is native to Borneo. When the humans examined it with care, they saw it had long, reddish-brown hair, a face that reminded Zela of Van Scolpvelt and arms half again as long and powerful as those of a man.

Losing their desire to see any more of Borneo, the group returned to their own island, and there had the first of many picnics. Only Zela was sorry it had been necessary to kill the orangutan. Trelawny was too busy eating the oysters one of the men had gathered, and found them superior to those anywhere else on earth.

The carpenters were making such good progress that Trelawny was able to spend much of his time with Zela, whose health was gradually restored, as were her naturally high spirits. Fresh food was abundant, she enjoyed a daily swim in the harbor, which was protected from sharks and barracuda by a thick coral reef, and the discovery of a grove of date palms delighted her, as dates were her favorite fruit.

Trelawny regained his perspective, too. His wife was whole again, her health unimpaired, so he could put the loss of the baby out of his mind. The schooner would be sturdier than ever when the carpenters were finished with her, and the addition of ducks and geese to the larder, along with vast supplies of birds' eggs, would be welcome when he put to sea again. De Ruyter had gone off for a few days to dispose of the booty, selling it to a merchant from Amsterdam whom he knew, a man who lived in the islands and often acted as an intermediary. And Trelawny's share was far larger than he had anticipated. Displaying his customary reticence when dealing with financial matters, he did not reveal the sum to the readers of *Younger Son*.

De Ruyter proposed a holiday excursion before the ships went to sea again, and a chief of the Bajaus offered to take a party on a hunting expedition. Its members were De Ruyter, Trelawny, Strong, the rais and Zela, who refused to carry any weapons. All were mounted on tame elephants and traveled through deep forests festooned with orchids. They dismounted when they came to the Plain of Elephants, an open area where the tracks of wild elephant herds could be seen in the mud. It was a necessary precaution to walk, the chief of the Bajaus explained, because some of their mounts might bolt and join a herd if they should encounter any wild elephants.

Out of deference to the tender-hearted Zela, the men killed only for food. But they remained in the interior of Borneo for a week, where they saw many strange birds and animals. Among the latter were several kinds of apes, clouded leopards and honey bears, the only beasts the Bajau chief feared. They also saw the rhinoceros, which the amazed Trelawny described in detail, flying squirrels and mouse deer, tiny, graceful creatures about the size of a rabbit. They saw a strange little badger and the so-called "flying snake," as well as toads larger than small dogs.

Trelawny was the first Westerner ever to describe these creatures, and many of his contemporaries condemned him for his too vivid imagination. But the beasts were real, as was the flying snake. All of them truly existed in Borneo, and his descriptions indicate beyond all doubt that he saw them and spent time there.

Zela wept as she kissed her elephant good-by, and Trelawny made two rings from a tuft of hair taken from the elephant's ear. He gave one to Zela and slipped the other onto his own finger. It remained there to the end of his days, and when he died he was buried with it still on his finger.

The holiday having ended, the two ships prepared to go to sea again, and De Ruyter sat down with Trelawny, the rais and Strong for a council of war that promised more loot and adventure.

## XII

## *"The widow was a hideous caricature of womanhood."*

De Ruyter was making new, ambitious plans more daring than anything he had previously contemplated. British merchant shipping in the Far East had assumed considerable proportions, and he proposed to disrupt it. But the attacks had to be launched immediately, because he had been informed that a Royal Navy expedition was being mounted in Bombay to sweep the South China Sea of all pirates—a formidable undertaking. So he intended to begin his campaign without delay. He instructed Trelawny to sail to Batavia for the purpose of carrying letters to the Dutch governor there. He was to buy provisions such as wheat, that were unavailable elsewhere, and if possible, purchase several more 12-pounder cannon, which would equalize the odds somewhat in any battle that might occur with British frigates or sloops of war. It was agreed that Louis would accompany Trelawny in order to attend to the food buying. De Ruyter named a new rendezvous, Seahorse Island, which lay off the Philippines.

The voyage began auspiciously. Trelawny halted a small Brit-

ish merchantman and relieved her of her cargo. That night,
Louis cooked one of his fancier dishes to celebrate the event; the
dish consisted of pigs' feet, sharks' fins, deer sinews, plovers'
eggs, mace, red peppers and cinnamon. It was a great success.
And as usual, the grossly overweight Louis was his own best cus-
tomer.

After only a few days at sea the schooner reached Batavia—
later known as Jakarta—the capital of Java. One of the largest
and most sophisticated cities in the Far East, it had a population
of more than a half million and was under Dutch rule, as were a
number of neighboring islands. The Dutch had first entered the
area in the fifteenth century, and the architectural styles were an
odd blend of two cultures. In some respects Batavia was a larger
version of other Malay communities, and in other ways it closely
resembled Amsterdam and The Hague.

The raw materials of the islands had made the Netherlands
one of the wealthiest nations in Europe, and Batavia's harbor
was ordinarily one of the most crowded on earth. Only a few
ships rode at anchor when Trelawny arrived, however, and he
and Louis learned the reason when they went ashore. A cholera
epidemic was raging, and most European captains were giving
Batavia a wide berth.

By the time Trelawny and Louis discovered the situation,
however, it was too late. Louis contracted cholera and was so
badly overweight that even the best of the Dutch physicians
could do nothing for him. He died after an illness of only a few
days, and Trelawny put out to sea to bury him.

The young captain wanted to conduct an appropriate funeral
service but could find no copy of the Book of Common Prayer on
board the schooner. He made do, however, by saying the Lord's
Prayer, augmenting it with some impromptu prayers of his own.
A volley of three shots was fired as Louis's body was heaved over
the side, and everyone agreed that—from beginning to end—the
ceremony had been impressive.

Bucking finality, however, or maybe succumbing to its own
weight, Louis's body rose to the surface twice. The weights attached to it had proved insufficient, and so Trelawny ultimately
admitted defeat; the body was taken back to Batavia for burial
on land.

We might note at this point, though we will be departing somewhat from the central story here, that Louis's death and the tragicomedy of his burial wrought lasting effects on Trelawny. He vowed never to bury anyone at sea if it could be helped, and he kept his promise. More important, he took to heart the word of the physicians who had told him that they might have been able to save Louis had he weighed less.

From that time, Trelawny was careful of his weight and saw to it that he remained slender. He had always loved food and because of his youth had gained very little, no matter how much he ate, but now he changed his whole approach to diet. He ate only lean meat, vegetables and fruit, and throughout his long life nothing could ever induce him to change this regimen. He wrote that it was the greyhounds, those who were lean, who escaped plagues and fevers, while those who were fat and red-faced died. His comments in *Younger Son* made his feelings on the subject emphatically clear:

*I rejoice in the extermination of the great feeders and fat-but-tocked—all except poor honest Louis, the beating of whose warm heart no mounds of suet could impede. I loathe greasy and haunchy brutes as Moses and Mohammed loathed swine. I salute and revere gout, apoplexy and the stone, for they are in their nature fierce radicals; slayers of kings and priests, the grasping wealthy and the greedy gluttons.*

Zela ate only fruits, vegetables and such natural sweets as honey, and the death of Louis so impressed her husband that he adopted her diet, adding fish or lean meat to it. For all practical purposes he also gave up alcoholic beverages, although—for the next few years—he occasionally abandoned that resolve and indulged in an evening of heavy drinking. Thereafter he was firmer with himself, drinking only coffee and tea, and when served wine in the homes of friends, poured a few token drops into a goblet of water.

He was one of the first of his era to recognize the dangers of obesity, and later in his life, when he tried to persuade other members of a gluttonous generation to eat and drink less, he was regarded as an eccentric. He persisted, however, never wavering in his stand against overweight, and by the end of his long life had won a number of converts to a way of thinking that became general in the next century.

The Dutch authorities in Batavia were anxious to be rid of foreign vessels until the cholera epidemic subsided, and the lack of warmth in their welcome made it difficult for Trelawny to buy his provisions there, so he put out to sea again immediately after burying Louis. Within a few days the validity of his new way of life was emphatically demonstrated: a number of the Western members of his crew came down with cholera, but he and Zela, along with the Arabs on board the schooner, remained in good health.

Trelawny was forced to act as physician and gave the ailing crewmen doses of opium and ether; those who survived the disease and his treatment were fed finely ground cinchona-tree bark, later known as quinine, but which, when used by Trelawny, was dissolved in wine. The medication was effective, and he lost only four sailors—a remarkable record.

The ship was becalmed again, and for days the sails drooped beneath a blazing tropical sun. Morale sagged, which was almost inevitable under the circumstances, so the captain ordered a sail lowered into the sea, and the men went bathing without risking attack by sharks. The appearance of several small Portuguese gunboats provided a temporary diversion and offered targets for gunnery practice; one of the boats was hit, but managed to withdraw before sinking, and her crew went aboard other vessels in the fleet.

Before the schooner was able to get under way again, Trelawny was threatened by the first serious mutiny in his career as a ship's master. He knew something was amiss when the European members of the crew were surly, obeying his orders with reluctance, and after a few days he realized the principal troublemaker was the bos'n. This man, who was French, tried to convince the others that the captain was too young and inexperienced, and that they would fare far better if they took command of the ship themselves and entered a life of piracy.

The bos'n was canny, making it difficult for Trelawny to prove he was stirring up trouble, but the continuing inactivity, combined with the heat, made the man reckless. One morning, as the young captain was making his way to the quarter-deck, he saw the bos'n threatening First Lieutenant Strong with a long knife. It was typical of Trelawny, the man of action, to react instantly and without hesitation. Drawing the *kris* he habitually carried in his belt, he drove the blade into the bos'n's heart, then unceremoniously dumped his body overboard and summoned the rest of the crew to watch the sharks at work. That ended the mutiny, and Trelawny suffered no regrets. He had killed without emotion, knowing the drastic punishment he had inflicted on the bos'n had been just, and although he mentioned the incident only briefly in the autobiography of his early years, he admitted the experience was crucial to his achievement of greater leadership and responsibility.

The voyage was resumed when a breeze sprang up, and Trelawny sailed along the coast of Java, putting into native towns and villages for supplies whenever possible. It was not easy to accumulate the provisions De Ruyter wanted, but he persisted and gradually filled the schooner's hold. In one of these towns he became friendly with the local Javanese chieftain, who invited him to take a day's holiday and go into the interior on a hunting trip.

Trelawny accepted, but before he could mount the horse the man had provided for him he was surrounded by the party of Javanese, and he realized, too late, that he had been trapped by enemies who intended to kill him for his clothes, weapons and pocket watch. He fought hard, even though outnumbered, and for a time held his own, although it was obvious to him that he would be overwhelmed.

Zela, who was watching his departure from the deck, immediately alerted Strong, who went ashore with a party of sailors, rescuing the captain, killing the Javanese chieftain and routing his followers. Trelawny was safe, but his life was in danger, because he had been wounded in the leg by a pistol fired at close range and the wound was filled with powder which it was impossible for him to remove.

Again Zela saved him, applying a poultice soaked in the yolks of raw eggs, which drew out the powder. After allowing the poultice to remain in place for several hours she washed out the wound with hot wine, then repeated the process, and by the following day Trelawny felt so much better that he was able to resume his full duties. He was more in Zela's debt than he knew at the time; many years later, when he suffered a far more severe wound while serving as a volunteer in the Greek Revolution, he remembered her treatment and it saved his life a second time.

Having gathered all the provisions he needed, Trelawny set sail for the rendezvous with De Ruyter. Before he could reach Seahorse Island, however, the schooner and the grab came together during a storm. The latter had been battered by a typhoon and was in need of repairs, so De Ruyter signaled a change in plans. Instead of going on to the Philippines, they would return to the secure harbor of the little island off the coast of Borneo.

The local Malay chief welcomed his friends, and the crews were delighted to go ashore again. Trelawny and Zela went on picnics in their favorite places, and he amused her by building her a two-room hut near the beach. Their existence here was so idyllic that he thought of settling permanently on the island, but Zela demurred. She regarded the Île de France as a Utopia and wanted them to make their home there when he gave up his life at sea. Trelawny was so eager to please her in all things that he agreed.

De Ruyter soon discovered they could combine business and relaxation by their headquarters on the little island. The native Malays earned their living by fishing, and occasionally reported that they had sighted a merchant ship at sea. So the crews of the grab and the schooner were summoned, and the ships went out to take prizes. They captured a number of merchantmen, the men happy to receive their share of the booty, and one day they returned from a raid with a prize of enormous value, a copper-bottomed brig that had been sailing from Bombay to China with a cargo of cotton, opium and pearls.

De Ruyter decided he and his subordinates could cash in only by selling the brig and her cargo in a major port, even though it meant sharing the prize money with local authorities. The Dutch governor, who made his headquarters in Batavia, was amenable to such deals, asking no embarrassing questions, so Trelawny and Zela had to give up their island hut. The rais led a prize crew aboard the brig, and she sailed to Batavia, escorted by the grab and the schooner.

The cholera epidemic had subsided, and the entire company was granted shore leave. De Ruyter indicated that the sale of the brig and her merchandise would take some time to accomplish, so Trelawny rented quarters in the city for himself and Zela, and they spent hours each day wandering around the bustling city.

Batavia, they discovered, was three cities in one. The industrious Dutch conquerors had re-created Amsterdam, and the houses, canals and cobbled streets made the visitors think that a portion of Holland had been transplanted to the opposite side of the earth. The Chinese, who owned most of the shops and bazaars, lived and worked in their own quarter, speaking their own language and clinging to the customs of their ancestors. De Ruyter, one of the few Westerners who had visited Shanghai and Canton, swore that the quarter was as completely Chinese as any city on the mainland. The third quarter, which was the poorest and most crowded, was the home of the gentle Javanese, who performed hard labor in return for infinitesimal wages.

Trelawny again demonstrated his humanitarian instincts, rare in an age when the exploitation of the weak by the strong was taken for granted. He was outraged and disgusted by the treatment accorded the Javanese by both the Dutch and Chinese but was sufficiently mature by now to recognize his own impotence. There was nothing he could do to alleviate the suffering of the natives, but he accomplished more than he realized when he wrote *Younger Son*, publicizing their plight and embarrassing the government of the Netherlands, which was forced to increase the wages paid the Javanese and improve their living conditions.

Batavia may have been the wealthiest city in the world during the first decades of the nineteenth century. Most of the tea and coffee consumed in Europe came from her plantations, she grew almost all of the world's pepper, and she exported vast quantities of other spices. There was such a great demand for her diamonds that the island's mines would be exhausted by the middle of the nineteenth century, and her fabrics, particularly muslin, were highly prized in Europe and North America, Western women considering the cloth superior to any made in India.

De Ruyter and his young friend were warmly received by the governor and the merchants of the Dutch community, international politics making the welcome a matter of course. The Netherlands had been Great Britain's traditional ally for more than two hundred years, but Napoleon had changed the balance of power, conquering the Low Countries and placing his inept but inoffensive young brother, Louis, on the Dutch throne. So London had become Batavia's enemy overnight, and men whose ships flew the French flag were received as intimate comrades.

Many of the wealthier citizens had maintained close business relationships with De Ruyter for years, but now they could enjoy their friendships in the open. He thence spent many nights at country homes in the mountains. Trelawny and Zela shared these invitations and soon developed a number of their own friendships, the tall Englishman and his tiny wife being recognized as an exceptionally attractive and interesting couple. Zela, although she had enjoyed no formal education, proved even more adept than her husband in learning Dutch.

No one showed a greater interest in Trelawny than the landlady in whose house he and De Ruyter had rented apartments. She was an extraordinary person, the subject of one of Trelawny's most fascinating descriptions. A native of the province of Jug, she was said to be one of the wealthiest Javanese in Batavia. Twenty-four years of age, she was no longer considered young but had no lack of suitors, because she was so rich. Her reputation was unique because she had already been married to ten husbands, shedding six of them via divorce. One had died a natural death, two had been murdered and another, who had disappeared on a trip into the interior, was conveniently assumed to be dead. The widow, as Trelawny called her, was seeking her eleventh mate.

Judged by Western standards, the lady was repulsive. She stood slightly over four feet in height, and was very heavy. Her skin was orange-yellow, and she burnished it with coconut oil, which not only made it glisten but gave her a rank odor, as she rarely bathed. Her body resembled a fat ball, and her head looked like a smaller but equally fat ball balanced on it. She was so badly overweight that mounds of flesh concealed her eyes, which resembled two tiny dots. Her nose was so small that it seemed to sink into the ball of flesh, and only her thick, heavy lips protruded. Her head was shaved and was completely bald except for a tuft at the crown reminiscent of De Ruyter's mustache; in it she put a number of jeweled pins for purposes of decoration. She wore thin gowns of muslin, and her walk—which resembled a waddle—was considered by the lady to be provocative.

She compensated for her lack of beauty with a supreme self-confidence. Her next husband, she declared, would be a veritable prince, the proprietor of vast estates complete with plantation houses. She grew rice, tobacco, sugar and coffee, which she shipped in her own merchant fleet, and she owned hundreds of slaves. All this property would belong to her eleventh husband.

The widow first cast her net for De Ruyter, who made it very clear to her that he had no interest in her or her money. She accepted the rebuff with good humor, and told De Ruyter she would be satisfied with his young friend. It did not matter to her that Trelawny was already married. His wife, in her opinion, was a pale, scrawny creature, unworthy of the love of a real man. It would be easy for Trelawny to get rid of her, divorce in Java being a simple matter. All that was needed was for one partner to appear before a Javanese priest, who would dissolve the marriage by cutting a small length of twine with his golden scissors.

The amused De Ruyter told Trelawny and Zela what had happened, and they, too, were entertained. Zela thought the joke particularly hilarious and teased her husband so unmercifully that he told her, with a straight face, that he returned the widow's interest. She refused to believe him.

Thereafter, whenever he left his lodgings or returned, he found the widow waiting for him in her apartment, which was directly below the quarters he and Zela had rented. He tried to prolong the joke by spending a few minutes at a time chatting with the hideous woman, but Zela knew him too well to believe that his interest in the creature was genuine.

The widow, however, took Trelawny's alleged courting in earnest, and returned the favor of his brief conversations by deluging him with gifts. She sent him bags of coffee, whole roasted pigs, sacks of tobacco, a steady stream of fruits, cakes and candy. The situation became embarrassing, and Trelawny tried to snub her; she refused to acknowledge his rebuffs, however, and sent him still more gifts.

At last De Ruyter completed negotiations for the sale of the copper-bottomed brig and her cargo, Trelawny's share being ten thousand pounds, then the equivalent of one hundred and twenty-five thousand dollars. He had more than enough money now to buy a plantation on the Île de France and build a house there for Zela. When the present cruise ended he planned to retire there with her, and they would spend the rest of their days in Paradise.

On the day the schooner and the grab left Batavia, the widow of Jug became desperate. She had herself rowed out to the schooner, and standing in the small boat, called up to Trelawny on his quarter-deck. She was not permitting him to escape, she shrieked; he was her man, and she intended to marry him.

Trelawny called down to her that he was happily married and had no interest in anyone else.

The widow had a fit of hysterics, and as the schooner left the Batavia harbor, her sails slowly filling, Trelawny could see the rotund widow lying on the deck of her little boat, her chubby legs flailing as she screamed and cursed. That, he thought, was the last he would ever hear of the woman, but he soon discovered he had made a fatal error.

## XIII

## *"Ours were no common ties."*

Not yet twenty years old, Edward John Trelawny had every reason to be satisfied with his life in the early months of 1812. He was the master of his own ship, an experienced and accomplished sailor; he was married to a girl to whom he was devoted and who returned his love. He had earned a small fortune, and he intended to spend it buying the home that would make his happiness complete.

But as the schooner put out from Batavia in the wake of the grab, bound for new adventures in the Indonesian Archipelago before returning to the Île de France, the young Englishman felt an increasing sense of uneasiness he could not define.

That night, he had a dream so frightening and vivid that he never forgot it. There were four figures in the nightmare: one was the Javanese chieftain who had tried to trick him and whom he had killed; a second was the widow of Jug, no longer ludicrous, but vicious and menacing; a third was the Blue Angel of Death, an evil skeleton. All three were closing in on a figure he could not identify at first, and then his blood ran cold when he recognized the frail, gentle figure of Zela. She was asleep, unaware of her danger.

Trelawny awakened, brushed the cold sweat from his eyes, and felt infinite relief when he saw Zela, serene in her sleep beside him. No harm had come to her, and he knew he had been dreaming.

But that nightmare haunted him for the rest of his life, and he had the identical dream on a number of occasions. Discussing it in somber terms in *Younger Son*, he wrote:

*That vision has haunted me through life. Often since then I have arisen from bed, haggard, sick, suffering such agonies as only devils can inflict. Ever, as it recurs, it is the more frightful. Always, it assures me of some horrible change.*

At the time, however, he could dismiss the matter from his mind, in part because of a meeting at sea the following day with three French warships. He and De Ruyter went on board the flagship for a meeting with the three captains, who were in high spirits because they had fought, disabled and almost captured a British frigate. Trelawny heard her name and knew she was the frigate from which he himself had escaped.

At first he laughed with the French captains, relishing their story and enjoying the humiliation they had inflicted on their enemy. By that night, however, he was relieved the frigate had escaped and, his patriotism mounting, observed that three French warships were not the equal of one Englishman. He later noted with great pride that the French flagship was eventually captured by the British and became a Royal Navy warship, playing a major role in driving the French out of the Indian Ocean.

Surely Trelawny's joyful reaction to the British Navy's success in this matter—a navy he had seen fit and necessary to run from—leads us to believe that Trelawny was not, at this time, "his old self." The dream of Zela's death may have absented itself from Trelawny's conscious mind, but certainly anxiety was afloat.

The grab and the schooner soon caught a number of small prizes, and one day they encountered a longboat in which they found the mate and four crew members of a shipwrecked English merchantman. Van Scolpvelt immediately treated the starving men, who had been exposed to the elements too long, but in spite of his ministrations two of them died.

One of the survivors was the mate, Darvell, who joined Trelawny on the schooner as his own second officer; they became good friends. They shared a concern for the oppressed people of the world, and they had the same love of adventure; in addition, Darvell was English, like Trelawny's other good friends with the exception of the American De Ruyter.

The voyage through the Indonesian islands, then known as the India Islands, was one of the most pleasant excursions ever made by the schooner. Again and again De Ruyter and Trelawny went ashore for water and wood, sometimes landing on uninhabited islands, at other times finding natives who had never before seen white men. Sometimes the visitors saw animals and birds that, unaccustomed to humans, regarded them without fear and made no move to escape. Trelawny was afraid the Île de France would be the first British target but kept his fears to himself because he didn't want to disappoint Zela unless it became necessary.

Lieutenant Darvell and the two merchant seamen who had survived the ordeal in the longboat with him parted company with Trelawny and De Ruyter in Celebes after finding passage to Bombay on a Portuguese vessel that intended to stop there. Trelawny said a reluctant good-by to his new friend, neither realizing they would meet again in England.

Van Scolpvelt was particularly busy in Celebes and fumigated both the schooner and the grab in order to rid the ships of rats, roaches and such dangerous tropical insects as scorpions and centipedes. He did his usual thorough job, and when he was done the ships were cleaner than they had ever been. The grab also underwent major repairs in Celebes, so the stay there was prolonged, which gave Trelawny and Zela unexpected opportunities to go ashore, visit the pretty town and go on picnic excursions into the countryside. They agreed that, after the Île de France, Celebes was the most attractive island they had ever seen.

The repairs were made in a harbor that faced the huge Gulf of Bone, and Trelawny built a little hut for Zela similar to the dwelling he had made for her on the island off the coast of Borneo. A cliff high above the beach promised him a view of the surrounding countryside and sea, so he determined to climb it with a small party. Zela wanted to accompany him, but the climb was so steep he felt she would be safer below, and went without her.

The view was magnificent, and as Trelawny and his comrades watched they saw a number of little dots moving in from the sea. These were sharks, a native guide told the young Englishman, who watched, through the glass, a fight to the death between a shark and a swordfish at the entrance to the harbor. The school of sharks managed to overcome the barrier of the coral reef and enter the harbor, and when the native guide explained this meant bad weather was coming, Trelawny returned to the beach below. His men were shooting at the sharks with their muskets and pistols, so he left them amusing themselves and strolled on in the direction of the hut he had built for Zela. As he drew closer he could hear Adoo sobbing and weeping, so he broke into a run.

To his horror he found Zela stretched out on a grass pallet, semiconscious and bleeding from a dozen severe cuts and gashes. Dropping to his knees, he kissed her, and she regained consciousness for a moment, long enough to smile at him. Van Scolpvelt was nowhere in the immediate area, so Trelawny went to work himself in an attempt to stem the flow of blood and save his wife's life.

The sailors gathered outside the hut, and Trelawny ordered them to launch the longboat without delay so he could take Zela back to the schooner. They refused to obey him, however, pointing to the harbor, now filled with sharks and troubled with turbulent water. He knew they were right—the storm would break at any moment. It was better to wait it out than to have the longboat capsize in a turbulent, shark-infested sea.

The men erected a sail over the hut, creating a makeshift tent, and Trelawny spent the night there, guarding Zela and keeping close watch over her. The winds howled, sometimes threatening to tear away the tent and subject them to the driving tropical rain that fell steadily all night. Zela remained unconscious and unmoving, was so still, in fact, that Trelawny repeatedly felt her heart to assure himself she was still alive. The Blue Angel of

Death seemed to be hovering nearby, and through the long hours his nightmare seemed very real to him. He recalled his feelings years later when he wrote:

*I knew that the spring tide which had borne me on to perfect happiness was turned, ebbing back to the sea, and that mine and my happiness would be left a stranded wreck. I wished that the lightning would rend the rocks about us till they crumbled down, filled the bay, and buried us together. The invocation I made then I have never revoked—would that it had been accomplished.*

When dawn came, a trace of color reappeared in Zela's cheeks, she awakened and was able to take a little nourishment, bits of the picnic fare she and Trelawny had brought ashore the previous day. She was able to speak, haltingly, and she and the frightened Adoo told him their story. The two girls had gone swimming together and suddenly had realized that sharks had entered the harbor. They had tried to scramble ashore over sharp rocks, and Zela had been more dead than alive when she had reached land. Even now neither she nor Zela knew whether her gashes were the rocks' or the sharks' doing.

The storm subsided after sunrise, and by the time the crew launched the longboat the last clouds were disappearing. Trelawny took his wife back to their quarters on the schooner, then hurriedly sent a message to the grab, asking Van Scolpvelt to come without delay. He dreaded the old surgeon's touch, but Van Scolpvelt proved to be surprisingly gentle as he applied medication to Zela's wounds and bandaged them. He gave her a dose of laudanum, and she dropped into a deep sleep.

Trelawny resumed his watch over her, not moving from her bedside, and had no idea how many hours passed. Then a messenger from the grab appeared, summoning him to an immediate conference with De Ruyter. He hated to leave the sleeping Zela but could not disobey the order.

De Ruyter greeted him with news of primary importance. An Armenian merchant from Bombay, whose ship had dropped anchor near the grab less than an hour earlier, had just told him, during a courtesy call, that the British were planning to launch

an overwhelming surprise attack on the Île de France. The largest flotilla of warships ever gathered in the East would participate and would be accompanied by ten thousand soldiers and
marines. It was essential that the authorities at Port Louis be
notified at once, so the grab and schooner would sail that same
evening, as soon as they could be made ready.

Trelawny returned to the schooner and went to work with a
heavy heart. He did all that was required of him but performed
his duties mechanically, indifferent to the crisis that threatened
the French rule of Mauritius. Nothing mattered to him except
Zela, and if she died he had no desire to live, either.

Van Scolpvelt remained on board the schooner to take care of
Zela, and the old man was kinder and more gentle than
Trelawny had ever known him to be. He refused to promise mir-
acles, but said Zela had a good chance to recover. Trelawny was
further heartened when a local chieftain, prior to the sailing of
the ships, sent Trelawny a gift of the most precious of the
Celebes' healing unguents, a jar of Macassar oil.

There was little change in Zela's condition as the two ships
crowded on sail. They made a brief stop at Batavia for munitions
and provisions, and Trelawny had to supervise their loading
while De Ruyter hurried off to tell the governor the news. Then
they put to sea again, and when they reached the open waters of
the Indian Ocean, Zela began to improve.

For the first time, Trelawny was heartened. When they
reached De Ruyter's house on the Île de France and Zela was
comfortably installed in the primeval garden she loved, she
would be certain to recover her full strength and health. Little
by little he dared to allow his hope to swell.

The Île de France drew closer. And when the ships were only
twelve to fifteen hours from their destination Zela surprised
Trelawny by dressing in one of her prettiest Arab gowns. Her
health was so improved that she sang him one of the songs he
loved. Her recovery was almost complete, she assured him; her
convalescence would be brief after they landed. The relieved
Trelawny left his wife in Adoo's care and went off to the small
cabin in which he had been sleeping since they had left Celebes.

Almost as soon as he dropped off to sleep he suffered a recur-
rence of the nightmare in which the Javanese chieftain, the

widow of Jug and the Blue Angel of Death appeared. He was awakened by the sound of Adoo's frightened voice, calling him.

Trelawny raced to his wife's cabin and found Zela half conscious and in great pain. The hysterical Adoo pointed to a jar of green nutmegs preserved in syrup, and even as Trelawny summoned Van Scolpvelt he knew the widow of Jug had won her victory. The Javanese were noted throughout the East for their ability to concoct deadly poisons, and Trelawny guessed what the widow had done.

Van Scolpvelt confirmed his hunch. The nutmeg was poisoned, and the surgeon could offer no hope from the outset, even though he worked through the night, giving Zela antidotes. The girl's agony became worse, so Van Scolpvelt finally gave her a sedative to ease the pain, warning Trelawny, however, that it was unlikely she would survive.

At dawn the lookout in the crow's nest sighted land, and First Lieutenant Strong sent word to Trelawny that they were approaching the Île de France.

Trelawny saw that Zela was awake and bent down to tell her the news, cradling her in his arms and bending close so he could hear her barely audible words.

"I am glad, love," she murmured. "But I am too weak to walk. You will have to carry me." She smiled at him. And then she died in his arms.

The schooner and the grab put into the quiet harbor of Port Bourbon, their crews learning at once that news of the impending attack had already been received and that feverish defense preparations were being made at Port Louis. De Ruyter and most of the others hurried ashore, but Trelawny, his grief paralyzing him, sat beside Zela's bed, staring with tearless eyes at the body of the girl who had meant more to him than anyone else on earth. Never again would he love or be loved so much, never again would his life be the same.

Late in the day, De Ruyter returned and tried to arouse his friend with gloomy news. The British invasion fleet was already at sea, and according to reports that had reached Port Louis was too powerful to be resisted. The governor was thinking of surrendering without a fight rather than letting men die in a hopeless cause. More than the loss of the Île de France was at stake, De

Ruyter said; the day of the French in the East was coming to an
end, and Britain would rule supreme in India and the waters of
the Indian Ocean.

The words made no impression on Trelawny, who could think
only of Zela's burial. He had thought of burying her at sea, but
remembered the fate of Louis and could not bear to watch the
sharks attack her. He had thought of burying her in the garden
outside De Ruyter's house, the garden she had loved, but the
possibility that tropical insects would attack her lifeless body
overwhelmed him.

Yet another idea had occurred to him. Perhaps they might
prepare a funeral pyre, similar to that of the ancient Greeks. He
was not a truly religious man, but perhaps, as the flames consumed her body, her spirit would return to the elements.

De Ruyter promised that he, the rais and Van Scolpvelt would
take care of the details and would send a signal from the shore
when the necessary preparations had been made. Trelawny, still
in anguish many years later as he recalled the fateful day, told
the story best:

*The utmost human nature can endure and survive, I suffered.
Ours were no common ties. She had been as a bird driven by
tempest from the land that sought refuge in my bosom, and like
a darling bird too delicate to be entrusted to others' hands, I
alone fostered and cherished her.*

*I robed Zela in the richest costume of her country. Her yellow
vest was spangled with little rubies, and her chemise and flowing
drawers, of sea-green Indian crepe, edged with gold; her outer
garments were of the finest muslin of India; her slippers, and the
embroidered kerchiefs which bound up her hair and concealed
her bosom and the lower part of her face, beaded and embossed
with pearls. I preserved one braid of her long, dark, silken hair. I
placed it in my breast and kissed her eyelids, cheeks and lips.
Carefully folding her in a large Arab barbican of white camel's
hair, I conveyed her onto the boat.*

*I was a mere machine. The blood in my veins was stagnant. I
got over the boat's quarter into the sea, and pressing my precious
burden to my breast and warily preventing the water from
touching her, I walked through the surf to the shore. Its coolness*

*strengthened me, and I was able to stagger to the spot where stood the funeral pyre. A black iron furnace, like a coffin, was placed upon it; figures flitted about like spectres. I paused, realized the necessity of going through with what I had undertaken, and placed the body within the iron shell as tenderly as a mother lays her sleeping child in its cradle.*

*De Ruyter drew me back. Oil, spices, musk, camphor and ambergris were thrown in. Dry bamboo and reeds covered all: so that, when ignited, I could see nothing but a dark, impenetrable pyramid of smoke. I tried to speak; then entreated by signs, for my throat was dry as death, that they would unhand me. But they held me fast, and my strength had totally fled, else I would have cast them off and followed my beloved onto the pyre. But De Ruyter knew my intent, and they would not release me.*

*Owing to some confusion, the cause of which I did not then ascertain (it was the rescuing of Adoo, who had thrown herself into the flames), I found myself unfettered. With the intention of doing this same thing, I sprang forward, but, stumbling from weakness or over some object in my way, I fell on the sand, so near the fire that my outstretched hands were severely burned. What followed I know not, for I remained insensible. When restored to reason, I was swinging in a cot on the deck of the schooner.*

De Ruyter had gone to Port Louis for urgent consultations with the governor and had left First Lieutenant Strong in command, giving him strict orders to maintain an adequate guard over Trelawny at all times. Van Scolpvelt was there too and, unable to persuade his listless, grieving patient to eat, forced him to take a sedative. Trelawny had no idea how long he slept, but by the time he awakened he felt hungry and, despite his grief, was able to choke down small quantities of food.

De Ruyter returned after an absence of two days, perhaps three, after making drastic plans for the future. He himself intended to sail to Europe with messages from the governor for the Emperor Napoleon. Then, having taken with him as much of his personal treasure as he could comfortably carry, he would return to the United States. War was threatening to break out between America and Great Britain, and he intended to offer his services, those of Strong and the schooner itself to the U. S. Government. Van Scolpvelt, who would sail as far as Europe with him, planned to return to his native Holland; completely apolitical, he didn't care whether it was governed by the house of Orange or the Bonaparte usurpers.

The rais, to whom De Ruyter was giving the grab, would return to his own home on the eastern coast of Arabia, taking with him the twelve surviving members of Zela's tribe, whom he intended to "adopt" so they could become integrated with his own people. He also planned to take Adoo with him, give her her freedom and make her a member of his tribe.

That left the problem of Trelawny's own future. He could remain on the Île de France, but De Ruyter strongly urged him not to consider the possibility. Not only would he become involved in the fight between the English and the French, but his life would be in grave jeopardy when the island fell. The frigate on which he had served would undoubtedly participate in the invasion, and if he were captured and recognized, he could be put to death as a deserter in wartime. At the least, he would face a long term of imprisonment.

A second possibility was migration to the United States, accompanying De Ruyter and Strong. But this idea had its drawbacks too, since it appeared inevitable that America and Britain soon would be at war. Many years had passed since De Ruyter had last seen his home, and he admitted he did not know the temper of his fellow Americans. But he remembered the strong feeling against Tories during the War of Independence, and he was afraid an enemy alien, regardless of his personal sympathies, would not be accorded the warmest of welcomes.

That left the third possibility, a return to England. Trelawny could sail in the schooner with De Ruyter and Strong and be dropped off at some isolated point on an uninhabited stretch of coast. The chances that he would be prosecuted as a Royal Navy deserter were remote, there being several thousand others in the same position. It would be embarrassing for the government to take action against one and not all.

For all practical purposes Trelawny had been disowned by his family, so it was impossible to predict whether he would be able to re-establish relations with them. As De Ruyter pointed out, it was also questionable whether Trelawny would even want to be on friendly terms with his father. To go it alone, then, in some area of England new to Trelawny might be the answer, De Ruyter surmised.

As to his vocation, he was an experienced ship's captain and could probably find a satisfactory position for himself in the merchant marine. On the other hand, he had enough money to support himself for a long time if he wanted to live the life of a gentleman and do no work at all. The choice was his.

Trelawny was still so dazed by the death of Zela that he didn't care where he went or what he did, and only when prodded by his friend did he finally decide he would return to England. But, he insisted, he would take Adoo with him. She and Zela had been devoted to each other, so he was under a lifelong obligation to look after Adoo himself.

The notion was so impractical that De Ruyter was horrified, realizing that the young Englishman had absented himself from Western civilization for so long that he had no concept of the reality of life there. It would be difficult enough for a young man on the eve of his twentieth birthday, an ungainly, ill-mannered youth who looked like an Arab, to make his way in polite society. He would create the worst kind of sensation if he appeared in the company of a Malay slave girl, and no one in England would be able to accept the true state of their relationship.

Trelawny waved aside the protests. He would be faithful to Zela's memory, and for her sake he would not abandon Adoo. Nothing could persuade him to leave her at the mercy of others.

Trying to exercise patience, De Ruyter finally presented an argument to which the younger man was willing to listen. Adoo would not be able to survive in England. The climate, food and customs were alien to her, the way of life there beyond her ken. It would be unfair to the illiterate Malay girl—no matter how great the loyalty she had transferred from Zela to Trelawny—to take her to the most advanced of Western nations, where civilization was far too complicated for her.

At last Trelawny gave in, but a new problem arose. If Adoo learned he intended to leave without her, he knew, she would refuse to remain behind. De Ruyter promised to handle that aspect of the matter, and the fact that Trelawny would sail to Europe on the schooner would be concealed from her.

Preparations for the voyage were made with great haste, as the British attack on the Île de France was expected momentarily. Ample food supplies were available on the lush island, although no munitions could be spared, but this presented no real difficulties, as the schooner's magazine was still filled. The hiring of a crew proved to be remarkably easy, as there were many English sailors on the Île de France who had good reason to wish themselves elsewhere when the British war fleet captured the island. So the procurement of a Western crew was accomplished within a few hours.

On the day of departure Trelawny said good-by to the rais and to the faithful Arab seamen who had sailed with him on so many voyages, but he lacked the courage to bid farewell to Adoo. So she remained with the rais, confidently believing that Trelawny would remain behind with her.

The schooner sailed from the Île de France at sundown, and Trelawny and De Ruyter stood together in silence on the quarter-deck. The young Englishman strained in vain for a last glimpse of Zela's funeral pyre. De Ruyter, who was giving up his magnificent home, on which he had lavished so much care and attention over a period of many years, was busy with his own thoughts.

Not until a year later, when Trelawny received a letter from the rais, did he learn what became of Adoo. When the Malay girl realized he was sailing without her, she had dashed down to the harbor, jumped into the water and started to swim after his ship. The rais had organized a search for her, but it proved impossible to find her in the dark. It was not until the following day that her body was found floating in the water near the coral reef.

All Trelawny knew as the schooner headed westward was that he was leaving his youth behind. He had only his memories of Zela, whom he had loved with such passionate devotion, and he faced the most uncertain of futures in a land where he had never known a moment's happiness.

XIV

*"In six months we meet again."*

The westward voyage was uneventful, and Trelawny recovered a
measure of his equilibrium. He and De Ruyter spent long hours
in conversation, devoting most of their discussion to abstract
philosophical questions, and the young Englishman again was
filled with a desire to improve his education. It was the last service De Ruyter performed for him.

When they reached European waters off the coast of Spain
and Portugal, they saw many vessels of the Royal Navy on pa-
trol, and only then did they realize how tight was the sea blockade of France that Great Britain was maintaining. All of De
Ruyter's skill was needed to avoid British warships, and the
problem became worse when the schooner reached the English
Channel, where there were "more Royal Navy frigates and
sloops than fish." But De Ruyter demonstrated his consummate
cunning and managed to reach the French fishing port of Saint-
Malo without once having been challenged on the high seas.

It had become obvious, however, that there had to be a
change in plans. Van Scolpvelt left the schooner to return
overland to Holland, and De Ruyter, knowing his luck would not

last forever, abandoned his idea of sailing Trelawny to the coast
of England. Instead he paid two French fisherman a handsome
sum to smuggle his young friend across the Channel.

The time had come for Trelawny's farewell to De Ruyter, and
it was particularly hard for Trelawny, as De Ruyter appeared to
have been the only person who had ever loved him besides Zela.
The parting was so painful that, even when writing *Younger Son,*
the better part of two decades later, he devoted a minimum of
words to the subject—brevity helping to dam the flow of tears.

"In six months we meet again," De Ruyter said, but a nagging
premonition made Trelawny doubt it. His feelings proved correct. De Ruyter reached Paris safely and delivered the letters
from the governor of the Île de France to Foreign Minister
Talleyrand. Then, the United States and Great Britain having
formally declared war, he was entrusted with dispatches to President James Madison. He maneuvered the schooner through the
English Channel without incident. But a British frigate pounced
on him in the mid-Atlantic, and he was killed by a shot that exploded on the quarter-deck as he was burning communications
the French Government had given him. The enemy respected
him in death, and he was buried at sea, wrapped in the flag of
France.

Trelawny knew nothing of the fate that awaited his friend as
the fishermen conveyed him to England in short hops, hiding by
day in Channel Island coves, then resuming their voyage again
at night. He waded ashore through the surf, his sea chest on his
shoulders, then walked to the nearest town, which proved to be
Bournemouth. Going to the nearest inn, he remained there for
several days, buying an English wardrobe and trying to accus-
tom himself again to the land of his birth. The autumn weather
was cold, a thick fog rolled in from the Channel, and he felt
bereft, totally cut off from the life he had known and loved.

At this juncture *Adventures of a Younger Son* suddenly skips
the period of the ensuing year and a half. Trelawny made no
mention of his homecoming, his establishment of a new way of
life or his resumption of relations with his relatives. The little
that is known about these months must be gleaned from his subsequent correspondence and that of various members of his family.

Piecing together the puzzle, it appears that he went from Bournemouth to London. His funds being ample for the purpose, he took lodgings in a handsome house off the Strand, his quarters consisting of a sitting room, a small library and a bedroom. Eventually he got in touch with his uncle, who had presumed him dead, and thereafter he saw his mother, brother and sisters, who came to the city for a grand reunion with him.

At no time, even in his letters, did he mention his father, nor did he say whether he ever visited the family home again. Consequently two theories have been advanced. According to the first, Charles Trelawny had mellowed and greeted his younger son with civility if not with warmth; he was to have settled an allowance on him. According to the second version, Trelawny never saw his father again, never set foot under the family roof and continued to live on his share of the booty he had acquired in the East. All that can be said with certainty is that Trelawny's total silence on the subject seems to indicate that the relationship must have been painful and strained.

Gradually the young man took his place in a society to which his ancestry and the money he had himself earned entitled him. But the spirit of the country had changed from so many years of war. The struggle with Napoleon promised to go on forever, and the new conflict with the United States further strained the nation's resources and manpower. All classes were weary of war but were united in their stubborn determination not to stop until they had achieved victory. The Royal Navy was the most powerful armada ever built by man, and Britain was building her land forces for the climactic showdown with the French emperor that would be fought at Waterloo.

Each man sought his own individual escape from reality in day-to-day living. The poor drank vast quantities of cheap gin and raw beer, and lower-class girls tried to get money by streetwalking. Members of the middle class built exorbitant new homes, and dined in expensive taverns, inns and restaurants that sprang up in response to their demand. They spent their funds on theater, bear-baiting, cock fights and other entertainments. The aristocrats led even more frivolous lives, attending endless rounds of parties, assemblies, routs and balls, paying visits to Bath and Brighton, traveling non-stop from town houses to coun-

try seats and back. Morals declined. Young ladies imitated the
enemy court of Napoleon and wore as few clothes as possible,
and young gentlemen garbed themselves in such outlandish cos-
tumes that they looked like overdressed peacocks. Fortunes were
lost at gaming tables, and the bluebloods, like the poor, drank
themselves to alcoholism or death.

In literature, music and painting, the romantic movement was
in the air, artists escaping from the grim world around them by
seeking the pure, the ideal and the unsullied. Such radical philosophers as William Godwin dreamed of new Utopias, and
women, tired of being regarded as chattels, were writing books,
seeking careers and demanding the right to lead lives of their
own.

Edward John Trelawny, far more worldly than the stay-at-
home members of his generation, fitted uneasily into this changing society. He was so handsome that the young ladies of London fawned over him; he clung to memories of Zela, and his
interest failed to become aroused. The companionship of his
male contemporaries was equally unpleasant. These gentlemen
were childish in comparison to Trelawny, who had become inti-
mately acquainted with death, and with travel. Trelawny's distaste for those things his society was glutting itself on—drink,
common wenches and even gaming—made him something of an
outsider.

But the demands of the philosophers for a new world, the
yearnings of the poets for equality and brotherhood among men,
the insistence of the liberal politicians that the principles of justice be applied to all men, took root in England at the same time
as these excesses were threatening to destroy her. Trelawny discovered that men other than De Ruyter and Aston shared his humanitarian instincts, and he read everything he could find by
kindred spirits. He was particularly impressed by the works of
Godwin, soon to become the father-in-law and spiritual mentor
of the yet unknown young poet Percy Bysshe Shelley.

The fact that Trelawny was a Royal Navy deserter in no way
militated against him. The Navy's brutality was regarded as a
necessary evil, and no one blamed the man who had been courageous and cunning enough to escape from the system and its
rigid discipline. In later years Trelawny's correspondence would

indicate, with some amusement, that even admirals who were somewhat familiar with his background did not hesitate to greet him cordially when they met in fashionable drawing rooms.

Apparently the thought of seeking either naval or military service for the final phase of the war against Napoleon did not occur to him, and no one thought less of him because of it. Having already fought under the French flag against Britain, Trelawny would have been worse than a mercenary had he changed sides now. His situation was personal, and he viewed it in no other terms. He had seen enough of death and suffering and needed time to heal.

Not only did he continue to grieve for Zela; he now was doing the same for De Ruyter. A letter from Strong, the war having set back its delivery for many months, told him of De Ruyter's death. Almost immediately thereafter he suffered a third blow, learning that Lieutenant Aston had been killed in action, too. He was more isolated now than he had been at any time since he had left England a frightened boy.

His relationships with his family, although much improved, were curious. He and his brother were on amicable terms and remained friendly for many years thereafter, but they had led such different lives that a wide gulf separated them and neither ever understood the other. Trelawny was somewhat closer to his sisters, but suspected—with justice—that they did not entirely approve of him.

His mother stood apart from all the rest. It was true that she had ignored him for many years, but when he was middle-aged he confessed to Claire Clairmont that he could not really blame her for her seeming indifference to him in his childhood. Convention had forced her to accept the dictum of her husband, and she had neglected her younger son because she had been ordered to have nothing more to do with him. So, after they resumed relations, he went through the motions of being devoted to her. Certainly he showed her respect, and if he did not love her any more than she loved him, if they were never close, their association was at least correct.

Whether the young man and his father ever saw each other or communicated in any way remains a mystery. Several of Trelawny's biographers have suggested that he received an allowance from his father, but offer no substantiation of the claim. It seems more likely that, prior to the older man's death, Trelawny continued to support himself on the proceeds of the sales of the various prizes he had taken during his years as a privateer in the East. Neither in his correspondence nor in his personal associations with others did he ever reveal more about his father than he wrote in the early chapters of *Younger Son*. Thereafter, until the end of his life, he acted and spoke as though Charles Trelawny had never existed.

In spite of Trelawny's worldliness in essentials, he had few social graces at the age of twenty-one, and in many ways was less sophisticated than most of his contemporaries. He himself later revealed that he had never slept in a four-poster bed, lifted a crystal goblet to his lips or attended a concert. Until his return to England he had never visited a salon, chatted with his peers or engaged in a mild flirtation with a lady. He may have looked like a wicked philanderer, but his only relations with women thus far had been his pure love affair and marriage, and a number of evenings spent with Eastern harlots.

Seen in that light, it seems almost inevitable that the lonely young Trelawny should find himself ready bait for involvement with a young lady of his own class. The girl was Caroline Julia Addison, two years his junior and daughter of a gentleman who had been prominent in the affairs of the East India Company. Julia, as the girl was called, had been born in India.

Trelawny met Julia in Bath, which he visited in the early months of 1813 with a new friend, a Captain White. Julia and Trelawny were drawn to each other immediately. She was described as being "rather handsome," but this is probably an understatement, as Trelawny's tastes in women were very demanding. She was, furthermore, extremely "fascinating and well-educated." She spoke and read French fluently. Interests seemingly meshing and love seemingly strong, Trelawny and Julia were soon engaged.

On May 17, 1813, they were married in St. Mary's Church, Paddington. No details of the ceremony are known, and no information is available to indicate whether any members of the bridegroom's family attended.

For a time the young couple lived in Denham. Thereafter they moved from one lodging house to another at fairly frequent intervals. All of their homes were modest, although there was no particular need for them to stint. Their combined income from Trelawny's investments and Julia's dowry amounted to approximately five hundred pounds per year.

Their first child, Maria Julia, was born about a year after the marriage. And at the beginning of 1816, when Julia was pregnant with her second daughter, Eliza, they were living in a house owned by a Mrs. Prout on College Street, in Bristol. Their downstairs neighbor was Captain Thomas Coleman of the 98th Regiment of Foot, a man who owned a large library and knew how to work this in his favor. Realizing that Julia Trelawny loved to read but could not afford to buy many books, he offered her the use of his.

Before long he was slipping short notes between the pages of the books. These were followed by longer letters, which the housemaid delivered, and during the frequent absences of Trelawny he became her lover. Trelawny suspected nothing, but one afternoon, when he came into the building by the back entrance, he saw his wife hurrying up the stairs, trying to conceal a book. He persuaded her to show it to him, and a love letter dropped onto the floor. Julia, however, managed to convince him that it was addressed to the landlady.

Mrs. Prout and the housemaid knew better, of course, but went to great pains to keep the secret from Trelawny. He was, the landlady quickly learned, a man of violent disposition, her private name for him being "the Turk." She was convinced Trelawny would kill his wife and Coleman with the kris he kept on the mantel, if he learned the truth. Mrs. Prout was so afraid scandal would descend on her house that she refused to renew Trelawny's lease in the late spring, using as her excuse the fact that she didn't want couples with more than one child in the place.

So Trelawny and Julia went with their children to Bath, where they lived with Captain White and his family. During this period Trelawny formed a friendship with White's daughter, Augusta, who was about five years his junior, and they remained close for the rest of their lives, often confiding in each other but never becoming lovers.

If Julia had been sensible she would have broken off her affair with Captain Coleman at this time, and Trelawny might never have learned of the relationship. But she insisted on seeing him and found excuses to travel to London, where she met him surreptitiously. Her mother learned of the liaison, and during a visit to Julia and Trelawny during the Christmas season, she tried to persuade Julia to give up her lover. Julia refused; they quarreled. And Trelawny came into the room while the argument was raging.

For the first time now Trelawny discovered his wife had been unfaithful to him. He had become a man of the highest principles, and declaring he could not remain under the same roof with Julia, he left her, on the last day of 1816, immediately filing suit for divorce. The case was dragged on for more than two years, Julia's family trying to protect her by repeatedly petitioning the courts not to permit some portions of her correspondence with Coleman to be admitted as evidence.

These requests were denied, and the full facts were printed in the London newspapers throughout 1817 and 1818, the families of both principals being sufficiently prominent for the letters to warrant such attention.

Mrs. Prout testified that the couple were affectionate but reserved, and spent most evenings at home, where they read quietly. Undercutting this, though, was the discovery of a letter Julia sent to her husband after beginning her affair. It not only demonstrated her ability to deceive him but helped satisfy the court that Trelawny was being kept in ignorance of the liaison:

*How kind are your arrangements, but I am very well off for money; your last was not expected, tho' my expenses are enormous in the aggregate they are amply supplied by your generosity.*

*Do not, my own John, think of seeing me a moment before you can, with perfect convenience, undertake a winter's expedition. Your letters are my eternal solace from sorrow! How happy I am, and how grateful I ought to be for enjoying such a blessing. Heaven spare my husband to return to his children, who are all perfection in my eyes.*

According to some of the defense witnesses, Trelawny rarely showed his wife affection, was brusque and demanding, and absented himself for long periods. But the courts discarded this evidence when Trelawny himself took the stand and said that his investments in stocks and real estate required his personal attention, as he attended to them himself rather than utilize the services of a banker or business manager.

The judge who first heard the case and the three justices on the bench of the higher court to whom the defense appealed were unanimous in granting Trelawny his absolute divorce. He agreed to allow Julia to keep custody of the children, and he was granted the right to receive visits from them whenever he wished. He also pledged to support both daughters, but Julia was required to pay the court costs and the fees of the attorneys representing both parties.

Trelawny's correspondence with Augusta White during this trying period was a harbinger of things to come. Throughout his life he had the rare talent for establishing and maintaining a warm but totally Platonic relationship with sympathetic women. Certainly it is no exaggeration to say that they gave him the comfort that had always been lacking in his relationship with his mother and that only Zela, who was so rudely taken from him, had offered him. A letter he wrote Augusta in the difficult days of 1817, when he had returned to London and taken lodgings in Soho Square, illustrates not only his facility as a correspondent but illuminates his deep emotional needs:

*Your love and sympathy soothed my wizened soul and bid me hope—think then my friend should you ever be less kind and affectionate what I should suffer, the very thought is madness—thus have exemplified the following lines*

> *Trust me they are no idle hours*
> *That love determines dear*
> *Oh, when misfortune rudely lours*
> *How kind a woman's tears*
> *And what when pleasure wildly charms*
> *Oh what is half so sweet,*

*As clasped in Woman's faithful arms*
*Her thrilling lips to meet.*

*How often I long again to enjoy the felicity of your society, to pour into your faithful bosom the sensations of my heart, to feel that heart beat in unison with mine—do not conceive my sorrows can depress my soul—I am armed with fortitude to withstand the shocks of my evil destiny, but your undeserved, unlooked for kindness have entirely subdued the stubbornness of my nature, the retrospection of which has brought tears into those eyes—that no grief or sorrow ever could—O my dearest sister could you but see my heart, you would wonder it should be inclosed in so rough a form—my study through life has been to hide under mark of affected roughness, the tenderest, warmest and most affectionate sensibility.*

Even when suffering from the crushing blow to his ego and masculinity caused by his wife's infidelity, Trelawny could already walk the almost invisible line that separated friendship from something more. Those who accused him, in later life, of deliberately making subtle love to every woman he met, including those with whom he formed only friendships, were to some extent mistaken.

It is unlikely that his flirtatiousness was deliberate. His own needs were so pressing that, even in his dealings with a friend, he sometimes offered and simultaneously sought more than a friend could offer. He was not flirting in the true sense of the word but was reaching out for the warmth he had never known prior to his relationship with Zela, a feminine understanding and sympathy that was strangely lacking in the women he subsequently married or took as mistresses.

His verbal gropings were not offensive, and most of his correspondents, Augusta White among them, were flattered. Not many men could sound passionate yet respectful at the same time, and prove harmless, when such was the extent of the relationship, in face-to-face confrontations.

For more than three years after the dissolution of his marriage to Julia, he drifted. His bachelor lodgings at 9 Soho Square were simple, and his expenses were few. He ate sparingly, drank no alcoholic beverages and, having been twice burned, did not become involved in any romances—despite his pursuit at the hands of many aspiring ladies. He satisfied his physical needs by taking harlots to his rooms for brief visits but was the first to admit that he ran whenever an unattached woman of his own class developed an interest in him.

As he was handsome, a spirited conversationalist and a man of rapidly developing intellect, he had many acquaintances and never lacked dinner invitations. He actually needed extraordinary friends to admire, men like De Ruyter and Aston, women like Zela, but he did not find them. Consequently he formed no close relationships, other than that with Augusta White, from 1817 through 1819.

His principal form of relaxation was reading, and he bought or borrowed books of every description. So many things had happened to Trelawny already, it is not surprising that he would encounter the man who would become the most influential of all his friends through the mere pages of a book. A journey Trelawny would soon make to Switzerland would, in effect, become a turning point in his life.

## XV

## *"Who can control his fate?"*

Edward John Trelawny was the first to admit that a never-ending restlessness, caused by the journeying-about of his adolescence, was the curse of his existence. No matter how much pleasure or satisfaction he found in any one place, he soon became dissatisfied with it and had to move. When he was in London he yearned for a life in the country, and when in a rural retreat he wanted the excitements of the city. Only because he was finding himself was he content to remain in England for the seven and one half years following his return in 1812.

By the early spring of 1820 his wanderlust became overwhelming, and he decided to pay his first visit to the Continent. He spent a month in the country with his daughters, renting a cottage for the purpose, then returned them to Julia and went off to Paris.

Like thousands of other Anglo-Saxon visitors, Trelawny was dazzled by the physical beauty of the French capital, but life under the restored Bourbons depressed him. The former governor of the Île de France was living in Paris in retirement, and several others whom Trelawny had known in the East were also in the city. Consequently he saw more of the place than most outsiders, and everything he saw angered him.

The Bourbons, he said, were would-be despots who lacked the strength of real tyrants and compensated for their inability to rule in scores of little ways that harassed Parisians. The press was censored, and people either read alleged news they could not believe or were kept in ignorance. Even books were subjected to the censors' pencils, so no literature of consequence was being published. People did not dare to speak their minds freely in the streets or cafés, and only in the privacy of their homes did they dare unburden themselves to trusted friends.

The spirit of France he had known in the East was somnolent, but, giving the French the generous benefit of a doubt, he presumed it was not dead. He predicted that "the most spirited of people" would rise again. Apparently he had seen fit to forget or bury the contempt he had felt for France and all things French which had made him so indignant at the victory banquet held in the governor's palace on the Île de France.

From Paris Trelawny went to Switzerland, at the time the mecca for visiting English aristocrats, authors and artists. The political air was freer than anywhere else in Europe, the forces of repression that were rampant elsewhere after the fall of Napoleon being held in check. The scenery was incomparable, and most tourists having failed to discover the country yet, prices were reasonable. By late May he had found comfortable lodgings in Geneva and settled there for a protracted stay.

In the next few weeks Trelawny became friendly with a local bookseller whose shop he visited regularly, and one day he found the man indignant because a priest had protested the presence of a slender volume on his shelves. Trelawny told the story in virtually identical wording in both of his later books, *Recollections of the Last Days of Shelley and Byron* and *Records of Shelley, Byron and the Author*, in which he quoted the bookseller as saying:

*I am trying to sharpen my wits in this pungent air, which gave such a keen edge to the great historian (Gibbon), so that I can fathom this book. Your modern poets, Byron, Scott and Moore, I*

*can read and understand as I walk along, but I have got hold of*
*a book by one now that makes me stop to take breath and think.*

*To my taste the fruit is crude but well-flavoured: the writer is*
*an enthusiast and has the true spirit of a poet: they say he is but*
*a boy, and this is his first offering: if that be true, we shall hear*
*of him again.*

The poet was Percy Bysshe Shelley, and the book was *Queen Mab*, a poem regarded as shockingly radical by many of his contemporaries because of its plea for social justice, its rejection of Christianity and its strong stand in favor of the workingman as opposed to the vested interests of the period. Trelawny read it avidly and was stunned because so many of Shelley's views were similar to his own. He, too, did not regard himself as an orthodox Christian but nevertheless believed in the existence of a Superior Being, one who had created and ordered the universe. He, too, felt contempt for men of wealth and power who became richer and stronger at the expense of the poor. And he, also, dreamed of a new world, clung to the optimistic belief that it could be created by men of good will. Never had he read anything that made such a deep impression on him, and this own work convinced him that its author was a genius. In the light of all that followed, it is essential to one's understanding of Trelawny that he was one of the first men, anywhere, to become aware of Shelley's worth and uniqueness as a philosopher and poet.

While still absorbing *Queen Mab* and mulling it over, Trelawny met his first prominent English poet. William Wordsworth, generally recognized as the pioneer in the romantic movement that was sweeping English letters, was traveling in Switzerland with his wife and sister. Trelawny, eager to corroborate his own views of Shelley, asked Wordsworth his opinion of the younger poet and was startled when Wordsworth replied that he thought nothing of Shelley, adding, "A poet who has not produced a good poem before he is twenty-five, we may conclude cannot and never will do so."

The disappointed Trelawny pronounced his own verdict on William Wordsworth: "I could see no trace in the hard features and the weather-stained brow of the outer man, of the divinity within him."

He did not permit Wordsworth's views to dim his own enthusiasm for Shelley, however, and with the aid of his bookseller friend conducted a search for other works published by the virtually unknown young Englishman. *The Cenci* confirmed his opinion that Shelley was a rare genius. By the time he also read some of Shelley's short lyric poems he had become a devoted follower and was eager to meet the poet.

His stay in Switzerland was, in part, marred, however, by disturbing news about his old friend Lieutenant Darvell, the young officer who had been shipwrecked in the Indian Ocean. After the final defeat of Napoleon, Darvell, with whom he had continued to correspond, had become so taken with the sea that he had been either unable or unwilling to make a life for himself on land and had gone off to South America to explore and map portions of the coastline that had never before been charted. His ship foundered on hidden rocks, and all hands drowned. Trelawny believed Darvell had been killed in a naval engagement with a Spanish flotilla and that he had actually gone to South America to help some of the Spanish colonies there win their independence. He is the only authority for the allegation, which may have been true; it is, at any rate, as feasible as the other. In any event, the death of yet another friend reinforced his belief that all his intimates, luckless before fate, died violently and before their time. He expressed his view in a touching epitaph:

*Darvell's life was a short one. It has been so with all those to whom I have linked myself. His riper judgment shook off the fetters that had manacled him in boyhood; his daring spirit forced him on from danger to danger. On his return to Europe he became a leader of the forlorn hope of the heroic few who are to be found in the van of those fighting for liberty. No sooner was the flag of freedom unfurled in the New World by spirits like his own, than he hastened to join their ranks. His bleached bones may still glitter on the yellow sands of Peru. . . .*

While brooding over the death of Darvell and yet simultaneously rereading the few works of Shelley in his possession, Trelawny bumped into an old friend from London, Captain

Daniel Roberts of the Royal Navy. That meeting changed his
life. Roberts, like Captain White, was an officer retired on half
pay, and Trelawny, a navy deserter, was, nonetheless, on close
terms with him. Roberts had nothing better to do than travel for
pleasure and was staying in Lausanne. Unlike most navy men, he
was exceptionally well read, shared Trelawny's love of nature
and was a talented, if occasional, artist sketcher.

The two friends dined together, and after they had exhausted
the subject of ships and the sea their conversation turned to literature and authors. Trelawny was elated to learn that Roberts
was acquainted with both Lord Byron and Shelley, and was
eager to learn all he could about both.

Roberts' opinion of Byron was less than glowing: the man
reputed to be the most handsome of all living Englishmen was
short, overweight, his face ravaged by dissipation. He was something of a poseur in his personal relations and pressed too hard
in an attempt to make himself appear a dashing, reckless adventurer. He discussed poetry with great reluctance, but when he
warmed to his subject he praised his own work immoderately
while speaking with unveiled contempt about the poems of
others.

Shelley, however, was all that Trelawny had hoped and imagined. Roberts declared, "Never were manly wit and sense combined with such ingenuousness, or trust in mankind and unac-
quaintance with the world, as in Shelley." Roberts agreed with
Trelawny's estimate of Shelley's genius and filled in details about
the man himself. He was a superb pistol shot and a good horse-
man, although he sat his saddle in an ungainly manner. He was
married to the former Mary Godwin, the daughter of Trelawny's
favorite philosopher, William Godwin, and Mary was the author
of one of the most popular novels of the day, *Frankenstein.* The
Shelleys were devoted to each other, but Roberts was forced to
admit that the poet was something of an eccentric. For example,
he loved the sea and was a sailing enthusiast, taking many risks
that made an experienced sailor shudder. He could not, furthermore, swim a stroke.

Roberts promised to arrange a meeting with Shelley as soon as
it was convenient, and with that Trelawny was content. Soon
thereafter, in the autumn of 1820, he received an invitation from

a man who had been a boyhood friend in Cornwall, Sir John St. Aubyn, to visit his estate near Geneva. A number of other guests were present, among them two army officers who had recently returned from India, Captain Thomas Medwin and Lieutenant Edward Ellerker Williams. Both were retired on half pay and, with nothing better to occupy them, were seeing the world until they found new vocations. Williams, a robust but sensitive young man, was accompanied by his very pretty common-law wife, Jane, a sweet girl who played the piano and harp and had a good voice. Trelawny enjoyed Williams's company and went sailing with him on Lake Geneva, happy to discover that Williams also liked boating. He was drawn to Jane, although it was his private opinion that she was not too intelligent.

Trelawny reminisced about India with the two officers, and one day was electrified to learn that Tom Medwin was Percy Bysshe Shelley's cousin and had gone to school with him. Thereafter he pumped Medwin for every bit of information and gossip about Shelley he could and eagerly read Tom's copy of Shelley's *The Revolt of Islam,* a work published in a very limited edition.

Medwin was typical of army men who had served in India. He drank heavily but could hold his liquor well. He told lengthy stories about life in India, the jolly fellows who had been his messmates there and the hunting trips he had taken. He knew virtually nothing about Indians or their lives, had rarely visited the bazaars and had tasted native food only a few times. As all the literary persons who would make his acquaintance in the months and years ahead would emphatically agree, Medwin was "a crashing bore," but Trelawny tolerated the man and his endless, pointless stories because he knew so much about Shelley—and would be an even better intermediary than Captain Roberts in arranging an introduction.

It developed that Medwin was planning to visit the Shelleys in Pisa that winter. Williams and Jane were thinking of going there too, and Trelawny leaped at the suggestion that he accompany them. But the Williams baby was ill, so they decided to go to nearby Chalon-sur-Saône instead, and Trelawny's own plans were changed at the last moment when he received word that his father had died and that his presence was required in England for the settlement of Charles Trelawny's estate.

He hired a carriage, offering Edward and Jane Williams a ride to Chalon, and got to know them very well on the seventy-five-mile journey. Bad weather delayed them; they were forced to spend four days on the road. They hoped to meet again in Pisa and agreed to correspond.

It was October by the time Trelawny reached England, and the weather had turned foul. That and a visit to his family's estate combined to depress him more severely than at any time since the death of De Ruyter. His admission of his gloom is his only reference to the effect his father's death may have had on him. In none of his three autobiographical books did he mention Charles Trelawny per se, nor did he indicate his own feelings about the father who had, to all intents and purposes—and, without a doubt, emotionally—disowned or, better, denied him.

Harry Trelawny, as the elder son, inherited his father's estates and the bulk of his wealth, although provisions were made to insure the widow's independence and comfort for the rest of her days. Charles's will provided for his daughters, too, and somewhat to Edward John's surprise, he was also remembered. Neither in his autobiographical works nor in his correspondence does he mention the details of his inheritance, but he was left the income from a sufficiently large sum to support him for the rest of his life. Thus, it was unnecessary for him to do any work other than that which struck his fancy. He never gave credit to his father for outfitting him economically, perhaps because he realized he had been remembered only because he might have filed a lawsuit, and caused problems for the other heirs had he been omitted.

If he offered comfort to his widowed mother, he did not write about it. But the family's country home and London town house, now Harry's property, were open to him again, and thereafter he visited them freely. He also saw something more of his sisters during the winter of 1820–21, but he resisted their efforts to present him to various young ladies they regarded as suitable mates for him. He saw his daughters regularly; they were reminders enough that there was nothing more troubling for a man than a failed marriage. He still dreamed of Zela and felt certain he would never encounter her equal again.

In midwinter he received a letter from Edward Williams that

fired his imagination and made him eager to leave England once more. Williams and Jane had found Chalon so dull they had gone on to Pisa, where they had become close friends of Percy and Mary Shelley. In fact, they had taken lodgings in the same building.

Shelley, Williams wrote, looked like a poet, spoke like one, and was appropriately eccentric although the oddities in his nature were amiable and harmed no one. He was surprisingly athletic and, by far, more vigorous than Lord Byron, who had moved into a villa across the road with his mistress. He had a lively sense of humor, rarely displaying solemnity unless he was discussing philosophical or political subjects. He could deal brilliantly with abstractions, but even his conversation on prosaic matters was "akin to poetry; he sees everything in the most pleasing and singular light."

Shelley's principal joy, Williams wrote, was a little boat that had been made for him in Leghorn, and Williams, an enthusiastic sailor, if an amateur, often sailed with him. They had suffered an accident when they picked up the boat in Leghorn, intending to sail her to Pisa; a heavy wind was blowing, and by the time they discovered their sail was too large the craft capsized. Shelley almost drowned before Williams could haul him to the riverbank. The boat had been saved but needed a smaller sail.

Trelawny's reply indicated his amusement, yet there was a hint of condescension in it. Real seamen looked down their tanned noses at fresh-water sailors. Still he indicated he would give Williams and Shelley lessons in boat handling when he joined them.

Mindful of his responsibility to Maria and Eliza, he delayed his departure from England to bring his children to the Trelawny estate for a visit of six weeks so they could become acquainted with their paternal grandmother, uncle and aunts. Then, having fulfilled his obligations to his daughters, he made plans for his coming holiday, writing:

*Having become tired of society, I determined to pass the latter part of the winter in the wildest part of the Maremma, in the midst of the marshes and malaria, with my friends Roberts and*

*Williams; keen sportsmen both—that part of the country being well stocked with woodcocks and wild fowl. For this purpose, I shipped an ample supply of guns, dogs and other implements of the chase to Leghorn. For the exercise of my brain I proposed spending the summer with Shelley and Byron, boating in the Mediterranean.*

Trelawny felt his only ties to England were his daughters, whose support he was able to increase because of the new income left him by his father. His sixth sense, always acute, told him that the past few somnolent years would soon be thoroughly behind him and he would be making another major change in his way of living. He looked forward to its challenges. Above all, he was excited by the prospect of meeting Shelley, apparently having already decided that the poet would prove a major force in his future.

He was in no hurry to reach Pisa; it was as if he wished a period of due reflection to prepare him, as it were, for his coming "rite of passage." Again he traveled by way of Paris and Geneva, spending a few days in each city; then he went on to Chalon to pick up the horse and carriage he had purchased prior to his departure. Taking up his path again, at a leisurely pace, he went first to Genoa, where he visited the palaces and spent hours on the waterfront inspecting the merchant ships of many nations. He, likewise, had a brief affair with a widowed but still young countess to whom he had been introduced the previous year in Switzerland. Finally, his preparations of sorts for the meeting with Shelley completed, he drove to Pisa for the most important encounter, maybe even *epiphany,* of his entire life.

# XVI

## *"He comes and goes like a spirit, no one knows when or where."*

Until Edward John Trelawny began his association with Shelley and Byron, soon thereafter expanding it to include other literary figures such as Leigh Hunt, Walter Savage Landor and Charles Brown, he was known only to a handful of fellow British aristocrats, a sprinkling of artists and the friends of dubious character whom he had known in his youth. Suddenly, after catapulting himself into the company of articulate people, men and women of letters, he became a public figure. His striking appearance, his charisma and his willingness to relate his bizarre adventures made him a center of attention, which he loved. And thereafter his activities were constantly observed and criticized, his character praised, analyzed and damned by some of the most astute minds of the nineteenth century.

His own account of his doings was but one of many. His claims were usually corroborated but sometimes denied by fluent writers of prose and poetry. Even his feelings and motives were subjected to close scrutiny, and he was no longer the sole authority on his own existence. The interest he aroused everywhere was

astonishing, and people who became his followers were fascinated by him for the rest of their lives. For twenty-nine years
he alone wrote about himself; for the next sixty years, as Robert
Browning—who didn't care much for him—once remarked, no
self-respecting English person of letters wrote much about anyone else.

Perhaps the most remarkable aspect of this phenomenon is
that most of these observers spoke with one voice. Regardless of
whether Trelawny exaggerated the exploits of his youth in the
pages of *Younger Son*, he had become a compulsive upholder of
truth by the time he was in his thirtieth year, and the accounts of
others substantiate the accuracy of his own accounts.

Seen in retrospect, his earlier life seems to have been a prepa-
ration for the day when he would walk onto a larger stage. He
was equipped for it, ready to become a chronicler of the little-
known duo of Shelley and Byron—about whom all England gos-
siped but few people really knew. He was ready, too, to become
a celebrity in his own right, to perform great deeds and be admired for them, to write books that would subsequently become
classics, and be praised for them. . . .

His six-foot frame was still lean, but the body of the mature
man was rugged and powerful; his stamina inspired awe, and his
glowing health inspired others to follow his regimen. He had
grown a long, thin mustache which curved upward at the ends in
imitation of De Ruyter's; his tan had become permanent, in part
because he spent so much time out of doors. His charm was infectious, attracting others because it was natural. He had seen,
done and suffered so much that he had acquired a supreme self-
confidence, recognizing his limitations in some spheres and constantly trying to exceed his own achievements in others. But he
was never arrogant, and although humility was not one of his
virtues, he allowed himself to boast only when dealing with
friends who knew the substance behind his claims. He had
learned to curb his quick and violent temper, but he had no patience with sham, absolutely despised poseurs and refused to
waste his time and efforts on fools. His loyalty to his friends
knew no bounds, and he would do anything for them; con-
versely, he loathed his enemies and would stop at nothing to
humiliate or injure anyone stupid enough to cross him.

The people into whose world he moved were even more complex. Percy Bysshe Shelley, a few months younger than Trelawny, was a member of the same, aristocratic class as Trelawny and had rejected it just as emphatically, or so he thought. He was even more violent than Trelawny in condemning injustice, hypocrisy and cant, and his opinions of Christianity, English government and social morality were so radical that his father had broken relations with him. Romantic in his personal approach to life as well as in the philosophy he had been taught by Godwin, he loved nature, idealized his relationships with women and was what a later generation would call a loner, not only craving but needing solitude. His brilliance as a poet recognized only by a few people, he was something of an outcast. He had alienated a number of friends and colleagues after the suicide of his first wife, whom he had abandoned for Mary Wollstonecraft Godwin.

Mary Shelley was equally complicated. Her mother, the first real pioneer of women's rights in England, had died in childbirth. And Mary had been reared to a state of undeniable intellectuality by her genius father, who was, nonetheless, emotionally unstable, and by a stepmother whom she loathed. A gifted, exceptional person in her own right, Mary became more famous than her husband with her first book, *Frankenstein*.

Passionately devoted to Shelley, with whom, to the public's alarm, she had lived openly prior to marriage, Mary was, however, even moodier than her husband. Mary Shelley needed the social companionship her husband shunned; she had a superstitious belief in ghosts and omens, and lurking behind her ultrafemininity were a masculine drive and common-sense attitudes that brooked no nonsense. She was also one of the most beautiful women of her century.

George Noel Gordon, Lord Byron, was a man in whose personality and work so many intricate strains were woven that even today he inspires controversy. He was universally regarded as the most handsome man of his time, a clubfoot surprisingly adding to the aura of manliness that emanated from him rather than detracting from it. His poetry was the epitome of romantic melancholia, and his life became a symbol of political liberalism. He was wealthy but sometimes miserly, self-indulgent except for those periods when his self-imposed austerity became awe-inspiring. He was the romantic ideal of thousands of women but treated Lady Byron abominably and had many mistresses. His incestuous affair with his half sister was one of the most scandalous, ill-kept secrets of the Victorian Age. He liked to picture himself in a heroic mold but did little that was truly heroic until he went off to fight for Greek independence from Turkey, a move that cost him his life.

The link between the Shelleys and Byron, and a woman who became important in Trelawny's life for a time, was Mary Shelley's stepsister, Claire Clairmont. Like Mary, she was five years younger than Trelawny. Intensely romantic herself and living in the shadow of the brilliant Mary, Claire, who at one time had wanted to be an actress and singer, threw herself at Byron. She had a brief affair with him, gave birth to a daughter whom he insisted on keeping, and became his bitter enemy. The child died, increasing her hatred for Byron, diminishing her desires to ever marry or tie herself to one man again. Claire, long a member of the Shelley household, now lived and worked as a governess in Florence. She was anything but pretty, although she exuded an air of sexuality; she was so combative and interfering that Mary loathed her, but she was fiercely independent, and although impractical in handling money, developed a sensible attitude toward life.

By the time Trelawny arrived in Pisa, Edward and Jane Williams had become the intimate friends of the Shelleys, and the poet, who always needed an imagined heroine to whom he could address his lyrics, was engaging in a mock romance with Jane. Mary, who had seen him through a number of other pseudo affairs, was undisturbed, as was the down-to-earth Williams, who was Shelley's confidant and boating companion.

Night was falling when Trelawny found lodgings at an inn for himself and a stable for his horse. He ate dinner, one of the few meals he would consume alone in Pisa, then went to the Williams apartment. They greeted him with joy, and before they could exchange more than a few words, someone else arrived, "swiftly gliding in, blushing like a girl, a tall thin stripling [who] held out both his hands."

The astonished Trelawny could not believe this person with a "flushed, feminine and artless face," a man who resembled a "mild-looking, beardless boy, dressed like a boy in a black jacket and trousers he seemed to have outgrown," was the "veritable monster at war with all the world, excommunicated by the Fathers of the Church, deprived of his civil rights by a grim Lord Chancellor, discarded by his family and denounced by rival sages of literature as the founder of a Satanic school." Surely Edward and Jane were joking. This inoffensive creature could not be the immortal Shelley whose image had been growing in Trelawny's mind.

The two were introduced, but each had been told so much about the other that both were embarrassed. Jane was equal to the occasion, and noted that Shelley was holding a book in his hand. She asked what he was reading, and when he replied that it was Calderón's *Mágico Prodigioso,* some passages of which he was translating, she begged him to read to them.

Shelley needed no further urging, and promptly launched into a spirited reading, translating as he read. His performance was so brilliant, so filled with deep emotion, that Trelawny no longer doubted his identity.

A few moments after he finished reading, Trelawny said something to Edward, and when he turned back to speak to Shelley, he discovered the poet had disappeared. "Where is he?"

"Who, Shelley?" Jane Williams asked. "Oh, he comes and goes like a spirit, no one knows when or where."

A short time later, the poet reappeared with his wife, and Trelawny was drawn to Mary at first sight, impressed by her antecedents as well as her obvious beauty. She was attracted to him too but erected immediate barriers and fenced with him, asking innumerable questions about London, the state of the theater, the weather and the few acquaintances they had in common. Trelawny admired her quick wit and her bright spirits. He later wrote:

*Like Shelley she could express her thoughts in varied and appropriate words, derived from familiarity with the works of our vigorous old writers. That night she brought us back from the ideal world in which Shelley had left us, to the real, welcomed me to Italy, and asked me the news of London and Paris, the new books, operas and bonnets, marriages, murders and other marvels.*

Mary Shelley's reaction to the newcomer was somewhat reserved; she liked him but found him overwhelming and, in her private journal, called him "extravagant." Soon thereafter, in a letter to her friend Maria Gisborne, she tried to describe him:

*He is a kind of half-Arab Englishman, whose life has been as changeful as that of Athanasius, and who recounts the adventures as eloquently and as well as the imagined Greek. He is clever; for his moral qualities I am yet in the dark; he is a strange web which I am endeavoring to unravel. I would fain learn if generosity is united to impetuousness, probity of spirit to his assumption of singularity and independence. He is 6 feet high, raven black hair, which curls thickly and shortly like a Moor's, dark grey expressive eyes, overhanging brows, upturned lips, and a smile which expresses good nature and kindheartedness.*

Shelley did not reduce his impressions of Trelawny to paper, but there was no need for him to do so. The egocentricity of the poet had long been stunted in exile, and he had been forced to subsist on a diet of only a few crumbs of the praise he so badly needed. Here, suddenly, was a well-read giant who exuded masculinity and self-confidence, a man of the world whose words and eyes indicated his admiration of the shy poet.

Shelley frequently retired early, but that night he remained in the Williams apartment until long after midnight. When they parted he made an engagement with Trelawny for the next day.

Trelawny arrived as planned, and Shelley said he intended to pay a call on Lord Byron. He wondered if Trelawny wanted to accompany him; of course Trelawny accepted eagerly. They went to Byron's rented palace, and Shelley led his new friend through a mammoth great hall, then climbed a flight of marble stairs, where Byron greeted them in a billiard room.

Trelawny, at home anywhere and awed by few men, noted with private glee that Byron was uneasy in his presence and made stilted conversation. But the always exuberant Shelley could not be restrained, and the atmosphere became easier when he suggested a game of billiards. Byron played to win but was trying even harder to impress Trelawny, some of whose exploits he had learned from Tom Medwin and Edward Williams. He related in detail his swimming of the Hellespont and spoke at length of other adventures, each anecdote more extravagant than the last. Trelawny pretended to concentrate on the game of billiards, which he won without difficulty, but in actuality he was listening to and watching the poet who was the storm center of English and Continental gossip.

The picture of Byron he rendered thirty years later was as fresh and original as though the meeting had taken place the previous day. Trelawny wrote in his *Recollections*:

*In external appearance Byron realized that ideal standard with which imagination adorns genius. He was in the prime of life, with regular features, without a stain or furrow on his pallid skin, his shoulders broad, chest open, body and limbs finely proportioned. His small highly finished head and curly hair had an airy and graceful appearance from the massiveness and length of his throat; you saw his genius in his eyes and lips. In short, Nature could do little more than she had done for him, both in outward form and in the inner spirit she had given to animate it. But all these rare gifts, to his jaundiced imagination, only served to make his one personal defect the more apparent. He brooded over that blemish as sensitive minds will brood until they magnify a wart into a wen. His lameness certainly helped to make him skeptical, cynical and savage.*

*There was no peculiarity in his dress, it was adapted to the climate; a tartan jacket braided—he said it was the Gordon pattern, and that his mother was of that ilk. A blue velvet cap with a gold band, and very long nankeen trousers, strapped down so as to cover his feet; his throat was not bare as represented in drawings.*

Byron happened to be relatively thin at the time, and was subsisting on a diet he had devised himself. He ate only cold potatoes, served with vinegar, hard biscuits and soda water, and Trelawny, the advocate of fitness, heartily approved. Not only

did Byron have the slightly strained look which seemed appropriate to a great poet, but Trelawny believed that "by starving
his body he kept his brains clear; no man had brighter eyes or a
clearer voice."

Trelawny considered Byron somewhat old-fashioned in his
outlook on life, however, and recognized that the poet was adept
at adapting to various roles—depending on what his audience
expected of him at any given moment. He was not insincere,
though, in taking such parts; indeed, all were parts of his own inordinately complicated nature. Trelawny wrote:

*The character he most commonly appeared in was of the free
and easy sort, such as had been the fashion when he was in London and George IV was Regent, and his talk was seasoned with
anecdotes of the great actors, boxers, gamblers, duellists, drunk-
ards, etc., appropriately garnished with the slang and scandal of
that day. Such things had all been in fashion and were at that
time considered accomplishments by gentlemen, and of this tribe
of Mohawks the Prince Regent was the chief and allowed to be
the perfect specimen. Byron, not knowing the tribe was extinct,
still prided himself on having belonged to it; of nothing was he
more indignant than of being treated as a man of letters, instead
of as a lord and a man of fashion.*

The description was not an overt attack on Byron, as some of
his supporters angrily charged, although the portrait was anything but flattering. Trelawny was a trifle condescending to
Byron, it is true, but he understood human frailty better than
most and felt great sympathy for Byron, whose work he praised
unstintingly. His attitude is best expressed by a quotation from a
conversation in which the poet said to him:

*Now, confess, you expected to find me a "Timon of Athens" or
a "Timur the Tartar"; or did you think I was a mere sing-song
driveller of poesy, full of what I heard Braham at a rehearsal call
"Entusamusy"; and are you not mystified at finding me what I
am—a man of the world—never in earnest—laughing at all
things mundane?*

Byron was equally shrewd in his description of Trelawny. A few days after their first meeting, by which time they had seen each other several times, he said to Countess Teresa Guiccioli, his mistress of the moment, "I have met the personification of my Corsair. He sleeps with the poem under his pillow, and all his past adventures and present manners aim at this personification."

Trelawny's friendship with both Shelley and Byron progressed rapidly and became increasingly close, but he and Mary Shelley still continued to feel somewhat ill at ease in each other's company. Perhaps both were aware of their mutual attraction, but there is no evidence to suggest they had a love affair, as some of Trelawny's late-nineteenth- and early-twentieth-century critics charged. In her journal Mary noted one day that "a whim of his led him to treat me with something like impertinence, but I forgave him." They came no closer.

Perhaps the rumors came into being because Trelawny escorted Mary to a number of social functions her privacy-loving husband refused to attend. On other evenings he accompanied the couple on long walks; the relationship of the Shelleys was somewhat strained at the time, and no less an authority than Mary herself wrote that the kindness, warmth and sympathy of their new, mutual friend was instrumental in healing the breach.

Trelawny continued to join Shelley and Byron on their daytime excursions, and the group again was enlarged when Captain Roberts arrived for a visit. One afternoon, they practiced their marksmanship with pistols, shooting at coins, and Trelawny, showing unusual modesty, later wrote that he, Shelley and Byron achieved approximately the same scores. But Roberts' memory of the occasion was different. No one was a match for Trelawny, he said, and the adventurer unfailingly hit a coin with every shot. Shelley was a close second, his hand steady and his aim true, but Byron was a poor third.

On various excursions the two poets fell into professional discussions that Trelawny found fascinating. Byron was didactic, stubborn and closed his mind to argument, while Shelley, who would not be swayed from his own opinions, was unassuming and diplomatic, refusing to quarrel when his colleague expressed views he believed false. Only on one occasion did Shelley's patience desert him. Byron declared that Murray, his publisher, was urging him to return to his old *Corsair* style because it was favored by the ladies who were the principal buyers of his books. Shelley retorted that a "bookseller's logic" should not be permitted to influence an author's work. On this occasion it was Byron who kept silent.

One day Byron, who was out of sorts, quoted a line from a Coleridge poem calling the western sky yellow-green, and asked, "Who ever saw a green sky?"

Shelley, who knew that his colleague saw nature as he did people, in bold relief, made no reply.

Trelawny dared to intervene: "The sky in England is oftener green than blue."

Byron had no intention of tolerating an outsider's interference. "Black, you mean," he said in a firm tone that ended the discussion.

Many of the two poets' contemporaries believed that the virtually unknown Shelley was a satellite at the court of the internationally renowned Byron, but Trelawny made a major contribution to posterity by setting the record straight. While it was true that Byron sometimes spoke contemptuously of Shelley behind his back, as he did of almost everyone he knew, he fully realized what few others yet grasped, that Shelley was one of the greatest lyric poets in the history of all literature and may, in fact, have had no peer. So it was he who voluntarily took the lesser place in their relationship, deferring to the younger poet except on those occasions when he was in ill humor. Frequently Byron took Shelley's advice.

Shelley, who was already eclipsing De Ruyter and Aston as Trelawny's hero, displayed powers of concentration and an appetite for hard work that astonished the observer. He read incessantly, pondered and analyzed in solitude for endless hours, and in the process damaged his health. One day, for example, when Trelawny paid a morning call at the Shelley apartment, he found the poet standing before a fireplace, reading a book he had placed before him on the mantel. Not wanting to disturb him, Trelawny departed; returning that night, he found the poet standing in the same spot, still absorbed in his contemplation of the same book.

Another anecdote illuminates the domestic relationship of the

Shelleys and reveals something of the day-to-day difficulties that Mary encountered. The poet disappeared, and his upset wife, accompanied by Trelawny, went out to search for him. At last they came across a peasant working in a clearing beside a deep stretch of pine woods; the man indicated that the "melancholy Englishman" could be found somewhere in the woods. The narrow path was strewn with brambles, so Mary waited while Trelawny went on alone.

Eventually he came across the poet, sitting beside a pool, with papers littering the ground around him. He was lost in the throes of composition, unaware of the existence of anyone else on earth. When Trelawny interrupted him, however, reminding him he had a wife on the verge of hysteria, Shelley immediately became contrite.

Stuffing the papers carelessly into the pockets of his jacket, he said, "Poor Mary! Hers is a sad fate. Come along; she can't bear solitude, nor I society—the quick coupled with the dead."

He was so apologetic when they rejoined Mary that she felt compelled to halt his self-abuse by teasing him gently until his mood improved and harmony was restored.

Trelawny could not resist teasing Shelley in his own way. On one of their journeys to Leghorn he took the poet for a visit to the cabin of the captain of an American merchantman with whom he was acquainted. They spent an hour or two chatting, drinking and smoking, and the experience was more than Shelley could tolerate. The smoke made his eyes water, and he coughed so much that he became alarmed—principally because he was convinced he was suffering from consumption and would permit no one to dissuade him. For the first and last time in his life he drank a glass of grog, strong rum slightly diluted with water, and it made him ill.

On this same visit to Leghorn, Trelawny also contrived to take him aboard a Greek merchantman, since Shelley was an uncritical admirer of Greece and all things Greek. The poet was horrified when he saw the members of the crew squatting and lolling on the deck, shouting obscenities and quarreling loudly in the course of ordinary conversation, gambling furiously, littering the deck with spilled food and wine as they ate and drank and, in general, behaving like barbarians.

When the two Englishmen returned to shore, Trelawny kept a

straight face as he asked, "Does this realize your ideal of Hellenism, Shelley?"

Shelley shuddered as he said, "No, but it does of Hell."

In spite of his ultrasensitivity, however, the poet was fearless and sometimes displayed a reckless disregard for safety. On an excursion into the countryside outside Pisa one day, they came to a deep pool made by a bend in the Arno River. Trelawny went for a swim, the day being warm, and Shelley felt envious as he watched. He became depressed and finally said that swimming looked so easy he couldn't understand why it was impossible for him to do it.

Trelawny replied that the problem was in his mind. He couldn't swim only because he thought himself incapable of it; if he jumped into the water he would rise to the top, and after flipping onto his back he would "float like a duck."

Shelley immediately removed his jacket, trousers and shoes, then "took a header" into the water. To Trelawny's consternation he did not rise to the surface; instead "he lay there stretched on the bottom like a conger eel, not making the smallest effort to struggle or save himself."

Trelawny dived back into the pool and hauled him out.

But the poet showed no gratitude and seemed sorry he had been saved. "They say Truth lies at the bottom of the well," he said. "In another minute I should have found it, and you would have found an empty shell. It is an easy way of getting rid of the body."

The shocked Trelawny asked, "What would Mrs. Shelley have said to me if I had gone back with your empty cage?"

Apparently Shelley had forgotten that he had a wife and infant son. "Don't tell Mary! Not a word!" he exclaimed, then reconsidered. "But it's a great temptation. In another minute I might have been in another planet."

Although Trelawny found it difficult to understand his new friend, they drew steadily closer, and Shelley explained something of his approach to his work. The first draft of a poem, he said, was usually a crude scrawl that no one else could decipher; he agreed when Trelawny, putting it in an artist's terms, suggested it might be comparable to a preliminary sketch.

"When my brain gets heated with thought," Shelley said, "it

soon boils and throws off images and words faster than I can skim them off. In the morning, out of the rude sketch, as you justly call it, I shall attempt a drawing. If you ask me why I publish what few or none will care to read, it is that the spirits I have raised haunt me until they are sent to the devil of a printer. All authors are anxious to breech their bantlings."

Within a remarkably short period of time Trelawny became an intimate member of the Shelleys' circle. Certainly, however, he had no idea of the role tragedy would force him to play with this cast.

## XVII

# "We will all 'suffer a sea change.'"

In the early stages of Trelawny's relationship with the Shelleys and Byron he was principally a listener and observer, saying relatively little about himself. As he came to know them better, however, he became freer in his discussion of his adventures and exploits. Byron was envious, his reaction sharpening the sense of competition that marred so many of his friendships. Mary was inclined to be skeptical, but softened when Trelawny, in his private talks with her, made her his confidante and discussed his romantic problems with her. She wept when he spoke at length of Zela, and being far more conventional than she appeared, she was properly indignant when he told her the story of his marriage to Julia.

Shelley was spellbound by Trelawny's tales of his youth, reacting to them like a small boy. He questioned his friend eagerly, demanding as many details as Trelawny could supply, even neglecting his precious reading in order to hear more stories. His imagination was particularly stirred by what Trelawny said of the sea, his own compulsive love of sailing driving everything else out of his mind.

His daydreams expanding, Shelley began to yearn for a new boat, something larger than the tiny craft in which he and Edward Williams had sailed the previous year. He wanted a vessel large enough to leave the Arno and move into the open waters of the Mediterranean, yet small enough to be manned by a crew of two.

His desires stirred envy in Byron, who said that he, too, wanted to sail, but he wouldn't be satisfied with an elongated rowboat. He wanted a craft big enough for comfort, for entertaining his friends, for making voyages of several days' duration —in brief, a yacht.

Gradually the daydreams took shape and direction, and Trelawny was in the center of the discussions. The entire group of friends would move to the seashore for the summer and would sail their boats. Perhaps Trelawny would help them by acting as captain of Byron's yacht. Perhaps Trelawny knew someone who would build their boats for them. Edward Williams thought of Captain Roberts, then living in Genoa, the leading shipbuilding town in Italy. Roberts, of all men, was well qualified to supervise the construction of the boats.

Trelawny happily co-operated in every way and in secret was amused by the enthusiasm of the amateurs. He took the lead in designing Byron's yacht, the poet wisely allowing him to make the final decisions. He corresponded with Captain Roberts, and the retired Royal Navy officer promised to take charge of the boats' construction.

Byron's large boat caused few problems, and work was started without delay, but Shelley and Williams created complications. They offered innumerable designs for their craft, many of them impractical, and they changed their minds with regularity. Trelawny spent uncounted hours with them, sitting on the banks of the Arno and drawing diagrams in the sand. At last the designs were completed, Trelawny satisfying himself that the boat would be seaworthy.

But that was only the beginning. Shelley and Williams obtained a number of charts of the Mediterranean, studied and discussed them by the hour, and insisted that Trelawny sit down with them and offer his professional advice. What islands should they visit? What courses should they follow? Precisely what pro-

visions should they carry? How much water? What ship's stores
would they need?

Trelawny helped them, gently guiding them back to reality
when they veered into the uncharted realms of fantasy, and en-
livened the sessions by telling them tales of the sea. Byron
frequently attended these sessions, saying little but listening
"with the smile of Mephistopheles" on his face. He was less skeptical than he appeared; his next long narrative poem, *The Island*,
was based on one of Trelawny's favorite, true sea stories, that of
Captain Bligh and the mutiny on the *Bounty*.

Mary Shelley and Jane Williams grew tired of the incessant
talk of the sea but tolerated their husbands' preoccupation with
relatively good humor. They attached no blame to Trelawny,
even though Mary made it plain that she regarded him as responsible for Shelley's mania. In a letter, she made her own tolerance plain when she wrote:

> *Trelawny came in one afternoon in high spirits, with news
> concerning the building of the boat, saying, "Oh, we must all
> embark, all live aboard, we will all 'suffer a sea change,'" and
> dearest Shelley was delighted with the quotation, saying he must
> have it for the motto of his boat.*

By the time Trelawny had spent a month or two in Pisa, his
relations with Shelley and Byron had solidified, and he had become the intimate friend of the former but was beginning to realize he and the latter would never be truly close. His association
with Shelley was based on mutual respect, and for the first time,
Trelawny was enjoying a relationship with someone unlike himself.

At first glance it would appear that he and Shelley were complete opposites, but that was not the case. Shelley was endowed
with unlimited physical courage, a quality Trelawny always admired, and even though the poet was the complete aesthete, he
rode well, was an expert shot and demonstrated astonishing
stamina on long walks through rugged countryside. Often he was
still fresh when Trelawny was beginning to feel the strain.

The need in Trelawny that Shelley filled demonstrated that
the one-time adventurer had, at last, come of age. The bizarre

exploits and feats of daring he had regarded, in his youth, as the measure of a man had given way to a yearning for recognition based on intellectual achievement. It was still true, to be sure, that he took pride in his ability to sail a ship in a storm, to climb the perpendicular face of a cliff, to hit a target with a pistol held in either hand. But he had learned that such exploits did not win a man lasting renown; one used one's mind to win enduring fame, and he was eager to be accepted as a peer by thinkers.

There was much of the immature schoolboy in Shelley, too. He was anxious to emulate Trelawny as a man of action, and at the same time he was delighted that his friend wanted to improve his mind, perhaps even become an author himself. The adventurer and the poet complemented each other; each was aware of qualities in the other that he himself wanted. They admired each other rather than competed with one another; they were happy to teach and be taught, and neither wanted to gain the upper hand. Shelley was openly shy; Trelawny's shyness was better concealed, but each had sounded the other's sensitivities and was respectful of them. Inasmuch as both were English gentlemen there were certain subjects they did not discuss together, but the bonds of their friendship grew stronger every day.

Trelawny's friendship with Byron was far different. There had always been something forced, if not synthetic, in Lord Byron's derring-do, and he felt like an impostor dealing with a man whose exploits had been genuine. Byron had told the world he was a swashbuckler and then had tried to live up to the role, but Trelawny had been a real man of action. This made Byron uncomfortable, envious and perhaps a trifle cheap in his own eyes.

What he failed to realize was that Trelawny felt genuine respect for him as an author and actually envied him. Here the situation was reversed. Trelawny knew, or at least sensed, that his own achievements were passing and even trifling, and it annoyed him that Byron was not satisfied with his own genius but was even inclined to decry it. Both were cynics, skeptically suspecting the motives and acts of others; both were rebels, thumbing their noses at society, yet demanding comforts and prerogatives that the more revolutionary Shelley rejected. In a sense Trelawny and Byron were brothers, and like members of the same family, they suffered sibling rivalries, felt contempt for each other's weaknesses and were slow to forgive faults. At the same time, however, each secretly admired the other's strengths and wished they were not being dissipated in frivolous pursuits.

The complexities of Trelawny's friendship with Mary Shelley were even more marked. They had established a surface rapport; Mary was happy to accept Trelawny as an escort when Shelley went into isolation, and they had even reached the point where they could tease each other without rancor. But something continued to hold them back, and the reserve that had been present from the outset had not disappeared. Perhaps Mary was too beautiful, intelligent, warm—the only Western approximation of Zela whom Trelawny had ever met. Perhaps he was too dashing, handsome and virile.

It has been suggested that Trelawny was in love with Mary and that she knew it, making both of them wary, but this idea is based on the relationship that developed much later and is absurd. While it is true, certainly, that Trelawny regarded all attractive single women as fair game, his sense of honor was too pronounced, his principles too high, to permit himself a conscious emotional involvement with the wife of the man he admired above all others. Under no circumstances would he have permitted himself to entertain romantic thoughts about Mary, and had he been aware of any such feelings he would have gone to great pains to conceal them from her. A man's honor was sacred, and he would have left Pisa had he thought he might be betraying Shelley's friendship and trust.

The one member of the Shelley circle whose path had not yet crossed his was Claire Clairmont, although he frequently heard her name in conversation. She was still in Florence, very much concerned about her daughter's future, and was using Shelley as an intermediary in her efforts to persuade Byron to modify his custody terms. Her reluctance to see Byron, which both Shelley and Mary thought wise, was responsible for her failure to visit Pisa. She did, however, plan to visit the family at the seashore.

The boating plans did not occupy all the circle's time and attention. Trelawny had fallen into a regular routine, spending at least a portion of each day with Shelley, Byron, Williams and the other men, but then dining at his own inn and finally returning to the Shelley apartment for an evening with the ladies as well as the men.

He did not lack invitations from Mary or Jane to dinner but politely declined. The others thought this was one of his eccentricities and accepted it as such, but there was more to the matter than met the eye. He had dined at the Williams house once, and nothing would have persuaded him to go there again. Jane, at best a sloppy housekeeper, could not afford a cook, prepared her own meals and scarcely knew what she was doing in the kitchen. The Shelleys were somewhat better off and had a cook, but Mary was so concerned with matters of the intellect, as was Shelley, that they rarely noticed what they ate, and the Italian peasant woman who cooked for them took full advantage of their indifference. Granted Trelawny had become something of an ascetic, but he liked his meat prepared to his taste; he could not tolerate vegetables that had been boiled for hours and was unwilling to eat fruit that was growing too soft.

Having satisfied himself at his own table, he was prepared for an evening of intellectual stimulation with his friends, and one night found Shelley, who frequently read to the company, bubbling with a new idea. They would give a performance of Othello for their own pleasure; Byron had offered the cavernous great hall of his palace as a theater. Their audience would consist of "all Pisa."

The entire group joined in the game of casting the various parts, and Trelawny was the unanimous choice for the title role. He looked the part, and it would be almost unnecessary for him to learn his lines, as he could recite the better part of the entire play from memory. Mary would play Desdemona, which pleased Trelawny, and Byron agreed to portray Iago. Shelley, who was far too shy to act in the presence of an audience, would stage the production, and Edward and Jane Williams would play minor roles, as would Tom Medwin, who had just returned to Pisa.

There were other distractions too, one of them demonstrating that Trelawny had not yet conquered his trigger-like temper. Among those who rode with Byron and his friends every afternoon were an Italian dragoon named Masi and an Irish count, Lord Taafe. There was bad blood between these two, and one day they had a fight. Masi galloped off, and in the ensuing chase Shelley was knocked from his horse. A wild scuffle followed, and Masi was shot by one of Byron's servants. The government, which already looked malevolently at the notorious Lord Byron, conducted an official investigation.

Depositions were taken, and all would have been well had not Taafe, trying to extricate himself, put the full blame on the others, telling some outrageous lies in the process. The other gentlemen were furious, and only the intervention of Byron, aided by Shelley, prevented Taafe from suffering sudden death. Writing a letter on the matter, Byron said that Taafe was very much in his debt, because "I prevented Mr. Trelawny, a truculent Cornish gentleman, from breaking his bones for his conduct on this occasion, and I assure you it was no easy matter."

Soon thereafter, Claire Clairmont arrived from Florence, even though the summer plans had not yet been completed. Trelawny liked her from the first, despite the fact that he found her emotional excesses somewhat wearing. He was not drawn to her as a woman at this time, contrary to popular belief. His later correspondence indicated that he saw through her surface façade of magnetism and realized she was really a cold woman with strong masculine tendencies, far less appealing than the seemingly cool, always self-assured Mary.

It was during Claire's visit that her five-year-old daughter, Allegra, died of typhus at the convent in which Byron had placed her for schooling. Trelawny took charge of the situation when the Shelleys, who were too close to both Claire and Byron, proved incapable of handling the delicate adjustments that had to be made. Byron, grieving in his own way, took out his frustrations on Claire by refusing to grant her permission to see her daughter's body.

Trelawny demonstrated tact as well as strength in a trying situation. He soothed Claire after breaking the news to her and with some help from Shelley persuaded her it would not be in the best interests of her own mental or physical health to visit the convent. He also kept her at arm's length from Byron, thereby preventing a confrontation that would have resulted at best in an ugly scene, at worst in physical violence.

This was the beginning of a curious relationship between

Trelawny and Claire that would extend over a half century. Claire underwent a dramatic personality change, and while the death of her daughter was undoubtedly the primary cause, it is impossible to determine the extent of Trelawny's influence on her. In any event, she modified her conduct, became reasonable, calm and self-controlled, and rarely gave in to the fits of depression and self-indulgent petulance that had been so trying to those around her.

Trelawny saw the change in her and admired her for it. He was even more impressed by her courage in tragic circumstances, a quality he always valued above all others, and he initiated a correspondence with her that, over a period of many years, would fill several volumes. A relationship that was born of necessity in an hour of grief developed into a lifelong friendship. As Claire grew older she became curt and even vicious with others but was always gracious and pleasant in her dealings with Trelawny. His own attitude was unselfish, and aware of his own need for sympathy and compassion, he recognized the same urgent need in someone else. He fulfilled it, receiving little in return, but he was satisfied. He did not realize that his letters to Claire would provide posterity with many of the details of his life and times.

The death of Allegra caused the cancellation of the plans to produce *Othello*, and everyone in the Shelley circle anxiously looked forward to a summer's rest at the shore. Trelawny went with Williams and Shelley to search for suitable accommodations, two small houses for the families of the pair and a mansion for Byron. It was taken for granted that Trelawny himself, now an accepted member of the inner group, would spend the summer with them, staying with one or another.

Everyone, Trelawny included, was looking forward to the holiday, and only Mary suffered premonitions of unprecedented disaster.

## XVIII

## *"I looked to seaward anxiously."*

The search for adequate summer housing was disappointing, and it soon became apparent that there were no large homes suitable for Lord Byron's purposes on the seashore. But Shelley, Williams and Trelawny persisted in their hunt, and eventually they were able to rent one ramshackle house, called the Casa Magni, which was situated near Lerici, a small fishing village. There was room for both families, although Mary and Jane would be forced to share the kitchen and would have to move in some furniture of their own to make the place habitable. Only Trelawny, who knew Mary's tastes, suffered any doubts; Shelley and Williams were making so many boating plans they waved aside any thought that their wives might not be satisfied with what they had done.

Mary had misgivings, and when Trelawny, who refused to lie to her, displayed little enthusiasm, she insisted on seeing the Casa Magni. It lived up to her fears, but Trelawny showed his loyalty to Shelley by trying to persuade her to accept the place. She argued that it would be foolish to give up comfortable quarters in Pisa for a house that was remote, isolated and cramped.

Trelawny countered by saying she would appreciate the Casa Magni when the weather in Pisa became unbearably hot, and reminded her how much Shelley was looking forward to his summer of boating.

At this point Mary confessed to him that she was suffering premonitions too dreadful to specify. She was unable to pinpoint her feelings but was filled with dread, and her instinct told her not to go to the Casa Magni.

Trelawny made no further attempt to urge her to spend the summer at the shore. He respected her feelings, even if he did not share them, and vividly recalled his own nightmares about the Blue Angel of Death prior to the tragedy that had ended Zela's life. Most members of the Shelley group were too sophisticated to believe in omens or feelings of premonition, but Trelawny knew from personal experience that there was more to such feelings than reason or common sense could admit. It was not his place to interfere, however, and knowing the matter was one that Shelley and Mary had to settle between them, he assumed a neutral position in their controversy.

But Mary fought a losing battle, and the die was cast when word was received, on May 1, 1822, that the boats were ready. The Shelley and Williams families left immediately for the Casa Magni, and Trelawny went to Genoa, where, during the final days of making the vessels ready for the sea, he indulged in a short affair with an Italian beauty named Gabriella Wright. Gabriella was the estranged wife of a Captain Wright, who owned the shipyard where the boats had been built.

When Trelawny got back to matters directly at hand, he immediately came to the conclusion that Byron's yacht, the *Bolivar*, was too sumptuous for sea duty. Her large saloon looked like a drawing room; there was a marble bath adjacent to the master sleeping cabin, and velvet cushions, made in Genoa according to Byron's specifications, were everywhere. Trelawny took her out on a trial run expecting the worst and found, to his happy surprise, that Captain Roberts had done his work well. She was a seaworthy craft and would perform ably in any weather.

He also liked the smaller boat made for Shelley and Williams, but he felt, on the other hand, that she might be a trifle topheavy. He found her difficult to handle for a day or two but soon mastered her peculiarities. After engaging a crew for the *Bolivar*, he hired two men and a boy to sail Shelley and Williams's vessel to Lerici and sent off a letter to Shelley. The boat was all the poet could desire, Trelawny said, but boats were like women— each had her own personality—so it would be wise, especially for those unaccustomed to the sea, to keep the men and the boy as a crew until Shelley and Williams had learned to handle her themselves. He felt sure they would need no more than a week or two to master her characteristics; in the meantime the precaution would be worth the expense.

The smaller craft reached Lerici first, and by the time Trelawny had cast anchor in the *Bolivar* he found his advice had been ignored. Shelley and Williams were so anxious to sail their eagerly awaited boat on their own that they had discharged the two men and retained only the services of the boy. Trelawny bluntly told them they were foolish, but he understood why they acted in this manner; they ignored his warnings because they were preoccupied with something else. Both were outraged by Byron's interference in a matter that was none of his business, and Mary shared their indignation. The Shelleys had intended to name the boat the *Ariel*, rejecting Byron's suggestion that they call her the *Don Juan*. But the latter name had been burned on her prow and was painted on her sail.

Shelley and Williams were unable to obliterate the name on the prow but scrubbed at the painting on the sail, and Mary came down to help them even though she disliked boats in general and had sworn she would not set foot on this one. The lettering would not wash out, so the piqued Shelley went to the expense of procuring another sail, with the name *Ariel* written on it, but Byron achieved a minor triumph all the same. No matter what the new sail proclaimed, Shelley and Williams began to refer to the boat as the *Don Juan*, and Mary called it by that name in her correspondence.

A complication in Shelley's vocational life provided only a momentary distraction. He had made elaborate plans for the publication of a new literary magazine which he and Byron would launch with the help of Leigh Hunt, publisher of another literary publication, the *Examiner*, which had now gone out of business. Hunt, his wife and large family had been expected since the previous autumn, but a letter just received indicated they would arrive momentarily.

Shelley solved the awkward problem in his own way. Perhaps Trelawny would pick up the Hunt family in the *Bolivar* and bring them to Lerici; Byron would not object, as he had shown no interest in sailing on his own yacht. In the meantime Shelley and Williams could get on with the business of sailing their own boat.

Jealous of their authority, the two proprietors of the *Don Juan* accepted no advice from Trelawny and made it plain that he could go to sea with them only as a passenger. He was amused, and agreed, but was privately prepared to take charge if they proved too inept. They were so deliriously happy they behaved like adolescents and even had the temerity to make a rash bet with Trelawny, recording it in Williams's handwriting:

*I, E. El. Williams, do bet a wager of five crowns, that Lord Byron's boat, the* Bolivar, *does not sail at the rate 11 knots the hour, during the first month after his arrival at Leghorn. I do bet, also, that the* Don Juan *will sail at this rate within the same span of time.*

Whether Trelawny won or lost the bet is not known, but he did sail with Shelley and Williams as a passenger and recorded the memorable scene in his *Recollections* thirty years later:

*As usual, Shelley had a book in hand, saying he could read and steer at the same time, as one was mental, the other mechanical.*

*"Luff!" said Williams.*

*Shelley put the helm the wrong way. Williams corrected him.*

*"Luff!" said Williams, as the boat was yawing about. "Shelley, you can't steer, you have got her in the wind's eye; give me the tiller, and you attend the main-sheet. Ready about!" said Williams. "Helms down—let go the fore-sheet—see how she spins round on her heel—is she not a beauty? Now, Shelley, let go the main-sheet, and boy, haul aft the jib-sheet!"*

*The main-sheet was jammed, and the boat unmanageable, or, as sailors express it, in irons; when the two had cleared it,*

*Shelley's hat was knocked overboard, and he would probably
have followed, if I had not held him. He was so uncommonly
awkward that, when they had things ship-shape, Williams, somewhat scandalized at the lubberly manoeuvre, blew up the Poet
for his neglect and inattention to orders. Shelley was, however,
so happy and in such high glee, and the nautical terms so tickled
his fancy, that he even put his beloved Plato in his pocket, and
gave his mind to fun and frolic.*

But Shelley was not as infantile as he appeared, in spite of his
juvenile pleasure, and he wondered how long Trelawny would
tolerate his behavior at sea before losing his temper. His single
comment on the subject speaks volumes: "How long the fiery
spirit of our pirate will accommodate itself to the caprices of the
poet remains to be seen."

Trelawny went for outings on the *Don Juan* as infrequently as
he could without being rude, and thereby preserved his nervous
system. He frequently invited the Shelley and Williams families
to make short cruises with him on the *Bolivar*, and Mary and
Jane sometimes went with him, enjoying the luxury of the yacht.
But Shelley and Williams refused, preferring to mishandle the
*Don Juan*.

For all practical purposes, the *Bolivar* was Trelawny's boat,
and he could do with it as he pleased, inviting anyone he wished
to sail up and down the coast with him. Byron appeared reluctant to leave Pisa, and had no intention of abandoning the comfortable routines he had established there for his mistress and
himself. Trelawny suspected he did not want to be regarded as
ignorant of sailing and inferior to Shelley and Williams, as well
as to a competent sailor who had been the master of his own
ship in the Indian Ocean.

The eccentricities of the poets entertained rather than annoyed
Trelawny, and the spring of 1822 was one of the happiest periods he had known since the death of Zela. Members of the literary circle had accepted him as an equal on his own terms; he
was close to Shelley and on friendly, if less intimate, terms with
Byron. Even Mary Shelley, the most critical member of the
group, approved of him. Trelawny was incapable of relegating
himself to the role of a passive observer, always needing an ad-

miring audience. His new associates awarded him applause and made him content. No longer feeling isolated, he settled comfortably into his role and was content to live each day for its own sake. He made no long-range plans but took it for granted that when the Shelleys returned to Pisa in the autumn he would accompany them.

In one sense, however, he did remain something of an outsider. There were tensions in the Casa Magni caused by the need for two families to live at such close quarters. Shelley and Mary alternately complained that Jane Williams was selfish and thoughtless of the rights of others, then promptly forgave her because she was so sweet, pretty and amiable. Most of the time, Shelley was lost in his own special world, so Edward Williams was forced to act as the mediator and peacemaker, soothing the women and enabling them to live under the same roof.

Trelawny did not participate in the petty quarrels that erupted almost daily, and was, on the surface, aloof. But in private he was a frank partisan of Shelley and Mary. In his estimation Jane was a greedy troublemaker, and years later, when Mary became disillusioned, he reminded her that he had never thought highly of Jane.

Claire Clairmont came to Lerici for a visit, and Trelawny saw her regularly, although she refused to set foot on board the *Bolivar*, because the yacht belonged to Byron. Claire never mentioned her daughter's tragedy and, determined to put her unhappy past behind her, was the gayest member of the group. Trelawny became her regular dinner partner, swam with her daily and was her escort on picnics and other outings, the rest of the group taking it for granted that they would be together.

In view of this developing relationship and the lifelong correspondence that followed it, some historians and biographers have assumed that Trelawny and Claire were in love, particularly in 1822 and 1823, when they exchanged a vast number of letters. But a sober appraisal indicates it was unlikely they ever contemplated either marriage or the establishment of a long-term liaison. Both spoke in extravagant terms, and their correspondence was no more and no less than an exaggeration of the ways in which a basically hard-headed man and an equally realistic woman engaged in friendship.

It is probable that Trelawny and the volatile Claire Clairmont had an affair in 1822 and 1823, the intimacy of their letters indicating they were something more than friends. Certainly, however, they regarded the relationship neither as serious nor as a prelude to something permanent. They enjoyed each other's company, and if they had an affair, they relished it for its own sake but did not regard it as being terribly significant.

They did not want to marry. Trelawny had been twice hurt; Zela still burned in his memory. Likewise, the fiercely independent Claire had already made it known that she had no desire to become any man's mate. So the affair or close friendship, whichever it may have been, must be seen as nothing more than the carefree association of two exceptionally free spirits, a sophisticated man of twenty-nine and a worldly, iconoclastic woman of twenty-four.

Ordinarily the other members of the Shelley-Byron following would have kept the relationship under close observation, commenting on it at length in their diaries and journals and analyzing it in minute detail in their correspondence. But other events that transpired in the summer of 1822 made them indifferent to the friendship of Trelawny and Claire Clairmont.

Leigh Hunt, along with his wife and six children, had been expected by the Shelleys since the previous autumn. But not until Shelley received Hunt's letter, postmarked June 20, did the Shelleys learn that the Hunts would be pushing right off to Leghorn, where they hoped to be met. They would be arriving at the most inconvenient of times: Mary Shelley, who had been in the throes of a difficult pregnancy, lost her baby and was seriously ill. There were no physicians in the vicinity of Lerici, and only the combined efforts of her husband, Claire and Trelawny saved her.

The problem of meeting the Hunts was resolved when Trelawny offered to sail to Leghorn in the *Bolivar* to greet them. It was necessary for Shelley to remain behind for another twenty-four hours, after which time he and Edward sailed in the *Don Juan*, leaving Claire and Jane to take care of Mary.

The Hunts were exhausted after their long journey and responded feebly to Trelawny's ministrations. Shelley arrived and escorted them to the quarters that had been prepared for them.

They disliked the alien atmosphere, hated the Italian food and lamented their departure from England.

Then Byron arrived, and matters became still worse. He had lost interest in the *Liberal*, the magazine that he, Shelley and Hunt were planning to publish, and greeted the Hunts with such cold indifference that they were crushed. Shelley, although anxious to return to Mary at the Casa Magni, delayed his departure for two days in order to soothe them.

Shelley's anxieties increased, and by July 8 he decided he could wait no longer to go to Lerici. Trelawny, who was still uneasy whenever he thought of Shelley, Williams and their assistant, young Charles Vivian, sailing alone in the open sea, arranged to escort the *Don Juan*. That morning, Trelawny and Shelley went shopping for food and other supplies needed at the shore, and then went on to Shelley's bank, where they were delayed for a time. They did not reach their boats until shortly after noon, and it was one o'clock by the time they made ready to sail.

Then, unexpectedly, a guard boat operated by the customs service appeared and requested the documents proving that the *Bolivar* had obtained clearance. Trelawny had never before been asked for such papers, but that did not matter to the captain of the port, who would not permit the yacht to sail without them and threatened to put Trelawny into quarantine unless he complied with regulations.

The wheels of Italian bureaucracy turned slowly, and Trelawny knew he would be delayed for at least an hour or two, perhaps longer. Shelley refused to wait for him, however, laughed at his fears and insisted that he, Williams and Vivian would sail at once.

Trelawny stood on his quarter-deck with his Genoese mate and watched the *Don Juan* through his glass. The mate remarked that they should have sailed earlier in the day, adding, "They are staying too much in shore. The current will set them there."

Trying to conquer his forebodings, Trelawny said, "They will soon have the land breeze."

"Maybe," the mate replied, "she will soon have too much breeze. That gaff topsail is foolish in a boat with no deck and no sailor on board." He paused, then pointed toward the southwest. "Look at those black lines and the dirty rags hanging on them out of the sky—they are a warning. Look at the smoke on the water. The devil is brewing mischief."

The humidity was increasing, making Trelawny sleepy, and he went down to his cabin for a nap while awaiting the clearance papers. He fell into a heavy sleep, which was interrupted by the crash of thunder directly overhead. He hurried back to the quarter-deck and saw that the sky overhead was black. The wind was heavy, thunderclouds continued to roll in and the rain fell in torrents. The crew of the *Bolivar* dropped a second anchor, and Trelawny's uneasiness increased when he saw many boats and small ships sailing into the harbor and battening down. The scene was still vivid in his mind three decades later, when he wrote in his *Recollections:*

> As yet the din and hubbub was that made by men, but their shrill pipings were suddenly silenced by the crashing voice of another thunder squall that burst overhead. For some time no other sounds were to be heard than the thunder, wind and rain. When the fury of the storm, which did not last for more than twenty minutes, had abated, and the horizon was in some degree cleared, I looked to seaward anxiously, in the hope of descrying Shelley's boat amongst the many small craft scattered about.
>
> I sent our Genoese mate on board some of the returning craft to make inquiries, but they all professed not to have seen the English boat. During the night lightning flashed along the coast. At daybreak, I resumed my examination of the crews of returning boats. They either knew nothing or would say nothing.
>
> Another day was passed in horrid suspense.

That suspense was shared by the women at the Casa Magni, and their anxiety increased when they received a letter from Leigh Hunt saying that he, too, was concerned, and was hopefully awaiting word that Shelley had returned safely to Lerici. Mary and Jane left their children in the care of Claire and made a long, tedious journey overland to Pisa. They arrived late at night and awakened Lord Byron out of a sound sleep, but he could tell them nothing. So they pushed on to Leghorn in spite of Mary's poor health, arriving at dawn. Trelawny would know what had happened, they felt sure, but he was not on board the *Bolivar,* having gone on to an inn with Captain Roberts, who had arrived the previous evening. The exhausted women went to the wrong inn, which further delayed them, but at last they came to a place called the *Globe,* whose clientele was made up almost exclusively of ships' officers.

Trelawny was seated at the breakfast table when Mary and Jane entered, and one look at his face told them that he, too, knew nothing of the *Don Juan*'s fate.

## XIX

## *"Is there no hope? None?"*

The ties of a close and lasting friendship were established between Mary Shelley and Edward John Trelawny the moment the
wan, bedraggled woman came into the dining room of the Globe
inn at Leghorn. Until then, Mary Shelley had maintained a certain degree of reserve in her dealings with Trelawny; she liked
him and enjoyed his company but felt somewhat uncomfortable
in his presence. The relationship changed drastically in her hour
of crisis, however, and thereafter he was her greatest comfort
and strength. Trelawny did his sincere best to help her; it was he
who became the central figure in the events of the following
weeks, and during that time bonds were forged that remained
firm until the end of Mary Shelley's life.

When he first saw Mary and Jane Williams, he did his best to
soothe them. Perhaps the *Don Juan* had been driven off her
course, and it was possible that she had found refuge in Corsica
or Elba. It was even more likely that, as the bad weather had
abated and the sea had become calm again, Shelley and Williams had, by now, made their way back to Lerici. In fact, they
were probably waiting there right now. He urged the women to

go to Lerici, finally escorting them to the Casa Magni himself. But there was no trace of either the poet or Williams.

Trelawny then returned to Leghorn and, aided by Captain Roberts, initiated an exhaustive investigation. A messenger was sent as far north as Genoa to make inquiries; the *Bolivar* went to sea under the command of the Genoese mate and cruised up and down the coast in search of the missing *Don Juan*. Meanwhile Trelawny and Roberts set out on horseback, pausing to search the beaches and ask questions of every fisherman and peasant they encountered.

Their hopes sagged, and at last they received word that confirmed their fears: a body had been washed up on the shore at Viareggio, part way between Lerici and Pisa. They rode there without delay and found the body had been in the water too long to be recognizable. But Trelawny knew it was the body of Shelley, because he found two waterlogged books in the jacket pockets, one of Sophocles' plays and the other of John Keats' poetry.

Soon thereafter, a second body was found three miles up the coast, at Migliarino, and Trelawny knew from bits of clothing that it was the remains of Edward Williams. Still later, a third corpse, that of the youth Vivian, was found at a still greater distance from Viareggio. Trelawny now had the difficult task of breaking the news to Mary and Jane; he tells us in his *Recollections* how he performed the chore:

*I mounted my horse and rode off to the Gulf of Spezia, put up my horse and walked on until I caught sight of the lone house on the seashore in which Shelley and Williams had dwelt and where their widows still lived. I paused—I had ridden fast to prevent any ruder messenger from bursting in upon them, and my memory reverted to our parting only a few days before.*

*They had all been in the verandah, overhanging a sea so clear and calm that every star was reflected in the water; the young mothers singing some merry tune with the accompaniment of a guitar. Shelley's shrill laugh—I hear it still—rang in my ears, with Williams's friendly hail, the general buona notte of all the joyous party, their entreaty to return as soon as possible, and not to forget the commissions they had given me. I was in a small boat beneath them, slowly rowing myself on board the* Bolivar *at anchor in the bay, loath to part from what I verily believe to have been the most united and happiest set of human beings in the whole world. And now, by the puff of an idle wind. . . .*

*As I reached the threshold the nurse Caterina crossed the hall and shrieked when she saw me in the doorway. Unannounced I went up the stairs and entered the room. I neither spoke, nor did they question me. Mrs. Shelley's large grey eyes were fixed on my face. I turned away. With a convulsive effort, she exclaimed:*

*"Is there no hope? None?"*

*I did not answer. I left the room and sent the servant with the children to them. The next day I prevailed on them to return with me to Pisa. The misery of that night and the journey of the next day, and of many days and nights that followed, I can neither describe nor forget.*

Trelawny took complete charge, and the widows turned only to him, perhaps because his masculinity and vigor were reassuring and soothing. Tom Medwin was Shelley's cousin and had been Williams's old friend, but it did not occur to Mary to seek his assistance. Leigh Hunt, himself grief-stricken, was so weak that no woman would have wanted to lean on him, and Lord Byron was not the type who inspired warmth, except in a far different kind of relationship.

"Tre did not try to console me," Mary later said, "but launched forth into an overflowing and eloquent praise of my divine Shelley, till I felt almost happy."

The bodies had been given temporary burial at the spots where they had been found, but both of the widows sought permanent resting places for their late husbands. Mary wanted Shelley to rest near the grave of a little son they had lost and had buried in Rome's Protestant Cemetery, while Jane Williams said again and again that she wanted Edward to lie in an English churchyard. But the situation was complicated by Italian law and the functioning of Italian bureaucracy.

Disinterment followed by the transfer of the body of a deceased person to a place outside the country was strictly forbidden. It was required that the body of "any mammal" washed up on the shore be burned, a precaution taken to prevent new outbreaks of the plague. But Roman Catholic law prohibited the burning of human bodies.

Trelawny vividly remembered the cremation of Zela and urged that the bodies of his friends be treated in a similar manner. The widows were stunned, but the malleable Jane Williams soon agreed. Mary Shelley demonstrated, even in her time of sorrow, that she had a mind of her own, and refused. Trelawny became persuasive. There was no ceremony more dignified than that of the ancient Hellenes, and he could think of no end more fitting for Percy Shelley, whose ideal had been ancient Greece. Mary finally agreed.

But that was just the beginning. Trelawny held endless meetings with Italian officials and signed scores of forms. He obtained the help of the British consul in Leghorn and of a friend, a Captain Shenley, who had moved to Leghorn after his retirement from the Royal Navy and had become a semiofficial adviser to the municipal officials. Ultimately the arrangements were made, and Trelawny promised to take complete charge of the ceremony but persuaded the widows not to attend. He knew from his own bitter experience that the scene would be ghastly.

His memories of Zela's cremation still haunted him, so his insistence that the bodies of Shelley and Williams be treated in the same manner is inexplicable unless one remembers Trelawny's basic nature. He was still an unabashed romantic and could think of no other end as dramatic.

The various arrangements took five weeks to complete. Among them was the purchase of an iron frame from a Leghorn blacksmith who charged him more than four hundred lire in silver, a price he paid out of his own pocket. He also purchased two boxes for the ashes, each of them "covered with black velvet and fastened with screws, a plate of brass attached to the top with a Latin inscription stating their loss by shipwreck, age, country, etc."

He sailed for Viareggio on the *Bolivar,* taking the helpful Captain Shenley with him, and on board were quantities of incense, honey, salt, sugar, spices and wine, which the ancient Greeks had used. Williams's body was to be cremated first, and new complications developed. The local officials protested, and Shenley had to quiet them. No wood was available in the vicinity and had to be procured. Men had to be hired to erect the iron frame and build the funeral pyre. And soldiers had to be obtained from the government of Tuscany to protect the site and keep curiosity seekers at a distance.

Lord Byron had indicated a desire to attend the cremation but did not appear, so Trelawny sent a messenger to Pisa, who brought back word that Byron and Leigh Hunt would arrive the following morning. They kept their word, reaching the beach soon after dawn. Trelawny described the place in his *Recollections:*

*We were facing the gulf where my noble friends' bodies were found. The situation was well adapted for a Poet's grave, fronted by a magnificent extent of the Mediterranean Sea with the Isles of Gorgona, Capraia, Elba and Corsica in sight and on the other side an almost boundless extent of sandy wilderness, uncultivated and uninhabited, covered with wood stunted by the sea breeze and the poverty of the sandy soil. At equal distances along the coast stood high square towers with flag staffs on the turrets, for the double purpose of preventing smuggling and enforcing the quarantine laws. This view was bounded by an immense extent of the Italian Alps which are here particularly beautiful; those in the vicinity being composed of white marble which gave their summits an appearance of being covered with snow.*

*As a foreground to this romantic scene was an extraordinary group—Lord Byron and Hunt seated in their carriage, the horses jaded and overpowered by the intensity of the heat reflected from the deep loose sand, which was so hot that Lord Byron could not stand on it. Captain Shenley and myself, with the officer and sergeant commanding the nearest lookout tower, stood around the grave. . . .*

The soldiers dug up Williams's body, which Trelawny placed on the fire, and then applied a match to. "The fire was immense," and Trelawny, Byron, Hunt and Shenley threw salt, sugar, incense, oil and wine into the flames, making them rise still higher. The Italian soldiers, who were superstitious, withdrew as far as possible.

Eventually the scene was too much for Byron, who plunged into the water and began to swim far out to sea. Trelawny and Shenley followed him, and when they were about a mile from shore Byron became violently ill but, nevertheless, rejected Trelawny's pleas to return to shore. Shenley suffered a severe cramp, and would have drowned had Trelawny not saved him.

When they returned to the shore, the body, which had been burning for two hours, had not yet been consumed, so the flames were built up again. Eventually Trelawny was able to scoop up Williams's ashes, placing them in the box he had brought for the purpose, and the iron frame was cooled in the sea. The day was so far advanced by the time these tasks were completed that the cremation of Shelley was deferred until the following morning.

The next day, August 16, the activities were repeated. A tremendous fire was made, but Shelley's body burned more slowly. It was four o'clock in the afternoon before the last remains—with the exception of his heart—became ashes. Byron later said to Thomas Moore, "All of Shelley was consumed, except the heart, which would not take the flame."

Acting on impulse, Trelawny took the heart from the fire, and sprinkled it with water; but in spite of this precaution it was so hot it burned his hand. After it cooled, he placed it in the box with Shelley's ashes, and the party then rode to the local inn in a buffalo-drawn carriage. The gruesome ceremonies were ended, and Lord Byron returned without delay to Pisa, while Trelawny went on board the *Bolivar* and sailed to Leghorn.

The emotional and physical strains would have exhausted a man of less stamina, but Trelawny could not rest until he had sat down in his cabin and written a complete, detailed account of all that had happened on the beach. It was the first of five such accounts that he prepared over the course of many years.

When he rejoined the widows, he tried to stress the dignity, solemnity and beauty of the occasion, but neither then nor at any later time could Trelawny fool Mary Shelley, who was sharp-eyed and alert in spite of her grief. "It was a fearful task," she later said. "He stood before us at last, his hands scorched and blistered by the flames of the funeral pyre and by touching the burnt relics."

The cremation out of the way, Trelawny and Captain Roberts

plunged into the task of dredging for what was left of the *Don Juan*. Mary knew that some of her husband's poems were on board in a supposedly watertight compartment, and as there were no copies of these works anywhere, they were valuable. Trelawny had reason of his own for conducting the search, however; from remarks made by various Italian officials, he suspected that the boat had been run down by a larger Italian ship, and the wreckage would either confirm or disprove this theory.

Meanwhile there were scores of other errands to be carried out. Claire was leaving Italy and was joining her brother, Charles Clairmont, in Vienna. Jane Williams was packing up her belongings and returning with her two small children to England. Mary Shelley decided to remain in Italy for a time with her son and intended to share an apartment with the Leigh Hunts in the little town of Albaro, near Genoa. Trelawny looked after everything, and Hunt later wrote:

*Mr. Shelley's and Mr. Williams's friends were indebted to Mr. Trelawny for every kind of attention; the great burden of the inquiry fell upon him and he never ceased his good offices, either then or afterwards, until he had done everything that could have been expected to be done, either of the humblest or highest friend.*

The dredging had to be interrupted at Mary's request so Shelley's remains could be buried in Rome. She herself lacked the fortitude for the task and depended completely on Trelawny, giving him the right to select a site if a place could not be made beside the grave of her son.

Her suspicion proved correct, so Trelawny found a spot he deemed appropriate, beside an old Roman wall in a remote corner of the Protestant Cemetery. There he buried Shelley, and with his own hands planted flowers around the grave and a row of young cypress trees in front of it. Although Mary did not yet know it, he bought a plot large enough for two graves, and immediately wrote his own will, stipulating in it that when he died he wanted his grave to be adjacent to that of Shelley.

"*We saw sorrow in other faces, but we found help only from you,*" the deeply grateful Mary later wrote to Trelawny. Certainly their friendship was cemented and was on a new basis now. The mutual reserves had vanished, both lowered their guards and there was no subject on which either was reluctant to speak. Trelawny regarded Mary as his closest friend, and she returned the compliment.

Claire was the first to depart, and Trelawny was so busy he scarcely realized he missed her. Lord Byron, as a gesture to Shelley's memory, not only agreed to finance the publication of the *Liberal* alone, but arranged to move into a villa in the neighborhood of Genoa himself. The general exodus from Pisa began, and everyone in the Shelley-Byron circle moved from Leghorn to Genoa in the *Bolivar*, with Trelawny shuttling back and forth.

He took Jane and her children first, then saw them off on the first stage of their overland voyage through France. He transported Mary and her little son to Genoa and then moved the entire Hunt family, which included several dogs, two cats and an infamous goat that immediately got into a fight with Lord Byron's bulldog. Then he moved Byron, his mistress and their mountains of belongings.

The thankless task finished, his responsibilities were ended and he took lodgings for himself in Albaro. He found the town drab but was motivated by a desire to remain close to his friends and to share their grief. Not until time began to drag did it finally dawn on him how much he had depended on Shelley and Mary for friendship and company.

The widow was forced to rebuild her life, a lack of funds making it necessary for her to write professionally, and she could no longer spare several hours daily for chats with Trelawny. She had to act as an intermediary between Byron and Hunt, too, and Trelawny, who had no desire for the surviving poet's company, was isolated.

Certainly Trelawny's continuing friendship with Claire was in part responsible for the change in his feelings toward Byron, whom he had admired and respected without serious reservation when they had first met. By now he had absorbed much of what Claire felt, and he developed a contempt for Byron's character which would persist for quite some time. His feelings were reflected in the books he subsequently wrote about the poets.

Nothing better reveals Trelawny's desolation at this time than

the letters he wrote to Claire and to Mary. With nothing better
to occupy him, he and Captain Roberts continued to dredge for
the *Don Juan* and finally brought her up from the bottom. She
bore no marks of a collision. So they promptly had her repaired
and sold her for salvage, the sale paying the cost of the dredging
expenses. Then the pair went duck hunting for some weeks, as
they had long planned.

Trelawny's mind remained active though, and he sent off
many letters to Mary and to Claire. He was patient and sympathetic in his relations with the former, but he could be realistic,
too. He could reply firmly when self-pity threatened to over-
whelm her:

*As to melancholy, I refer you to the good Antonio in Shylock.
"Alas! I know now why I am so sad. It is time, I think." You are
not so learned in human dealings as Iago, but you cannot so
sadly err as to doubt the extent or truth of my friendship.*

*As to gratitude for uttering my thoughts of him I so loved and
admired, it was a tribute that all who knew him have paid to his
memory. "But weeping never could restore the dead," and if it
could, hope would prevent our tears.*

He continued to urge her to curb her sorrow and, six months
later, wrote to her again:

*You need not tell me that all your thoughts are concentrated
on the memory of your loss, for I have observed it, with great
regret and some astonishment.*

At the same time, however, he sought to soften the blow with
kinder words:

*Dear Mary, of all those that I know of, or you have told me of,
as connected with you, there is not one now living has so tender
a friendship for you as I have.*

Hoping to distract her, he also told her the latest gossip about
one of his mistresses of the past year, a woman known to poster-

ity only as Rose. And hoping to distract her, he even asked her to do him a favor:

*I enclose a letter just received from my old friend, Rose, do favor me by replying in full to it—in my name—and direct it to her in Paris. Say everything, tell her what I have been doing, where I am—how unshaken is my attachment—how anxious I have been to hear from her—how delighted with her constancy —that henceforth I will not believe the tales of the French wanting stability—that I will take the first opportunity of coming to Paris to see her. Do, dear Mary, write her a long letter, for she is most [word smudged by seal].*

His therapy was effective. Mary Shelley not only wrote the letter but utilized her talents as a professional author to the utmost, with the result that Rose was elated. Not waiting for Trelawny to come to Paris, Rose visited him in Italy and for several weeks assuaged his loneliness.

He was far freer in his letters to Claire, developing a correspondence which, with only a few lapses, continued for more than a half century—until 1875. Claire preserved a number of his letters, which were subsequently published.

Trelawny addressed Claire in the same extravagant tone he employed in his correspondence with Augusta White, and one unfamiliar with Trelawny's exuberance, his exaggerations and his use of endearments would be justified in thinking he was truly in love with Claire. In one typical letter he wrote:

*You! you! torture me, Claire—your cold, cruel, heartless letter has driven me mad. It is ungenerous under the mask of Love to enact the part of a demon.*

*In the sincerity and honesty of my affection, I wrote unhesitatingly, unreflectingly, my vaguest, wildest thoughts. By the power of what I considered mutual and fervent affection you bared my heart, and gathered my crudest, idlest, most entangled surmises. You then sum them up together in a cold, unfeeling, arithmetical manner.*

*I am hurt to the very soul, I am shamed and sick to death. I fearlessly opened my heart, confessed my weaknesses, entreated your counsel, aid, judgment, looked to you as my destiny. You have used your unlimited sway over me with a remorseless and unfeeling hand.*

*You are right in withdrawing your fate from mine, my nature has been perverted by neglect and disappointment in those I have loved. My disposition is unamiable; I am sullen, savage, suspicious and discontented. I can't help it—you have sealed me so! You have made me hopelessly wretched.*

*Yet I long to see you, and will allow nothing to prevent me from joining you in Vienna the moment spring arrives.*

Trelawny knew he could let himself go with Claire, because she had no intention, ever, of marrying him or anyone else. Like Mary, she had been reared by William Godwin, and she practiced what Mary preached: that marriage was an outmoded form of slavery for a woman.

All the same, Trelawny had engaged in enough affairs by this time to have become wary of his misleading Claire—even despite her professed demands for independence. Claire knew the unwritten rules of their relationship, but he was sometimes afraid she would take him at face value when he used such terms of affection as "dearest," "darling," and "my own." So he built safeguards into even the most passionate of his letters to her, usually protecting himself by telling her in detail of the latest developments in his affair with Gabriella Wright. At loose ends in Genoa, Gabriella joined him in Albaro. And there they lived together publicly, causing such a scandal that Trelawny took an isolated villa on a rocky peninsula that jutted into the sea. At this haven, he told Claire, he and Gabriella could swim and sunbathe in the nude when they pleased, and no one could see and criticize them.

It becomes apparent that the biographers and historians who have claimed that Trelawny was in love with Claire have not read his letters to her in their entirety. In one sentence he could call her his "dearest angel, the custodian of my heart," and in the very next paragraph could tell her that Gabriella's erotic appetites overwhelmed him, awakening in him a greater lust than he had ever before felt.

Certainly Claire understood him, and although she played the game with him, her letters were more restrained. Eventually he tired of what may have been a form of self-mockery, and his correspondence became calmer.

Over the years, his involvement with Mary Shelley grew deeper and deeper. She returned to England about a year after her husband's tragic death and devoted herself to the twin tasks of rearing her son and making the world conscious of Shelley's genius. She wrote a half dozen novels, all of them financially successful, and also turned out a number of magazine articles and encyclopedia entries. Her financial struggles were grim, but she obtained an allowance from her father-in-law on the condition that she write nothing about her late husband.

She violated the agreement in spirit and had a number of unpleasant confrontations with Sir Timothy Shelley, but the old man became less bitter when his son's reputation started to spread. At this point his allowance became more generous.

Mary became increasingly conservative as she grew older. But she never wavered in her determination to trumpet Shelley's name, be it to such solid devotees as Browning, Coleridge and Lamb or to the general reading public, who would profit from having Percy Bysshe Shelley's works available.

Though Mary never remarried, Trelawny, the one man she would not hold at arm's length, proposed to her. It is difficult to assess this proposal, which Trelawny made during a brief visit to England after he and Mary had not seen each other for a long time. It is impossible to avoid the suspicion that he asked her to marry him for two reasons. First, she was the widow of the man he most admired in the world. Even more important, he may have thought she expected him to do so. Certainly he was relieved when she rejected him, and he made no secret of his feelings.

One of Trelawny's worst faults was his habit of talking out of turn as a way of allowing the world to share his exuberances, and he was indiscreet in telling people he was delighted that Mary turned him down. Mutual friends lost no time in repeating to her what he had said, and even a woman who had no intention of marrying a man could not help feeling he had scorned her. The friendship cooled when she told a friend, "Trelawny is

full of fine feelings and has no principles. I am full of fine principles but never had a feeling; he receives all his impressions
through his heart, I through my head. *Que voulez-vous? Le
moyen de rencontrer* when one is bound for the North Pole and
the other for the South."

XX

# "When was there so glorious a banner as that unfurled in Greece?"

Early in Trelawny's love-hate association with Lord Byron, the poet expressed his enthusiastic sympathies for the War of Independence being waged by the Greeks against the Turks, rulers of the sprawling and corrupt Ottoman Empire. The direct descendants of the glorious Hellenes, founders of Western civilization, were, unlike their Turkish antagonists, noble souls, Byron declared. And one day in the not too distant future, he asserted, he would mount and lead an expedition that would help the Greeks throw off the yoke of slavery imposed on them by cruel and barbarous masters.

Trelawny listened politely, even though he was convinced that Byron was indulging in dramatic daydreams far removed from reality. In his private conversations with the Shelleys and others, and particularly in his subsequent correspondence with Claire, Trelawny expressed his contempt for the idea and ridiculed the Greeks. He had known a number of Greek seamen and merchants during his long years in the East and had found them crafty, unreliable and corrupt. They were greedy, ignorant savages who were no better than their Turkish masters; they were totally unlike the ancient Hellenes whom Byron and Shelley admired. And in his private opinion they were not only cowards whose bid for independence was certain to fail, but they didn't deserve freedom.

He continued to humor Byron whenever the poet raised the subject, but the discussions bored him and he dismissed them. He had far more important matters on his mind, and not the least of them was money. His income was fixed, but his expenses were enormous during the second half of 1822 and the early months of 1823, and the drain seemed never-ending.

Everything happened at once. Julia was extravagant and sent him an urgent request for help; he was not obligated to assist her but continued to feel responsible for his daughters' welfare, so he sent his former wife the additional three hundred pounds she requested. He paid for the cremation of Shelley and Williams, knowing the gesture was beyond the means of Mary and Jane, and he refused to permit Mary to repay him for the purchase of the lot in the Rome cemetery.

Leigh Hunt, congenitally incapable of making ends meet, was having a very hard time paying his bills, thanks to Byron's niggardliness, so Trelawny, who liked any friend of Shelley's, quietly came to his aid. Mary Shelley needed funds too, and when life became intolerable for her in Italy in 1823 as a result of increasing strains in her relations with Byron and her distaste for the Hunts' slovenly housekeeping, she decided the time had come to return to England. Lacking the money for transportation, she humbled herself by applying to Byron for a loan. He promised to help but was slow in giving her the funds, so Trelawny came to her rescue, giving her more than she actually needed so she could travel in the style befitting a lady who was the widow of one of the world's great poets.

Claire was desperately poor now that Shelley was no longer alive to augment her income with occasional "loans," and Trelawny, who knew her circumstances, insisted that she accept help from him. Claire was too proud and demurred, but Trelawny insisted, telling her, "Give me proof of your belief in my entire friendship by freely using me in your service." Claire finally weakened, agreeing to accept money provided he would allow her to repay him, and Trelawny accepted her conditions, knowing he would never see his money again. Then, to his great embarrassment, he discovered he didn't have the fifty gold napoleons he wanted to forward to her in Vienna and had to borrow the sum himself from a Pisa bookseller with whom he had become friendly.

The winter of 1822–23 dragged interminably. Trelawny amused himself in dalliances with Gabriella Wright and Rose, but affairs occupied only a small portion of his time, thoughts and energies. He appeared to be drifting, something new in his experience, and he despised the feeling. He thought of taking a long sea voyage but was too poor and didn't know where he wanted to go. The idea of finding employment as the captain of a merchantman occurred to him, but he quickly rejected it. That life was behind him, and there was no excitement or pleasure in carrying cargo from one port to another.

He indulged in a daydream of his own and could not dispel it from his mind. He wanted to buy a sleek schooner or sloop, go to sea with a carefully selected crew of men who shared his zest for adventure, and return to the life of a privateer. But ships were expensive, sailors would have to be paid in cash pending such time as they captured prizes, and equally important, he would have to forgo the company of respectable people, piracy being beyond the pale in peacetime. So the scheme remained no more than an elusive dream.

On a practical level, he found it distasteful to play at being a sailor, and in December 1822 he told Byron to find another captain for the *Bolivar*. The poet, who had lost even a surface interest in the yacht since Shelley's tragic death, promptly sold the boat.

The realization gradually dawned on Trelawny that he had reached a new crossroads. His life lacked direction and purpose, and at the age of thirty he had no goal, nothing to occupy him. There were dragons to be slain in many places, to be sure; for instance, in his correspondence with Claire he violently condemned the institution of slavery in the United States. But, nonetheless, America seemed beyond his reach, and he had no clear idea of what he might be able to do to help the abolitionist groups that were forming in New York, Boston, Philadelphia and various other cities of the North.

A lack of purpose caused Trelawny to become lethargic, the only time in his life that he gave in to a feeling of indolence. He continued to observe his diet and rode horses, fenced and engaged in target practice to keep himself in physical trim, but, still, he was desperately unhappy. When Gabriella became convinced he didn't intend to marry her, she left him for someone else, and Trelawny began to spend his evenings at an officers' waterfront tavern in Genoa. He drank to excess, something he hadn't done in years, and inevitably became involved in brawls which he soon learned had lost their adolescent flavor.

He was not aware of it yet, but he was ripe for adventure, particularly for a campaign fought for a noble cause. He knew of no active crusades, he claimed, but was certain that he was still a man who needed activity rather than cerebral contemplation. Lord Byron was in somewhat similar circumstances: his mistress bored him, and the company of the high-born English ladies and gentlemen who called on him throughout the winter left him lifeless.

At this point fate intervened in the person of Captain Blaquiere of the London Anglo-Greek Committee, an organization formed for the purpose of helping Greece to win her independence. Blaquiere came to Genoa to ask Byron to join the committee and go to Greece as its representative. The poet was electrified and imagined himself leading an army of volunteers —certain his exploits as a soldier would shame the enemies who were spreading vicious stories about him in London.

He immediately approached Trelawny, requesting him to find a ship suitable for the purpose of transporting a stout company of freedom fighters to Greece. Trelawny said he would help but did nothing. He had listened to Byron on the subject of Greece too often, and he shared Mary Shelley's opinion that the poet was making speeches simply for the pleasure of listening to his own voice. Nothing could conceivably come of the scheme, so a search for a ship would be a waste of time and effort. He told Captain Roberts that, as always, the poet would "exhaust himself in planning, projecting, beginning, wishing, intending, postponing, regretting and doing nothing."

But Lord Byron was in earnest, and as early as April 1823 he was busy making definite plans for his expedition. Trelawny yawned behind his hand and, like most of the people who knew the poet well, remained skeptical. Unable to tolerate the eager talk, Trelawny went off to Rome to attend to other matters, one being the gardening of Shelley's grave plot.

During his absence, Byron surprised virtually everyone who knew him by purchasing the *Hercules,* a sturdy Genoese ship he was able to pick up at a bargain price. Then he began to recruit his company, his first volunteer being the young brother of his mistress. He wanted experienced fighting men, gunners, horsemen, a surgeon, a quartermaster, an ordnance expert. He was excited with plans for his expedition, but knew he was an amateur and often floundered. The man he most wanted to join him was Trelawny, and the poet sent him a warm letter of invitation.

By then Trelawny had left Rome, and with time still on his hands he returned to Genoa by easy stages, pausing to see the sights and visit acquaintances in a number of Italian towns along the way. He arrived in Genoa at the end of June and found a number of urgent messages from Byron awaiting him at his lodgings. He paid the poet a visit, was taken to see the *Hercules,* and his skepticism vanished.

The cause of the Greeks suddenly became transformed in Trelawny's eyes: they became a noble breed, the bona fide inheritors of the Hellenes, a people who deserved the help of every freedom-loving man. His change of heart has been regarded as opportunistic, as perhaps it was, but there was a vast difference between Trelawny and the unemployed veterans of the Napoleonic Wars and the other soldiers of fortune who made up the bulk of the volunteer regiments rallying to the banner of Greece. He was still endowed with enthusiasms, his love of liberty was real, and he was sincere in his turnabout, absolutely convincing himself that the cause of Greek independence was just, a crusade that demanded the help of honorable, freedom-loving men everywhere.

If any traces of his skepticism remained, they lingered in his

regard for Lord Byron. He apologized to Claire when he informed her of his new association, telling her bluntly that he was
well aware of her feelings. He was even more candid when he
confided to Mary Shelley that he was uncertain whether Byron
would actually accompany the expedition he was mounting. But
the poet's active participation was irrelevant. Trelawny—the ide-
alist, the man of action, the champion of the oppressed, the
crusader for justice—had found his cause, and it did not matter
in the least that he had adopted a completely new attitude toward the struggle in Greece.

He felt he had no personal obligations to anyone other than
his daughters—and Mary Shelley. Seeing her in Genoa prior to
her departure for England, he made an effort to persuade her not
to leave. The physical climate in England was miserable, the
emotional climate was hostile. Italy was warm and friendly, and
if she would stay he would gladly share his income with her. The
offer was typical of Trelawny, made without ulterior motives of
any kind.

Mary was grateful but had already made up her mind to
leave. It was essential that her son attend school in England, and
only there could she engage in activities that would make the
world aware of her husband's genius.

Trelawny was deeply disappointed that a good friend was
moving out of his immediate orbit, but busied himself with preparations for the Greek campaign. He bought two superb Hun-
garian cavalry mounts from a colonel in the Austrian Army, then
hired a black American groom. Certain that he had grown soft
from the past months of easy living, he went camping in the Italian woods, cooking his meals in the open and marching a minimum of twenty-five miles each day. It was gratifying to discover
that a man of thirty had the stamina and strength of a youth of
twenty, and when he returned to Genoa he felt ready for the future.

The *Hercules* needed work too, and he was meticulous in
readying the ship for her voyage. Ignoring Byron's complaints
that he was spending too much money, he had the vessel
overhauled, personally supervised the placement of her guns and
permitted no one else to buy her provisions and munitions. He

even took charge of the search for a surgeon. A letter he sent
Captain Roberts is indicative of his activity and thinking:

*I am collecting together the things necessary for the expedi-
tion. I am going with as few things as possible, my horses and
two very small saddle portmanteaus, a sword and pistol, but not
my Manton gun, a military frock undress coat and one for
superfluity, 18 shirts, etc. I have a servant who speaks English, a
smattering of French and Italian, understands horses and cooking, a willing though not a very bright fellow; he has been the
afterguard of a man-of-war.*

*Tell me if you wish to have all three dogs. But perhaps you
will accompany us. All I can say is, if you go, I will share what I
have freely with you—I need not add with what pleasure!*

*Lord B. has desired me to look after a surgeon. He has given
the same directions to Dr. Vacca and Dunn. I could have induced a clever gentlemanly fellow to have gone with us, an
Englishman, not for the salary but for the spirit of enterprise and
love of travel. But I am afraid to act as Vacca will most likely
have engaged some mercenary Italian.*

His enthusiasm still mounting, he became rhapsodic in a letter
to Claire:

*When was there so glorious a banner as that unfurled in
Greece, and who would not fight under it? I have long contemplated this, but was deterred by the fear that an unknown
stranger without money, etc., would be ill received. I now go
under better auspices. Lord B. is one of the Greek Committee;
he takes out arms, ammunition, money and protection to them.
When once there I can shift for myself, and shall see what can
be done.*

*It is only within the last few days that I have engaged myself
in this expedition, or I should have given you earlier notice. I am
sure you will approve the principle I am acting on, though you
may regret I am not accompanied by such a being as Shelley.
Alas, that noble breed is extinct. All others are nearly alike
indifferent to me. We are but drawn together to amuse, or serve
ourselves—I expect nothing more.*

Balancing Trelawny's flamboyant idealism was a new note of cynicism, a hint that behind the façade of his enthusiasm was a harder-headed approach than he was revealing to the world. He wrote to Mary Shelley in his farewell letter:

*You must from time to time let me know your wants that I may do my best to relieve them. You are sure of me, so let us use no more words about it.*

*I have been racking my memory to remember some person in England that would be of service to you for my sake, but my rich friends and relations are without hearts, and it is useless to introduce you to the unfortunate; it would but augment your repinings at the injustice of Fortune.*

*My knight-errant heart has led me many a weary journey foolishly seeking the unfortunate, the miserable and the outcast; and when found, I have only made myself one of them without redressing their grievances; so I pray you avoid, as you value your peace of mind, the wretched.*

Trelawny went on to say good-by to Mary and the Hunts, had a business session with Byron the day following the composition of Mary's letter, and then made a thorough inspection of the *Hercules*. But even though it had been repaired the ship did not suit him. "She was like a baby's cradle," he said. "Every touch of Neptune's foot set her rocking."

He told Byron he was uneasy, but the poet waved aside his complaints. It was his turn to be realistic, and he made it clear he had paid very little for the 120-ton ship. He also emphasized that he expected to fight no sea battles in her. He had purchased her for the sole purpose of transporting himself and his associates to Greece, and she would serve that end. And he laughed when Trelawny expressed his dissatisfaction with the surgeon, Francesco Bruno; the trouble with Englishmen, Byron said, was their belief that only their compatriots were capable of the practice of medicine.

Enjoying himself thoroughly, the poet had a Genoese tailor make spectacularly attractive uniforms of scarlet and gold for himself, Trelawny and one Gamba, who was upset because his helmet had fewer feathers and was smaller than the other two.

Byron was so pleased with his appearance that he willingly allowed a local artist to do his sketch.

But Trelawny, who knew the ugliness of war, "refused vehemently to wear the theatrical costume that had been made for him. Under no circumstances would he go off to Greece looking like an actor in a comedy. Byron cajoled and begged, but in vain, and Trelawny's costume was returned to the tailor.

On July 13 the poet, the adventurer, Gamba and the young surgeon set sail from Genoa, accompanied by eight servants, five horses, Byron's two pet dogs and a hold filled with provisions, munitions, medical supplies and two small cannon. Mary Shelley summed up the economics of their departure in a letter to Jane Williams, saying that Byron was carrying ten thousand pounds in cash, while Trelawny had no more than fifty pounds in his wallet. A small flotilla of American, English and Italian ships provided an escort of honor out of the harbor, and their crews lined the decks to cheer the departing heroes.

Then the wind died, and the embarrassed Trelawny had to creep back into port, where the *Hercules* waited for three more days. A breeze sprang up on July 16, and Trelawny promptly put out again, this time ignored by the other ships in the harbor. The seas were rough, the *Hercules* lived up to the captain's fears, Gamba was violently seasick and the frightened horses kicked down the partitions separating their stalls, damaging the superstructure.

For the second time, the ship was forced to go back to Genoa. Byron, Gamba and the physician went ashore, and Trelawny stayed on board to supervise the necessary repairs. Three English carpenters were hired, and by working around the clock they completed their task by the next day. For the third time the *Hercules* put out to sea, a Greek pennant flying from her topgallant, and the great adventure was under way.

## XXI

## "We sailed to Greece in the finest possible weather."

Relations between Trelawny and Lord Byron had never been better. In spite of their differences and jealousies, they had gained a greater understanding of each other. Certainly Trelawny was influenced by the fact that the poet was actually making the journey to Greece and was proving sincere in his desire to risk his life for a liberty-loving people. Byron, for his part, had changed his opinion after Shelley's death, when he had seen Trelawny's "devotion to the dead and kindness to the living." In a rare tribute to his companion, he wrote:

*I know of no comrade I would rather stand beside on our journey into the unknown. I know of no man more brave, and together we will sweep aside all obstacles in our path, together we will prevail.*

Trelawny recorded his changed opinion of Byron in equally glowing terms:

*You never know a man's temper till you have been imprisoned on a ship with him, or a woman's until you have married her. Few friendships can stand the ordeal by water; when a yacht*

*from England with a pair of these thus-tried friends touches, say,
at Malta or Gibraltar, you may be sure that she will depart with
one only.*

*I never was on shipboard with a better companion than Byron.*

In spite of the warm exchange of compliments, the *Hercules*
proved to be as inept a sailor as Trelawny had feared, and
needed five days to make the brief voyage from Genoa to
Leghorn. There several newcomers joined the party. One was an
observant young Scotsman, Hamilton Browne; a second was a
Greek adventurer who called himself Captain Vitali; the third
was a relative of Prince Mavrokordatos, who had taught Mary
Shelley Greek during his exile from his native land and was now
the leader of a large and vocal group of partisans fighting for independence. This man, who was called Schelizzi, was an eloquent complainer who soon made himself thoroughly unpopular
with the rest of the company.

The *Hercules* put to sea again, and while Trelawny was busy
on his quarter-deck, Lord Byron happily read newspapers and a
supply of books they had picked up in Leghorn. Trelawny later
noted that the poet was always cheerful, never interfered with
the operations of his ship and gave the captain a free hand to do
as he pleased.

Every day at noon, the two men jumped overboard "in
defiance of sharks and the weather" for a long, invigorating
swim. Every afternoon they practiced marksmanship at the fan-
tail rail and every bottle on board was in jeopardy for use as a
target, regardless of whether it was empty or full. They spent
long hours analyzing freedom and its abuses, and they soon discovered their mutual love of nature was bringing them closer.
Again and again, when sailing past one small island or another,
they noted identical beauties at the same moment. Trelawny was
surprised to discover that Byron shared his cynical opinion of
contemporary Greeks and intended to fight more for an ideal
than because of his admiration for the people who currently
wanted freedom from the Turks.

In his *Recollections* Trelawny wrote of the poet:

*He had an antipathy to everything scientific; maps and charts
offended him; he would not look through a spy glass and only*

*knew the cardinal points of the compass; buildings ancient or*
*modern he was as indifferent to as he was to painting, sculpture*
*or music. But all natural objects, and changes in the elements,*
*he was the first to point out and the last to lose sight of. We*
*lay-to all night off Stromboli, shrouded in smoke from its vol-*
*canic fires, the waves rolling into its caverns, booming dismally.*
*Byron sat up watching it. As he went down to his cabin at day-*
*light he said, "If I live another year, you will see this scene in a*
*fifth canto of* Childe Harold."

At times the poet-adventurer and the adventurer-future author
behaved like small boys. According to Browne's subsequent accounts, they placed small bets on their daily swimming races and
tried to outdo each other in swimming long distances. One day,
they made a larger than usual wager, and Trelawny insisted he
could swim indefinitely in the ship's wake. He jumped overboard
and kept up with the *Hercules* until the coming of night forced
him to climb aboard. He was elated, insisting he had won his
bet, but Byron refused to pay and teased him for hours, insisting
with mock solemnity that he had tired prematurely.

The *Hercules* responded violently to the slightest swell, the
faintest breeze, and most members of the company were
confined to their beds for the better part of the voyage. But
Byron, like Trelawny, never felt ill effects, and they spent most
of their time in the open, reading on deck even when the sky
overhead was leaden and a stiff wind caused the ship to pitch
and roll.

Byron had been the intimate friend of few men, but as he and
Trelawny grew closer he became increasingly confidential. One
night, as they were sitting together under the stars, Byron spoke
of the possibility that he might be killed. He had no fear of
death, he said, and would not protest if his life came to an
abrupt end. The one thing he could not bear was pain. Then,
mindful of the possibility that he was becoming mawkish, he
reverted to his usual sardonic approach.

"Mind you, Trelawny," he said, "don't repeat the ceremony
you went through with Shelley. No one wants my ashes."

Trelawny suggested that he would be buried in Westminster
Abbey.

Byron stared at him for a long moment, saw he was serious and burst into loud laughter. Any ministry that permitted such a burial would be voted out of office the next day. In fact, the famous who were buried in the Abbey would turn in their graves if the deputy of Satan joined them. It would not be implausible, he went on, for the Abbey itself to crash and fall in ruins. But, again turning serious, Byron mentioned a tiny, rocky isle off Maina—the "Pirates' Island" that had inspired *The Corsair*—and said he wished to be buried there.

When the others recovered from their seasickness and rejoined them on deck, Trelawny noted that Byron dispelled these gloomy thoughts and promptly reassumed his air of cynical, bored indifference. Trelawny perceived that he wore a mask because he felt it could somehow make him invulnerable to hurt.

On the morning of August 2, 1823, the *Hercules* dropped anchor in the harbor of Argostoli, the principal port of the island of Cephalonia. The voyagers were hungry for news, but what they learned quickly confused and bewildered them, conflicting rumors, making it impossible for them to learn the truth. Neither side was engaging in active fighting; the fighting everywhere was vicious. The Turkish fleet was inactive because of mutinies; the Turks were gathering a mammoth flotilla at Istanbul and soon would launch a large-scale invasion. Greek independence was assured; the Greeks would never win their independence, because various factions were engaging in a violent civil war that was tearing the country apart.

Byron and Trelawny were disgusted. Out of the welter of fact and fiction they finally gathered that three principal parties were struggling for Greek leadership. Prince Mavrokordatos did not have the support of the mainland population, as the Englishmen had assumed. The nobles were devoted to his cause, and most of the foreign volunteers and mercenaries were fighting under his banner, but many of the common people had little use for him. A second leader was a former cattle thief named Kolotrones, who was enthusiastically supported by peasants to whom he gave the lands of nobles—which he confiscated for this explicit purpose. The third group was made up of men from the mountains, and included the Macedonians, whose ancestors had formed the core of Alexander the Great's legions. These troops held Athens, and were led by a guerilla chieftain who called himself by the romantic name of Odysseus. The English officials who made their headquarters on Cephalonia knew virtually nothing else about him other than that he had won the most significant victories in the battles with the Turks.

Representatives of Mavrokordatos and Kolotrones appeared, clamoring for the food, arms and medical supplies Lord Byron had brought with him, but he refused to open the hold of the *Hercules* and would give neither faction the funds he had brought with him. He intended to take no action of any kind, he declared, until he learned the truth of the situation.

That meant inactivity, and when Byron began to stall it was difficult to prod him into doing something constructive. Trelawny suspected a time of procrastination was at hand, and had no intentions of rotting in Cephalonia, dining with the British there and spending his days on the beaches of fine sand. Byron agreed with Trelawny insofar as the political views that they had thus far been exposed to seemed too partisan to be trusted. It was thus arranged that the poet would wait at Cephalonia for news, which would be supplied by Trelawny and Hamilton Browne, both of whom would go to the mainland. In this way, a real study having been made of the political situation, Byron would be sure that he was giving monetary and physical support to the right people.

Trelawny was intrigued by the little he had learned about Odysseus and decided to go to Athens, where he would arrange a meeting with the guerilla leader. His parting with Byron was unexpectedly touching, the two men still savoring the solid, friendly rapport that had been lacking in their earlier relationship. Byron presented Trelawny with a sword, saying, "Take this—and use it." Then he spoke softly, a wistful note creeping into his voice as he added, "Let me hear from you often, and come back soon."

Browne and Trelawny traveled as far as Hydra together, then parted company, and the latter went on to Athens alone. The devastation of war which he saw everywhere about him was shocking—even to a man who had seen excessive poverty and misery in the East. Trelawny's description of the Greek countryside in his *Recollections,* an account that any war correspondent would have been proud to sign his name to, goes as follows:

*This country is so poor and barren that in the best of times there would not be plenty; now that war had passed over the land with fire and slaughter there was scarcely a vestige of habitation or cultivation. The only people we met, besides soldiers, looked like tribes of half-starved gypsies. Over our heads on some towering rock, occasionally we saw a shepherd with his long gun, watching us and keeping guard over small flocks of goats and sheep while they fed on the scanty shrubs that grew in the crevices above them; they were attended by packs of the most savage dogs I ever saw. Except in considerable force, the Greek soldiers dare not meddle with these warlike shepherds and their flocks. Many of the most distinguished leaders in the war, and the bravest of their followers, had been shepherds.*

*Every step of our way to Tripolitza and on to Argos was marked by the ravages of war. Our road to Corinth took us through the defiles of Dorvenskia; it was a mere mule path for about two leagues, winding along in the bed of a brook, flanked by rugged precipices. In this gorge, and a more rugged path above it, a large Ottoman force, principally cavalry, had been stopped in the previous autumn by barricades of rocks and trees, and had been slaughtered like droves of cattle by the wild and exasperated Greeks. It was a perfect picture of the war, and told its own story of the sagacity of the nimble-footed Greeks, and the hopeless stupidity of the Turkish commanders.*

*The Turks might have been a herd of bisons trapped and butchered in the gorges of the Rocky Mountains. There, grouped in a narrow space, we saw five thousand or more skeletons of men, horses, mules and camels; vultures had eaten the flesh, and the sun had bleached their bones. Detached from the heaps of the dead, we saw the skeletons of some bold riders who had attempted to scale the acclivities, still astride the skeletons of their horses, and in the rear, as if in the attempt to back out of the fray, the bleached bones of the camel drivers' hands still holding the hair ropes attached to the skulls of their camels—death, like sleep, is a strange posture-maker.*

*It was not easy to obtain enough food on the journey, and even had there been peace the journey over such rough terrain would have been tiring in the extreme. But there were compensations—ample food for the mind for those who love the haunts of genius. Every object we saw was associated with some great name, or deed of arts or arms, that still live in the memory of mankind.*

*The Greeks have been enslaved for long centuries, suffering untold miseries, yet they still have the strength and will to throw off the yoke of their masters. No people who retain their nation and language need despair. There is nothing constant but mutability.*

When Trelawny reached Corinth, he met a number of rebel leaders, but they failed to impress him. They were predators, he said, similar to the bandits he had known in the East. He and Browne sent a letter to Byron, dispatching it in mid-September. In it they warned him of the caliber of leadership in Corinth, and Trelawny urged him to persuade the Greek fleet to act without delay in an attempt to break the Turkish blockade of the country.

In Salamis he found the tribal leaders even greedier, and he reported to Byron that they were feuding among themselves so ferociously that government had broken down there and anarchy prevailed. Going on to Hydra, Trelawny met Prince Mavrokordatos and was charmed; he remembered, too, how much Shelley had liked him, and that Mary Shelley had been his good friend. These ghosts of past associations undoubtedly colored his thinking, and his report to Byron was so enthusiastic that the poet forwarded four thousand pounds to Mavrokordatos for the purpose of strengthening his fleet and breaking the blockade.

At Hydra Trelawny and Browne parted, the former going on to Athens and the latter taking two representatives of Mavrokordatos's government with him to the malarial plains of Missolonghi, where Byron had now established his headquarters. It was agreed that the two Greeks would go on to London to negotiate a substantial loan that would provide the funds necessary to win the war.

Trelawny's reaction to Athens, as he wrote Leigh Hunt, was

"more that of a soldier than scholar." He inspected the Acropolis, then caught a cold while smoking his pipe "seated on the damned cold Greek marble of the Temple of Minerva." He condemned the "barbarians of all countries" who robbed the Greeks of their ancient treasures and had carted them off to museums and the palaces of the wealthy in other lands.

Only once did he suggest that the ancient city truly and deeply affected him, saying he felt "a little sentimental" when he paused to admire the foundation stones of an old house and was informed that it had been the Palace of Timon.

Ever since his early youth, Trelawny had been a chameleon, and the romantic element ever present in his nature compelled him to become more Greek than the Greeks. He adopted the national dress, ate his meat direct from the skewer and chewed whole cloves of garlic without wincing. He was so dark that most people whom he met took it for granted that he was a Greek, and one day, word has it, he actually had difficulty in persuading two English volunteer soldiers that he was their compatriot. He felt at home in Athens, as he had in so many other foreign places. He soon perfected his Greek, speaking it without an accent, and even the local women he met—and some he bedded—did not guess he was an alien. It is almost needless to add that he enjoyed every moment of the deception. The consummate actor could ask for nothing more.

Immediately after his arrival in Athens Trelawny went to see Odysseus, and the two men of action struck up an immediate rapport. The guerilla leader was even taller than the Englishman and had a full head of hair, a large mustache and a powerful physique. His physical strength and stamina were said to be unmatched in Greece. He spoke his own tongue eloquently, using many literary figures of speech. And even though his education was limited, his manners were those of a gentleman. He enjoyed hunting; he treated his horses gently, and he kept a number of pet dogs, treating them as kindly as if they were members of his own family. He was quick-witted and laughed easily, but his temper was ferocious. He could kill enemies with his bare hands, showing them no compassion or mercy. He had gained his position of eminence in the independence movement in part because of his great courage but principally because he instinctively understood military problems and was not afraid to put his theories to the test.

In brief, he was a man after Trelawny's own heart, and the pair became close friends; it seemed that, within a few days, each could read the other's mind. Trelawny had found a new hero in the old mold of De Ruyter and Aston rather than of Shelley, and his letters were filled with admiration for this novel mentor. He told Mary Shelley that Odysseus was "glorious," and he wrote to Claire that the Greek chieftain was "brave, clever and noble." To other friends he described the guerilla leader as an indefatigable champion of liberty and predicted he would go down in history as "the George Washington of Greece."

Reluctant to join Lord Byron on the plains and inevitably become stuck in the marshes of Greece's complicated politics, Trelawny temporarily threw in his lot with Odysseus. He dipped into his half-empty purse, bought a number of weapons and hired a band of rough Greek-speaking Albanian mountaineers. He was joined by a group of Greek volunteers, giving him a total command of about fifty men. They then joined Odysseus for a campaign of harassment against a full Turkish regiment that was occupying the town of Eubea. They made their headquarters on Parnassus.

Trelawny had the time of his life. He and Odysseus planned ambushes, stalked Turkish cavalry, made swift forays against the enemy and then miraculously vanished into the heights above the town. He likened the sport to deer-stalking, and his cares fell away. This was the life for which he appeared to be destined, and his conduct as a fighting man was magnificent. He was as fearless as Odysseus, and as cunning. By the time he turned thirty-one, in November 1823, he had already become something of a legend. But he might have been less carefree, less reckless, had he known what lay in store for him.

## XXII

# "This is no private grief."

The winter of 1823–24 was one of the happiest times in Trelawny's life, reminiscent of the days when he had stood on the quarter-deck of his schooner in the Indian Ocean. He had never been trained as a soldier, but like Odysseus he relied on his instincts and they never misled him. His followers were convinced he led a charmed life and were willing to go anywhere with him, no matter how dangerous the mission. They succeeded in making life miserable for the Turks, who paid Trelawny the compliment of putting a price on his head—doubling the sum if he was captured alive.

He became a magnet for other volunteers, among them a Scotsman named Fenton who had been a captain of Royal Artillery in the Napoleonic Wars. It seemed a shame to waste his talents, so Trelawny obligingly conducted a daring raid on the Turkish garrison at Eubea, escaping into the mountains with six small cannon. Then, before the Turks could recover from the blow, he made a second raid to obtain ammunition and again succeeded. Thereafter his band enjoyed the luxury of artillery cover, and Trelawny's reputation spread, newspapers in England, France and other countries devoting long columns to his exploits.

By January 1824, he became Odysseus' second-in-command and took charge of the entire guerilla regiment when the chieftain made periodic trips to Athens, where other lieutenants kept the city under control, maintained order and administered the affairs of government. During this time Trelawny exchanged a number of communications with Lord Byron and, indeed, came to feel sorry for the poet, who had become the storm center of Greek politics. Byron had been joined by a prominent member of the London Committee, Colonel Leicester Stanhope, later the Earl of Harrington, a hard-bitten and realistic soldier who had come from England to help end the feuds between the various Greek factions.

Stanhope made a trip to Athens at a time when Trelawny was visiting the city, and they took an immediate liking to each other, establishing a friendship that would endure for the rest of their lives. They agreed that a meeting of the various Greek leaders for the purpose of ironing out their differences was essential, and both believed it was imperative that Byron attend the conference. Always romantic, Trelawny wanted to hold the meeting on historically and mythologically significant Parnassus; he convinced Stanhope that Byron would recover from the cold and persistent fever he had been suffering if they could persuade him to spend some time in the clear mountain air.

Byron agreed. But his habit of delaying asserted itself again, and he did not come. Trelawny wrote him repeatedly, urging him not to delay, but there was no sign of the poet. Trelawny did not know that Byron had suffered an attack of epilepsy that, combined with his persisting fever, had debilitated him.

Unwilling to wait any longer and convinced that the union of the various Greek factions was necessary if the Turks were to be beaten, Trelawny decided in April that he would wait no longer. Perhaps Lord Byron was afraid to travel eastward through a countryside infested with Turkish patrols and bands of Greek irregulars who shot at strangers without bothering to learn their identity. He would go to Missolonghi himself, accompanied by his ferocious Albanian and Greek partisans; he would escort Byron to Parnassus for the conference.

The idea was so simple he wondered why he had not thought of it sooner. Filled with confidence that the quarrels of the Greeks soon would be ended, that Odysseus would become commander-in-chief of the combined Greek armies and that he himself would be awarded a high military post, Trelawny set out for Missolonghi. The journey was without incident, but when they were less than twenty-four hours from their goal they encountered a messenger coming from the opposite direction, bringing news they could not believe:

Lord Byron was dead. He had expired on April 19, almost a week earlier, and Trelawny raced on to Missolonghi, later writing in his *Recollections:*

*With despondent thoughts I entered the town. It is situated on the verge of the most dismal swamp I ever saw. I marvelled that Byron, so prone to fevers, should have been induced to land on this mudbank and stick there for three months shut in by a circle of stagnant pools, a "belt of death."*

*I waded through the streets, between wind and water, to the house he had lived in; it was detached and on the margin of the shallow slimy sea-waters. For three months this house had been besieged, day and night, like a bank that has a run upon it. Now that death had closed the door, it was as silent as a cemetery. No one was within but Fletcher [Byron's valet], of which I was glad. As if he knew my wishes, he led me up a narrow stairs into a small room, with nothing in it but a coffin standing on trestles. No word was spoken by either of us; he withdrew the black pall and the white shroud, and there lay the embalmed body of the Pilgrim—more beautiful in death than in life. Few marble busts could have matched its stainless white, the harmony of its proportions and perfect finish; yet he had been dissatisfied with that body, and longed to cast its slough. How often I had heard him curse it!*

Byron's workroom was in a chaotic state, with papers, documents, fragments of poems, unfinished letters and personal mementos scattered everywhere. Many of those papers were valuable, so Trelawny set himself the task of creating order out of the mess. He collected every document, making a detailed list of each paper's contents. It was a day and a half before he was satisfied. Then he had to make arrangements for the removal of Byron's body. He wanted to bury him in Greece, but others intervened, insisting it would be more appropriate for burial to take place in England; Trelawny was forced to concede. That night, he wrote a letter to Colonel Stanhope that expressed his feelings:

*With all his faults I loved him truly; he is connected with every event of the most interesting years of my wandering life; his everyday companion—we lived in ships, boats, and in houses together—we had no secrets nor reserve and though we often differed in opinion, never quarreled. If it gives me pain to witness his frailties, he only wanted a little excitement to awaken and put forth virtues that redeemed them all.*

*I shall ever regret that I was not with him when he gave up his mortality.*

*Your pardon, Stanhope, that I have turned aside from the great cause in which I am embarked; but this is no private grief; the world has lost its greatest man, I my best friend and that must be my excuse for having filled a letter with this one subject. . . .*

The loss of Byron dimmed Trelawny's enthusiasm for the Greek cause. But the war went on and he remained faithful to his commitment, returning to his post in the mountains and rejoining Odysseus. His letters to various friends reflected his growing disenchantment: the Greeks were inefficient, the conduct of the war was desultory, the government failed to support the troops in the field and the union of the various forces was still remote. He was relieved, in the summer of 1824, when Odysseus decided to call a temporary halt in the guerilla warfare, and they went together to the chieftain's "home."

Odysseus and his principal followers lived in caves on the western slopes of Mount Parnassus, above the town of Valitza. No more romantic spot could have been imagined. The caverns could be reached only by climbing ladders bolted to the side of a sheer precipice, and at the top stood a trap door that could be closed and secured instantly. On an overhanging lip outside the

caves was a natural platform that commanded a breath-taking
view of the valley below. Guards were on watch on this terrace
day and night and on the roof of the caverns above it, where a
high wall had been built to give the defenders additional protection. Sentries were also on duty at lower levels of the mountain-
side, making the caves the safest of all homes for the families of
Odysseus and his lieutenants.

The interiors of these natural dwellings were surprisingly comfortable, the inhabitants having brought furniture, rugs, kitchen
utensils and complete wardrobes with them from their more
prosaic houses and apartments. A spring situated at the rear of
the largest cave provided a ready supply of pure water, and
large stores of food, wine and firewood were always on hand.
Odysseus boasted that he could withstand a two-year siege with
ease.

There were four women in the family of Odysseus: the first
lady of the strange community was his wife, Helen, to whom he
was devoted; he was also loyal to his half sister, Kamenou, to
his stepmother, Acrive, and to her exceptionally pretty daughter,
Tarsitsa, a lively girl of about eighteen or nineteen years. Her
hair was a burnished red-gold, she had enormous, dark eyes and
she wore flowing gowns, complete with jewels. In short, she
reminded Trelawny of Zela.

Tarsitsa was of course attracted to Trelawny, and Odysseus
encouraged the romance, eager to make the foreigner who had
served him with such valor a member of his family. Certainly
Trelawny was vulnerable. Byron's death had saddened him, victory in the war was still a distant goal, and he felt disillusioned,
lonely and out of sorts. A radiantly beautiful girl was in love
with him, and he succumbed to the inevitable.

He and Tarsitsa were married in the large cavern in the autumn of 1824, a Greek Orthodox priest performing the ceremony
in the presence of a sizable company of guerilla leaders and their
families. The newlyweds settled down in a small cave of their
own, eating their meals with the rest of the family.

Some weeks after their marriage, Odysseus was called to
Athens, and Trelawny was left in charge of the compound. His
responsibilities required little effort, as he had a company of
well-armed men with him and a subcommander in Captain Fen-

ton—the Scottish artillery specialist who now supervised the guerillas serving sentry duty on the slopes of Parnassus.

Life was pleasant and easy. Trelawny taught his wife English, spent several hours reading each day, sent off to Athens for additional bric-a-brac to beautify the caves and, never neglecting his physical exercise, climbed up and down the scaling ladders. He also found time to respond to the request of a fellow Englishman, who had encountered an unhappy situation in Missolonghi, where a number of slaves had been captured. For the sum of five pounds per slave, Trelawny could set these pitiful creatures free. He promptly sent fifteen pounds, all the English money in his possession.

He maintained a heavy correspondence with friends in the outside world. In a letter to Claire he hinted at his marriage but did not mention it in so many words; he was far more candid in a letter to Mary Shelley, telling her in detail about Tarsitsa. He also wrote a very long account of the caves and of the lives that were led there, suggesting she might send the material to a magazine for purposes of publication if she wished. But Mary was struggling too hard to establish herself as a breadwinner and did nothing with the article.

Months passed, and the tenor of life in the caverns remained unchanged. The news of the war was increasingly bleak. The Turks were growing stronger; Prince Mavrokordatos was gaining additional support at the expense of Odysseus, and the end of the struggle for independence seemed very remote. Odysseus, who hated stagnation as much as Trelawny, signed an armistice of three months' duration with the Turks. The Englishman, who was convinced no Turk could be trusted, thought he was making a mistake.

By the spring of 1825 the truce was coming to an end, and Odysseus went off to confer with other Greek leaders to determine whether they could unite when the fighting resumed. Again Trelawny remained in charge of the base, and one of the more curious interludes in his life drew toward its end. For the better part of a year he had remained in the caverns, rarely venturing beyond the terrace and the scaling ladders. He had read, exercised, written letters and made love to Tarsitsa, but had been strangely quiet for a man who required action and excitement.

It has been suggested that the death of Byron had numbed him, and that he went through a period of readjustment similar to his recuperation after the death of Shelley. This theory cannot be completely denied, but its validity is questionable. Trelawny was sincerely devoted to Shelley, the attachment was deep and his suffering was protracted after the drowning of his friend. His relationship with Byron was far different, although genuine. Only his letter to Colonel Stanhope reveals suffering; thereafter he seldom mentioned Byron in his letters, other than to condemn the leaders of various Greek factions whom he held responsible for the poet's death because of their insistence that he remain in a swamp-infested section of the country.

It has also been said that Trelawny wanted to reassess his life and determine his long-range future, but neither his letters nor either of his later biographies indicate that this was the case. The truth of the matter may be very simple to explain. He was living a romantic life in the cave high on the slopes of Mount Parnassus; the presence of his lovely bride assuaged his loneliness, and he appears simply to have been content with his lot. He had enjoyed his time spent masquerading as an Arab sea captain in the Indian Ocean, and he was equally happy as a Greek guerilla chieftain. In the course of history few men have shown themselves able truly to escape from their backgrounds, but one of Trelawny's principal fascinations lay in his ability to make his daydreams come true.

His Greek dream was shattered, rudely and violently, however, late in May 1825. Early in the month a personable and well-educated young English volunteer named Whitcombe arrived at Odysseus' headquarters, and Trelawny assigned him to Captain Fenton's command. The two became very friendly, and Trelawny occasionally invited them to dine with him on the terrace overlooking the valley.

One afternoon, after they had eaten, Trelawny suggested they practice their marksmanship, and his servant, an Italian, drew a figure of a man's silhouette on a board and placed it at the far end of the terrace. Fenton and Whitcombe shot at it with their carbines then moved back. Both shots were wild, and Trelawny remarked that his pistol was a more accurate weapon. He drew it and turned toward the target.

At that instant both Whitcombe and Fenton fired their carbines at him. Fenton's misfired, but Whitcombe sent two bullets
into Trelawny; one fractured his jaw, and the other smashed his
arm, then lodged in his chest.

As he slumped to the ground Fenton dashed toward him,
shouting that the shooting had been accidental, but before he
could reach his victim one of the guards killed him with a single
shot through the head. A huge watchdog pounced on Whitcombe and pinned him to the ground until the guards bound
him and hauled him to the lip of the terrace, intending to hurl
him to his death below.

The dazed Trelawny still had enough presence of mind to
order the men not to kill or torture Whitcombe. Instead they
were to hold him until a full investigation of the shooting could
be made.

Then, unable to walk erect, Trelawny crawled into the cavern
and propped himself against the rough wall. He spat out the bullet that made it almost impossible for him to move his jaw, but
the other lead pellet remained embedded in his chest.

The men were greatly saddened. They knew that it was impossible either to obtain medical assistance in the immediate area or
to move him, as the stretch of land they were on was controlled
by the Turks. Trelawny, they felt, would die before a physician
could be summoned from Athens. So Trelawny took charge of
his situation himself, and his display of courage was astonishing.

Remembering Zela's remedy, he had poultices of raw egg applied to his wounds at frequent intervals. Unable to chew, he
lived on nothing but raw eggs and water, insisting that the diet,
combined with sunlight and fresh air, would cure him. For three
weeks he remained propped against the wall of the cave, and
nothing could induce him to move.

During the first days, he was more dead than alive and was
often delirious, but the remedy was effective, and on the twenty-
first day he was able to eat a little solid food, bread that Tarsitsa
baked for him and a few bits of thinly sliced ham. The Greeks,
who had been sure he would expire, were astonished by his recovery, and a legend was born to the effect that he was inde-
structible.

Meanwhile Whitcombe, confined in a small cave and closely

guarded, sent message after message to the man he had tried to kill. Gradually Trelawny was able to piece together the whole story. Fenton and Whitcombe had conspired to seize the best of the supplies, the treasure chest of Odysseus and the more attractive women, then make their way to the coast and return to England.

Trelawny's reaction indicated he was still naïve. He later wrote he could not conceive it possible that "an English gentleman, my guest," could have conspired to assassinate him. A search was made of Fenton's headquarters on the slope, and various papers were brought to him, giving him another shock. Fenton, it developed, had been a spy in the pay of the Turks, and in an association that had lasted for more than a year, Trelawny had not once suspected the truth.

The guards and women were difficult to control, and the wounded Trelawny had to exercise all his moral authority to prevent the murder of Whitcombe, whom he regarded as Fenton's dupe. Each day, he had to repeat his order that the man was not to be harmed, but the Greeks swore they would roast him slowly over a fire if Trelawny died. Instead he became stronger with each passing day, and a month after the shooting he felt sufficiently recovered to order the release of Whitcombe, an act of charity that belied the claims of his critics who said he was himself a savage barbarian.

He was not yet fully recovered when he was shattered by an even greater blow: word was received to the effect that Odysseus had been captured, tortured and killed.

## XXIII

## *"Death thought me his own."*

The death of Odysseus, whose standing as one of the great heroes of the Greek War of Independence has been confirmed by posterity, was the final blow to Trelawny's hopes. A helpless cripple, his right arm paralyzed in spite of an improvement in his general health, he knew he could contribute no more to the Greek cause. There was little to envy in his practical situation: he was marooned in a cavern high on the side of a mountain, the Turks still had a price on his head, and members of rival Greek factions were eager to betray him to the enemy in return for cash.

A captured physician was brought to the mountain stronghold and performed surgery, but his attempt to find and remove the bullet from Trelawny's chest failed. The patient's suffering did not cease. Summer came, and although there was no relief in sight, Trelawny clung stubbornly to the hope that a miracle would save him.

He did not realize it, but his situation was well known to the British, who had established bases in some of the Greek Islands and were surreptitiously helping to fight the Turks. Word seeped back to England; the newspapers printed long—and frequently garbled—accounts of the Englishman's plight, and for the first time the name of Edward John Trelawny became well known to his fellow countrymen. His mother wrote a strong letter to His Majesty's Government, demanding formal intervention on her son's behalf. Strong speeches supporting this request were made in both houses of Parliament, and a motion was placed on the floor of the Commons authorizing the dispatch of a warship and a contingent of Royal Marines to rescue the heroic Mr. Trelawny. No one mentioned the fact that the hero had been a deserter from the Royal Navy.

Trelawny's friends were horrified when they heard the news. Everyone who knew him wrote worried letters to everyone else, and Mary Shelley was so upset she confessed that she wept herself to sleep every night.

But no acts of Parliament were necessary, and no formal orders were sent from London to Greece. Commodore Rowan Hamilton, the commander of the Royal Navy flotilla stationed in Greek waters, took matters into his own hands. He sent a major of Marines from his own staff, accompanied by a strong, armed escort, into the interior to rescue the Englishman and his wife.

It was late August by the time the major located Trelawny, climbed the precipice and asked him to leave. Trelawny refused, believing it was his duty to stay at the side of Odysseus' wife and stepmother. They tried to convince him he was wrong, the other lieutenants of the slain chieftain added their voices to the argument, and Trelawny agreed to depart only when they promised him they would remain in the caverns, guarding Odysseus' treasure, until it was safe for them to return to Athens and give the money to a new leader who would beat the Turks and assure the independence of Greece.

Trelawny and Tarsitsa, escorted by the uniformed English marines, began a long journey. They made their way to the coast, traveling by easy stages because of the hero's infirmity, and four different warships were pressed into service, one after another, to carry him to Cephalonia. The bride made a strong impression on almost everyone who met her, and a number of officers wrote that she was lovely, news that, again, was no surprise to anyone acquainted with Trelawny, who never displayed an interest in any but attractive women.

One man who was not impressed by the couple was the Reverend Charles Swan, the chaplain of the flotilla, who referred to them as "a pair of savages" in his book *Journal of a Voyage up the Mediterranean*. He stood alone, however, and among those who became friendly with Trelawny and his bride was Samuel Gridley Howe, an idealistic American doctor who had come to Greece to offer his services to the freedom fighters. Dr. Howe examined the patient, and then performed surgery; the operation lasted the better part of a day, but he succeeded in removing the bullet that was poisoning the patient's whole system.

Trelawny's arm was still paralyzed, however, and two more operations were performed over a period of months by English surgeons before he began to regain the use of his arm. Then a course of exercises was prescribed to stretch and strengthen the atrophied muscles, and Trelawny, loathing Cephalonia because of its ugliness, moved with Tarsitsa to a pretty house in Zante in May 1826.

Determined not to be crippled for the rest of his life, he worked with furious energy to restore his right arm to its full use. He dug, planted and weeded in the garden; he rowed a small boat for two hours every morning and again in the afternoon; he had a set of weights made, and even when reading he held his book in his left hand and lifted the weights repeatedly with his right. His improvement was steady, and he insisted he would confound the physicians who had told him he would never regain full use of his arm.

In the meantime his correspondence was piling up, so he taught himself to write with his left hand, and the steady flow of outgoing letters to Mary, Claire, Leigh Hunt, Captain Roberts and many others was resumed. Several books in which his exploits were mentioned at length were published in England at this time, among them the Reverend Mr. Swan's and another by an Italian lawyer named Palma. Trelawny believed he had been slandered and sent Mary a statement which he asked her to insert on his behalf in the London newspapers:

*Thank heaven my right arm is not so wasted of its strength but that it can chastise the liar who asserted it!*

Mary edited the statement, making it less vehement before forwarding it to the press.

Another flurry was caused in Zante when two of Whitcombe's brothers came from England to Greece to learn the truth of the scandal that had resulted in Trelawny's injury. Commodore Hamilton was afraid the irate Cornishman would do the pair bodily injury and sent a detachment of marines to Zante to keep the peace. But the precaution proved unnecessary. Trelawny had slipped into the role of an English gentleman again, treated the brothers with every consideration and assured them he bore no grudge against young Whitcombe, whom he regarded as a confused weakling.

In the late summer of 1826 Tarsitsa gave birth to a daughter, and Trelawny named the baby Zella, after his first love. Life should have been complete, but soon after the baby's birth the differences between husband and wife began to drive them apart. Trelawny read incessantly; Tarsitsa could neither read nor write. Trelawny enjoyed a social evening for its own sake, but Tarsitsa was a flirt who could not resist fluttering her eyelashes at any man who came to the house. Now that pressing dangers had passed and Trelawny was regaining the use of his arm, rifts in the marriage that otherwise might have become apparent sooner began to show.

A trifling incident ended the relationship. Trelawny loved to see his wife in native dress, believing that flowing gowns suited her. But Tarsitsa, exposed to Western influences for the first time, wanted to dress like other ladies she saw in Zante. Deliberately disobeying her husband's explicit order, she sent to Paris for a gown and wore it in his presence.

There are several versions of what happened next. According to one of the more spectacular, Trelawny had warned Tarsitsa that if he ever saw her in Western dress he would cut off her hair. As this story has it, he drew the short, sharp knife of the guerillas which he carried in his belt and chopped off her hair. If another tale is correct, he was even more violent: he lowered Tarsitsa from a third-story window and left her hanging by her hair until she promised to change her dress.

In all probability neither of the sensational stories is true, as Trelawny was never known to subject any woman to physical abuse. But whatever may have happened, Tarsitsa departed and took up residence in a convent, leaving her belongings—her clothes and her baby—behind. Soon thereafter she filed suit for divorce, and encouraged by various relatives who believed all Englishmen were wealthy, she asked the court to award her an enormous sum of money.

Trelawny kept the house in Zante, hired a nursemaid for the baby and continued to exercise his arm. Warped and exaggerated stories about his activities drifted back to England, among them a tale to the effect that he was living with a harem of three slave women he had purchased. When Mary wrote to him, repeating some of the stories, he sent a sharp reply:

*You err most egregiously if you think I am occupied with women or intrigues, or that my time passes pleasantly. The reverse of all this is the case; neither women nor amusements of any sort occupy my time, and a sadder or more accursed kind of existence I never in all my experience of life endured or, I think, fell to the lot of human being.*

His daughter kept him tied to Zante; the lawsuit filed by Tarsitsa made it impossible for him to travel, and he continued the dreary routine of exercising his arm. By the end of 1826 he had regained the better part of its use but wrote to Mary and to his mother, with whom he now corresponded occasionally, that he would not rest until he could write and shoot a pistol with his right hand again.

The year 1827 was an important milestone in the Greek War of Independence. The Czar Nicholas was giving the Greeks help because of Russia's rivalry with the Ottoman Empire, and France and Great Britain, determined not to lose influence in the area, openly offered assistance, too. A combined Anglo-French-Russian fleet won a decisive victory over the Turks in the battle of Navarino, fought on October 20; sixty Turkish ships were sunk and eight thousand of the Sultan's men died, while the allied forces did not lose a single vessel. For all practical purposes Greek independence was now assured, and after two years of intensive political jockeying the major powers finally recognized the Kingdom of Greece two years later.

Trelawny was pleased by the victory in Navarino Bay and offered his congratulations to Commodore Hamilton and other Royal Navy officers with whom he had become friendly. But his own tangled affairs so preoccupied him that he could not give the battle the attention it deserved. Less than a month later, in mid-November, he made a trip to the island of Corfu, where the district court was situated, in the hope that he could expedite the divorce case.

When he appeared before the court, a nasty story that had been circulating about him and Tarsitsa finally came into the open, and the true facts became known. Shortly after she entered the convent Tarsitsa gave birth to a second daughter and promptly sent her to Trelawny. He hired a wetnurse, but the infant was so sickly she died a few days later. The angry Trelawny sent the baby's body back to the mother, and the court fined him a token twenty dollars. Since Tarsitsa was a Greek, the court did not reprimand her for having sent the infant to Trelawny in the first place.

Unpleasant charges and countercharges were made in court, and Tarsitsa did her best to blacken Trelawny's name, but the court ruled that most of the evidence she submitted was inadmissible. The hearings dragged on for the better part of a month, delayed by many adjournments, and Tarsitsa finally was granted a divorce. Trelawny won a victory of sorts, too, obtaining custody of Zella and being required to pay Tarsitsa the relatively small alimony of twenty-five dollars per month—as long as he remained in Greece. The court stipulated that he would be relieved of this obligation if and when he left the country.

Tarsitsa promptly disappeared from Trelawny's life, and thereafter he mentioned her only once in his correspondence. In 1836 he wrote Claire to the effect that the third of his wives had obtained another divorce in the Greek Orthodox Church and had married "the son of a Greek chieftain." She was "thriving," he said, and was still "distinguished for her beauty." A few facts regarding her late life have been pieced together, thanks to her daughter's disclosure. Zella visited her a few times as an adult, found her to be still beautiful and established something of a tenuous rapport with her. Tarsitsa's husband was a Colonel Phillepetis, who owned a number of large properties which he rented to currant growers. When he died, he left his widow comfortably situated, and she continued his business. In 1870 she died from an illness that developed after she contracted a chill

while collecting rents from her tenants. She left the bulk of her
estate to Zella, but the daughter could not be located, as she was
married and living in South America with her husband. When
Zella returned to Europe, some years later, and learned of the
bequest, her husband went to Greece on her behalf in an attempt
to claim it for her. By that time, however, she had been assumed
to be dead and the estates had been given to the convent in
which Tarsitsa had grown up.

Trelawny appears to have been relieved by the dissolution of
his marriage, neither grieving as he had done after the death of
his first wife nor feeling the hostilities that overwhelmed him
during and after his divorce from the unfaithful Julia. He was a
free man again; he loved his little daughter and so began to
make concrete plans for their future.

He wanted to return to Italy, the land he had most enjoyed, to
establish a home there. He would take Zella with him, and he
also would send for Eliza, the younger of his daughters by Julia.
He had corresponded regularly with the child, who was now
about twelve years old. He would be thirty-six himself later in
1828, and he was ready to settle down, bring up his children and,
he hoped, find a new vocation that would keep him occupied.
He wished at the same time to have this fresh venture increase
his income and still bring him renown based on more than his
exploits as a buccaneer and guerilla fighter.

His correspondence with Mary and with Claire in the winter
of 1828 indicates he was beginning to think of writing the
biography of his early years. Everyone to whom he told the story
of his harsh childhood and his subsequent life in the East had
been fascinated, and he was shrewd enough to reason there
might be a market for a book on the subject.

He was particularly diffident in broaching the subject to Mary,
who was not only the widow of the man he regarded as the
greatest of all poets but was herself a highly successful and es-
teemed author. She was quick to encourage him, however, and
even suggested—but very delicately—that she would be happy
to edit his work for him. And he knew his spelling and punctuation were abominable, so he accepted with gratitude. Claire was
far less encouraging than Mary, her relations with Lord Byron

having soured her on writers. She mentioned the matter briefly in her replies and indicated indifference to the project.

Trelawny could forgive anything but a blow to his vanity, but he regarded his friendship with Claire Clairmont as something special and struggled to overcome his anger. Had she rebuffed him a few years earlier, he would have written her a nasty letter and terminated their correspondence, but he was growing somewhat more tolerant now. So he waited until his temper cooled before he wrote, and did not mention his projected autobiography to her again.

By the early spring of 1828 he had made his plans. He would leave the two-year-old Zella in Greece until he sent for her in Italy, and would pay a visit to England for "docking and repairing" before he settled down. He would see his daughters by Julia: Maria and his beloved Eliza; he would visit Mary Shelley and other friends, and he would make needed changes in his investments before going on to Italy.

His departure was delayed when he was felled by a bout of malaria; some of his English friends in Zante despaired of his life. But his constitution was so rugged that he recovered from the disease with a speed that astonished his physicians, and by early summer he was ready to travel. He made arrangements for the care of Zella and left in July, traveling in a manner that befitted a hero. The one-time Royal Navy deserter who had despised his life on board a frigate went back to England as a passenger on a frigate. He slept in a comfortable cabin which the first lieutenant vacated for him; he dined regularly with the captain, and he spent much of his time on the quarter-deck. Neither in his correspondence nor in any of his books does he mention his feelings on the voyage.

By the early part of August he was in England, and after a joyful reunion with his daughters he paid Mary a visit. From her he learned that Jane Williams had not only recovered her equilibrium but had found a new mate. He was Thomas Jefferson Hogg, the intimate friend of Shelley's college days and his sympathetic listener during Shelley's subsequent struggles as a poet. Hogg was one of the most complicated characters in the Shelley circle and had a penchant for falling in love only with women

who had interested Shelley himself. He had proclaimed his un-
dying affection for Harriet Westbrook Shelley, the poet's first
wife, then for Mary. Now he took Jane's tall tales of her romance
with Shelley at face value and fell in love with her, too.

Jane was not legally divorced, so her arrangement with Hogg
was similar to that which she had enjoyed with Edward Williams. She moved in with her new lover, called herself Mrs.
Hogg and, for all practical purposes, was married to him.

Trelawny met Hogg and did not like him, finding him pom-
pous and overbearing. In a letter to Mary, then in Hastings, he
referred to Jane's new association as a "degrading connection"
and referred to her lover as *a* Hogg because "he looks like a thoroughbred hog."

Jane subsequently complained that Trelawny had refrained
from giving her his opinion of Hogg; he had offered her no guid-
ance on the wisdom of this liaison's establishment. When Mary
informed him of this, he wrote:

*I have long ago learnt the folly of such presumption; advice is
nauseous as castor oil—and few stomachs are found gross enough
to retain it—notwithstanding every fool tells you he has a way of
administering it so disguised that the most delicate palate cannot
be nauseated—all I can say in answer is that the very mention of
the one or the other inclines to vomit. . . .*

He knew no restraint in expressing his view of Hogg in a letter
to Claire, whose return to England was expected at any time.
Hogg, he said, was

*. . . a man so repellingly cold and distant in his rudeness, that
in the short time I could have for the attainment of such a
herculean object as the becoming intimate with him which I certainly have not the slightest reason to believe, he either wished
or permitted,—for it seemed to me an age would hardly have
sufficed to have established myself on good terms with such an
icy man—the utmost that I thought would be achieved was that
there was a possibility that our acquaintance might beget an intimacy between our children—that the good understanding with
them might ripen under auspicious circumstances to a friendship
between our respective grandchildren.*

Claire did return to England at the end of the summer, and Trelawny, who had looked forward to her arrival and had anticipated a return to a comradely relationship, was shocked by her attitudes. The past six years of working and living as a governess in Vienna had changed her in every way, and she was barely recognizable. The tempestuous girl whose affair with Byron had created gossip to which she had once been supremely indifferent was now a thin-lipped woman, a "compleat prude." She was querulous and prim, argumentative and intolerant. Mary, who wanted no more to do with her stepsister under the best of circumstances, avoided her "as one would a carrier of the Great Plague."

Trelawny was kinder, and for the sake of the past he tried to understand her change, but the effort was almost too much for him. Her clothes were dowdy and old-fashioned, and she condemned all of the new fashions; she not only wore thick stockings but talked about them at length, saying how practical and comfortable they were. This was not the Claire whom Trelawny had known, and he wrote to Mary:

*She talked of nothing but worsted stockings and marrying—the only doubt to my mind is which is worse—but if I am condemned to one, I think I must take the former.*

Prior to Claire's arrival, he had thought seriously of asking her to join him in Italy as a governess, taking charge of Eliza and Zella, but he quickly changed his mind. Claire, he told Mary, now regarded him as being a scoundrel in a class with Byron. He had outlived his honesty, but he added with irony that had he died in Greece he would have been still blessed in her memory.

Not all of Trelawny's time in England was spent with the friends of his Italian sojourn. He was universally regarded as a hero of Greek independence, even though he was the first to insist that his contribution to the cause had been slight. Many prominent people were anxious to meet him, and when he paid a visit to the country estate of his uncle Sir Christopher Hawkins, Lady Hawkins wrote to a niece that ladies and gentlemen from whom she hadn't heard in years were begging for invitations to dinner, lunch or tea.

He spent some time with his mother, also visiting his brother for a week or two, and both were flattered when their friends and acquaintances called in droves. The prodigal had been rehabilitated, and they were delighted. But the famous Trelawny was not fooled by all the praise being showered upon him—much as he enjoyed the attention. Members of his family and many of his old friends urged him to settle in England; he rejected the idea. He made his feelings on the subject clear when he wrote:

*Time has not quenched the fire of my nature—my feelings burn fierce as ever and will until they have consumed me. "I wear the burnished livery of the sun."*

*To whom am I a neighbor? and near whom? I dwell among tame and civilized human beings.*

By the end of the year, he was anxious to leave. He said goodby to his friends, paid brief farewell visits to his relatives and obtained a promise in writing from Julia that Eliza would be permitted to join him as soon as he set up a home in Italy.

He left London on January 7, 1829, looking forward to his first voyage on a steamboat, having already made up his mind to study this new mode of transportation so he could qualify as the master of a steam-propelled vessel. He stayed overnight in Dover and was awakened at dawn by the howling of a gale. Looking out his hotel window, he saw a mixture of rain and sleet and assumed the Channel crossing would be postponed. He then went down to the docks—he was impressed and a bit surprised when he learned that the ship would sail regardless of the weather.

The captain proved to be too much of an optimist, however, and Trelawny, who stood with him on the bridge, couldn't help laughing when the man put back into port. That laughter goaded the captain, so he turned around and made the crossing despite himself, giving his passenger the wildest three hours he had ever experienced at sea.

As volatile as ever, Trelawny wrote to Mary Shelley the next day from Calais:

*On Sunday, its gloom entered my soul—it is in London a melancholy and mortifying day—my nature was changed—my*

*sluggish blood oozed along, slow and unready. I was no longer a
child of the sun whose blood was made of fire but as apathetic as
ever Trevanion [a literary critic whose brother was married to
Trelawny's sister Charlotte] could have wished to have made the
hero of his poem—but to me apathy is certainly anything but
rest or peace.*

*This morning I was determined to arouse myself.*

## XXIV

### *"Brown and Landor are spurring me on."*

By 1829 Florence had become the principal Italian magnet for the expatriate English poets, essayists and artists who were living in Italy. The undisputed leader of the group was Walter Savage Landor, a poet and prose writer who stood apart from the mainstream of English letters but, nevertheless, commanded the respect of his contemporaries. Seventeen years older than Trelawny, he had met the younger man at some point during the previous year or two, the exact circumstances being unknown. Trelawny reached Florence in March 1829, and only a few months later Landor's *Imaginary Conversation between Odysseus, Tarsitsa, Acrive and Trelawny* was published in London after being edited by the author's good friend Southey. It may have been Trelawny's developing friendship with Landor that brought him to Florence.

There were others he found interesting there, too. One was Charles Armitage Brown, an editor, author and critic who had been close to John Keats and also a friend of Byron's. Yet another was Seymour Kirkup, who was regarded by many of his contemporaries as the greatest English painter of his day but

whom posterity has regarded as second-rate. In all, the English
community in Florence was the largest in Italy and may have
been the biggest on the Continent; it included a great many
dabblers in the arts, men and women who were sympathetic to
anyone at all who wanted to write, as well as a number of the retired Royal Navy officers with whom Trelawny had special rapport.

After spending only a short time in the city, Trelawny decided
he wanted to live there and rented a villa near the Tower of
Galileo which he considered admirable for his purposes. It had
flower and vegetable gardens, an orchard filled with fruit trees
and a bathing pool, all perfect for rearing children. Then he
hired four servants—a cook, a housemaid, a governess and a gardener—and awaited the arrival of his daughters.

A brief, formal letter from Julia informed him that Eliza had
fallen ill of a mysterious malady and had died before the physicians who had been summoned could reach her bedside.
Trelawny was crushed by her unexpected passing, writing to
Claire:

*She was the only creature from whom I expected nothing but
sweet remembrances, perfect love. By her death Fortune has extended her utmost malice on me—Fortune never gave me anything—and those few good things I wrested from her by desperate adventuring she has most revengefully taken from me.*

Zella was now overdue, and the death of Eliza made him doubly apprehensive as he hurried off to Ancona to meet her ship.
Delay followed delay; six or seven ships arrived from Greece,
but she was not on board any of them. Finally he received a letter of explanation from the wife of a retired Royal Navy captain
in Zante, a woman who had promised to help look after the little
girl. He had held his renowned temper in check for a long time,
but now it exploded in a furious letter he wrote to a friend:

*An officious reptile had taken it into her head that "for the
honor of an English gentleman" the child should be clothed in
the English fashion before she could be sent to Ancona; consequently she had been landed at Corfu, and the graceful robes of*

*the Greek girl were exchanged for the unseemly doll-like shreds*
*and patches of the European. I have written to the lady that I*
*cannot comprehend what in the devil honor has to do with the*
*cut of a child's frock, and I shall most assuredly commit the Eng-*
*lish rags to the flames, and as the lady, though loose in her*
*morals, is tight-laced in her religion, I added that even if the Vir-*
*gin Mary herself made the dresses, it should not avert my*
*profane purpose.*

After another two weeks of restless waiting, the ship bearing
Zella finally arrived. Trelawny swept his daughter into his arms,
and by his own admission he wept for the first time since the
death of the wife whose name she bore. He carried her off to
Florence, where he gave a dinner party in her honor, and he
learned something new about the care of children when Zella,
now not quite four years of age, ate so much that she fell ill.
Soon thereafter he discovered she was suffering from a far more
serious ailment, malaria, but she was cured by the cool Floren-
tine air and by the quinine Trelawny's physicians prescribed for
her.

As soon as Zella was settled into the house, Trelawny was able
to devote his thinking to other matters. His friendship with Landor developed swiftly, and Trelawny discovered he could do a
great service for the reputation of Shelley. Landor had long held
his fellow poet in very low esteem, openly snubbing him because
he had accepted at face value the stories that Shelley had been
vicious in his treatment of his first wife, Harriet. Trelawny gave
the older man a new estimate of Shelley's character, and when
Landor, at his urging, read and vastly admired quantities of
Shelley's poetry, the new friendship was sealed.

Landor and Brown combined in prodding Trelawny to write
an account of his youthful adventures, the former assuring him
that if he wrote the story as he had many times told it, he would
enjoy an enormous success, the latter telling him that he could
achieve the same reputation as that of so many authors he admired. Trelawny threw out the opening chapters of the autobiography he had written to date, calling them "amateurish
drivel," and began again, with Landor advising him and editing
his work, Brown encouraging and pushing.

Trelawny's correspondence with Mary Shelley increased, and he besieged her with questions and requests for help. He hoped she would assist in finding him a publisher; maintaining a household for Zella was expensive, and he would breathe easier if he could get an advance of five hundred pounds for the book. He intended to write it anonymously and was somewhat offended when Mary replied that too many people would see through the disguise. She advised him to publish under his own name. He planned to call the work *A Man's Life,* and he felt hurt again when she told him the title was too drab. He also asked her to do the final editing and promised to accept any cuts and revisions she cared to make.

In his enthusiasm for his new profession he indicated that when he finished the book he planned to write a biography of Shelley, but indicated that he would save Mary embarrassment by not mentioning her in it. He also asked for her co-operation. She replied, sensibly, that it would be impossible to omit her from such a biography. She also refused her co-operation, saying she intended to write the book herself one day but that the subject was still too sore.

Momentarily irritated beyond endurance, he wrote to Claire that Mary's attitude was "a lot of mawkish cant."

Then he recovered his equilibrium and went back to work on his autobiography. Landor and Brown went over the manuscript page by page, and as he finished each chapter Trelawny sent it off to Mary. Her attitude toward his literary efforts had been slightly patronizing from the start, and now she outraged him, causing him to forget his promise that he would abide by her decisions. She criticized his language, saying that polite usage prohibited the use of certain words that had been acceptable in the eighteenth-century day of Henry Fielding. Again he exploded, writing to her:

*Landor, a man of superior literary acquirements: Kirkup, an artist of superior taste: Baring, a man of the world and very religious: Mrs. Baring, moral and squeamish: Lady Burghersh, aristocratic and proud as a Queen: and lastly, Charles Brown, a plain, downright Cockney critic, learned in the trade of authorship and has served his time as a literary scribe: all these male and female critics have read and passed their opinions on my narrative, and therefore you must excuse my apparent presumption in answering your objections to my book with an appearance of presumptuous dictation.*

In brief, he flatly refused to eliminate the words that had offended the increasingly conservative Mary.

She also disliked his title, and suggested he call it *The History of a Man*, *Young Son* or *Adventures*. Trelawny's judgment was better than Mary's when he told her all three were commonplace, that *A Man's Life* was better than any of them because it was simple, accurate and less hackneyed.

But, through no fault of Trelawny's, it was Mary Shelley who had the final word in the matter. He had hoped to go to London himself to negotiate with publishers, but the trip was expensive. Also he felt he could not leave Zella behind, and she was too small a child for him to take with him. So he was compelled to stay in Florence, and Mary represented him, in effect working as his literary agent. It was she who made the arrangements with the firm of Henry Colburn and Richard Bentley to publish the book, and when they asked her what to call it, no title page having been attached to the manuscript, she promptly dubbed it *Adventures of a Younger Son*.

Trelawny was disappointed by the advance royalty payment of three hundred pounds the publishers paid him, but not even he was prepared for the reception the book received from the day it came out. The first printing, of two thousand copies, sold out in a week, a second, of five thousand, followed in another two weeks, and a third, of ten thousand, was exhausted in yet another fortnight.

*Younger Son* was a sensational success, and at least three or four new printings appeared every year for the next decade and a half; it was still selling by the time the author was in his eighties and had lost count of the number of printings. It not only established him overnight as a leading literary figure of the period, but it confirmed what the newspapers had said about his activities in Greece, and he became one of the most celebrated personages of the age. Every literate man and woman in England read the book or wanted to read it, and almost without exception everyone wanted to meet the author. Few men in the history of literature have ever catapulted to such fame so quickly. In June 1831, Trelawny was vaguely remembered by newspaper readers as a hero of the Greek Revolution; in July, after *Younger Son* was published, he was one of the most renowned men in the British Isles.

The reviews of the book were extraordinary, and even the worst of them helped the sale and further enhanced the author's reputation. The *Times* called it "fascinating" and hoped "that some portion of it is the truth"; the *Spectator* flatly called it "the cleverest book of the season." The conservative *Literary Gazette* said it was "wild and reckless" and referred to the author as a "bold buccaneer." The *Quarterly*, an equally respected critical journal, lavished praise on the author and called him "a man of remarkable talents." The *Athenaeum* was shocked, attacked Trelawny for the "extreme grossness" of his language and said he was a ruffian. His favorite critique, from the *Military Review*, which he quoted at length in a letter to Claire, said *Younger Son* was "wild, libertine and eccentric, revolting yet attractive, savage yet sentimental." Romance could go no further, it declared, than the actual adventures of this "homicidal renegade and corsair."

England was in the throes of political, social and economic turmoil at the beginning of the nineteenth century's fourth decade, but Trelawny scarcely knew it, just as he was none too aware of the abortive revolutions on the Continent in 1830. The expanding Industrial Revolution was spreading at too rapid a rate, which caused a financial recession; the laboring classes were underpaid, were forced to work long hours under despicable conditions, and were rebelling. And the common man everywhere was demanding a greater voice in the affairs of government.

In 1830, Trelawny was too busy writing *Younger Son* to be directly involved in what was taking place in the world around him, and the shower of gold that descended on him in 1831 blinded him to the poverty of others. He had hoped his book would earn five hundred pounds; in the first months after publication, it brought him an unprecedented three thousand, and in 1832 that figure was doubled. Not even Sir Walter Scott, the most popular British author of the century, had earned such sums from any single book.

Trelawny's mail overwhelmed him, and he needed a secretary to help answer it. But he refused to hire someone for fear he would be accused of putting on airs. A score of London publishers wrote to him, asking if he had any other manuscripts on hand or was planning any new works. Newspapers wanted interviews, and one or two offered to send reporters to see him. Magazines besieged him for articles on any subject that might please him. Invitations to dinners, receptions and even weekend visits came from friends, acquaintances and total strangers, a few of whom he recognized by name because of their high place in society.

He was amused and flattered but did not lose his perspective. At the same time, however, he realized his presence was required in England if he hoped to take advantage of his great success and pursue his new career in earnest. He was reluctant to take Zella there, because England was socially inhibited, physically cold and damp—and he blamed the weather for the death of Eliza.

On the other hand, his little daughter was becoming something of a problem. Not only was he learning that he was not the perfect guardian for a little girl, but the child was making life even more difficult for him by demonstrating that his independent, stubborn blood ran in her veins.

The gardener was proud of his peach trees and directed Zella to stay away from them. One day, he caught her in the branches of a peach tree, hauled her down and tied her hands behind her back. But nothing daunted her, and her father, strolling through the property in search of her, found that she had managed to climb a wall and, standing on her toes, was nibbling the forbidden fruit. Remembering his own punishment when he had dared to take fruit from his father's garden, he immediately cut Zella's bonds, allowed her to pick as many peaches as she wanted and carried a basket filled with fruit back to the house for her. He could not inflict severe punishment on her, but at the same time he was afraid his indulgence would spoil her.

A serious incident took place soon thereafter. An old friend of

Trelawny's was the Marchesa Boccella, whom he had known as a child in Cornwall. She had now been married for many years to an Italian nobleman and was a prominent member of the court of the Grand Duke of Lucca, a widower, sometimes acting as his official hostess. One day Jane Boccella offered to take Zella to the court with her for a visit, and Trelawny agreed, with some misgivings.

His fears were justified. The little girl was invited to sit on the grand duke's lap, and promptly committed lese majesty, horrifying the court by deliberately tweaking the old man's nose. Trelawny laughed when he was told what had happened, but at the same time he was worried. He had paid for his own misconduct as a child and didn't want Zella to suffer; perhaps he should exert stronger discipline, but the problem of rearing a daughter bewildered, upset and frightened him.

Jane Boccella offered him a solution. She would take Zella into her own home and would educate her as she would her own daughter. The child would be free to visit her father whenever she wished and could make the final decision in the matter herself. Zella, who badly missed a mother, was overjoyed, preferring life with the gentle, warm marchesa to that with a father who boomed from a quarter-deck, could not be disturbed when he closeted himself in his study and, when he was not ignoring her, overwhelmed her with affection.

So the details were arranged, the Marchesa Boccella took unofficial custody of the little girl, and Trelawny, now in his fortieth year, returned in triumph to London. He reached England in time to share the reactions of his compatriots to the great Reform Bill of 1832, perhaps the single most important legislative measure furthering the democratic process in Great Britain. Virtually the entire middle class, which had been voiceless in the affairs of government, was enfranchised. The wings of the old aristocracy were clipped, and some of the worst abuses that condemned the workingman to a life of semislavery were ended. Still the humanitarian and liberal, Trelawny rejoiced.

Before he reached England, however, he felt compelled to pay a visit to Paris on his way home. A cholera epidemic was raging there, and the newspapers said ten thousand persons had died.

Foreigners were fleeing, no new visitors were coming to the city and the hotels were empty. That was all the more reason for Trelawny, always perverse, to pause there. He wrote to Claire:

*I have always struggled against the stream. I know not how it is, but if I see a crowd all marching one way, I feel myself impelled to jostle through them in a contrary direction. So many people advised me not to come that I began thinking of buying a house.*

Several pleasant surprises awaited him in Paris. A translation of *Younger Son* had just been published there, by the house of Galignani, and was creating as great a sensation in France as it had in England. Trelawny met Victor Hugo, already regarded as the leader of the romantic movement in French literature and as one of the great authors of the age. They dined together at Hugo's favorite restaurant, the Grand Vefour, the Frenchman insisting on ordering the food and wine because he considered the English barbarians in such matters. Then, amenities out of the way, Hugo told Trelawny he thought *Younger Son* was the finest autobiography and one of the best true adventure stories he had ever read. Trelawny's joy remained undiminished on the journey to London.

Before telling anyone else that he was home, he went to see his eldest daughter, Maria Julia, now a grown young lady. She had left her mother's home and was living with a Mrs. Burley, whose son, John, she would marry a few years later. Father and daughter spent a few days together, and Trelawny felt a vague dissatisfaction, feeling that Julia, as she liked to be called, was insufficiently cerebral. She read few books, was interested principally in clothes, gossip and frivolous pursuits, and knew little about matters of the mind. What she needed, her father decided, was a long visit with someone of Mary Shelley's caliber, someone who would give her new interests and a new direction in life.

He discussed the matter with Mary, who was pleased to be able to return Trelawny's many favors to her. But he didn't want Julia to become a burden and wrote Mary a revealing letter:

*I wish her to live as you do, and that you will not put yourself to the slightest inconvenience on her account. As we are poor,*

*the rich are our inheritance, and we are justified on all and every
occasion to rob and use them. But we must be honest and just
amongst ourselves, and therefore Julia must to the last fraction
pay her own expenses, and neither put you to expense nor inconvenience. For the rest, I should like Julia to learn to lean upon
herself alone—to see the practical side of life: to learn housekeeping on trifling means, and to benefit by her intercourse with a
woman like you; but I am ill at compliments.*

*As to your style of lodging or living,—Julia is not such a fool
as to let that have any weight with her; if you were in a cobbler's
stall she would be satisfied and as to the dullness of the place,
why, that must depend mainly on ourselves.*

*At all events, come we shall: and if you, by barricading or
otherwise, oppose our entrance, why I shall do to you, not as I
would have others do unto me, but as I do unto others—make an
onslaught on your dwelling, carry your tenement by assault, and
give the place up to plunder.*

His correspondence was light enough, but when he and Julia
arrived at Mary's country house he proved to be in an exceptionally solemn mood. He was worried about Julia, he missed little Zella, he hated the fuss being made over him by the celebrity
seekers of London and, aware at last of the social changes in the
air, he looked forward to the future with increasing fear. He was
restless—Mary assumed it was because there were no attractive
young women in the neighborhood to distract him—and he
could not sit quietly for more than a few minutes at a time.

Mary unburdened herself in a letter to Maria Gisborne, her
old friend. She confided that she wouldn't know what to do
when Trelawny left and she had to handle Julia alone; the girl
was frivolous, silly and childish, the complete opposite of her father. In some ways, she reported, Trelawny was unchanged: he
loved "good sense, liberality and enthusiasm above all things";
he was still completely unprejudiced, but at the same time his
political opinions were so violent that she couldn't discuss politics with him. She ended by saying, "If you have any *very* pretty
girl of your acquaintance, enchant him by showing her to him
when he visits you in Plymouth."

Maria Julia Trelawny's visit to Mary Shelley lasted for three
months, the girl succeeding in doing no reading and discussing

nothing of substance, the woman managing, with a great effort, to retain her sanity. Julia then returned to the London house of Mrs. Burley, and soon thereafter the son of the house, returning home from Oxford, became interested in her.

Trelawny went to Plymouth, where he saw various relatives, paid a visit to his mother and, in fact, became quite frustrated there because his mother could talk of nothing except his book. She made as much of a nuisance of herself, he complained, as did the foolish women he met in London drawing rooms.

Almost from the day of his return to England, Trelawny had been made conscious of a new phenomenon, a tidal wave of migration to the United States. Men of every class were going, and wherever he went he heard people talking about America. Laborers were migrating because they were underpaid, were forced to work cruelly long hours and had no future in Britain; farmers were going because the great landlords from whom they rented were squeezing them, and middle-class men were going because it appeared everyone in America had a chance to make a fortune—and many did.

Liberals whom Trelawny met in various drawing rooms were ecstatic: America was the land of opportunity; it did not matter that rumor had it that her president, Andrew Jackson, was a barbarian. The institution of slavery still thrived in the South, to be sure, but the liberals were sure the day of slavery soon would be at an end.

The enthusiasm was contagious; Mary Shelley told Maria Gisborne that "Trelawny is America-mad."

She was right. He had seen many other parts of the world, but had never visited the Americas. He was tired of the static life he had been living in Florence, the adulation of Londoners irritated him and, finally, that old familiar wanderlust overcame him. It did not take him long to make up his mind: he would go to the United States for a lengthy visit.

## XXV

## "The sovereign people . . . are working out this grand experiment."

Edward John Trelawny's behavior in the late autumn and early winter of 1832 was extraordinary. He had always required an audience and had basked in admiration, but now he shunned the limelight and actively sought solitude. He may have reasoned that *Younger Son* spoke for itself, or perhaps he was going through some inner crisis that caused him to withdraw from society for several months. If that is the case, no details are known. On the other hand, isolation may have been due to nothing more complicated than exhaustion: he had worked hard producing his three-volume book, and the problems posed by his daughters caused an unaccustomed strain. Whatever his reasons, he shunned the clamoring hordes who wanted to lionize him in London, and he retired for a rest to the Cornwall estate of his brother. The suspicion lingers that he was just being perverse; knowing how eagerly his company was sought, he elected to have nothing to do with other members of the human race.

By early January 1833, he was ready for his new adventure and went to Liverpool to obtain passage across the Atlantic. He was of two minds about America, writing to some friends that he wanted to see "the grand experiment in democracy" in action, while defensively telling others he felt certain he would be disappointed, that he was confident nothing in the New World would interest him.

He had chosen the worst time of year for travel, particularly as he intended to go first to Canada for a visit with his old friend Augusta White, now Mrs. Draper. Temperatures in the North Atlantic were bitterly cold and snow that was piled several feet high awaited him in Quebec, but he apparently did not mind the weather, however different it was from the warm climates where he had spent most of his life.

Steamships were not yet crossing the Atlantic, but Trelawny felt completely at home on a sailing vessel. He was not prepared for the luxury he found on every side, however. His stateroom was even larger than the main cabin on his beloved schooner, the passengers dressed for dinner every evening and then sat down to meals of six or seven courses complete with the appropriate wines. Ladies and gentlemen gathered in a handsomely appointed saloon to read, chat and play cards, and the atmosphere was like that of an aristocratic London reception.

Trelawny felt stifled and promptly rebelled. When his ship was only forty-eight hours out of Liverpool on a voyage that would last four and one half weeks, he deserted the dining saloon and ate his meals with the ship's officers, refusing to set foot in the main saloon. He spent most of his time either on the quarter-deck or exchanging sea stories with the captain and the first mate. Apparently he was in the same antisocial mood that had caused him to avoid London society all through the autumn. He enjoyed a vicious January storm that sent most of the passengers to their berths and was lavish in his praise of the captain and the crew.

Trelawny landed in Quebec in mid-February, when snow fell daily, but he did not appear to mind the weather, and after a stay of a few days he traveled to Montreal for his visit with Augusta White Draper. There was little in the town to interest him, Montreal at that time being little more than a collection of log cabins, but he enjoyed his reunion with his old friend.

The following month, he returned to Quebec and went by sea to New York, where he received a hearty welcome from the wealthy and was immediately accepted in artistic circles. No American edition of *Younger Son* had been published as yet, an oversight that was corrected in the same year. Scores of prominent persons had read the English edition, however, and Trelawny was greeted with the deference due a literary man of stature. By this time he was ready to be paid tribute again, and he happily attended the theater, went to concerts and was the guest of honor at many dinner parties.

He found old New York very similar to London. Although the poverty of the masses was less pronounced, he wrote Mary and Claire, nevertheless he was unhappily surprised to find sharp class distinctions in this supposed democracy.

All was not disquieting to Trelawny, however; quite the contrary. . . . The American political system was effective, and nowhere else could a frontiersman like Andrew Jackson be president. Trelawny was told on good authority that Jackson frequently dined at the White House in shirt sleeves and carpet slippers, and as we might have expected, the Englishman approved.

The women of America made a lasting impression on him, and he wrote repeatedly that they were the most beautiful in the world. He was surrounded by lovely women at every turn and naturally enjoyed a number of flirtations.

He was astonished by the attitude of Americans to religion. Protestants, Catholics and Jews were devout, practiced their faith with an earnestness that he had encountered nowhere else and permitted no one to make light of their beliefs. The sincerity of the women was even greater than that of their fathers, husbands and sons, and the churches were always crowded with worshipers.

Trelawny, the close friend of women's-rights advocates, disapproved of the approach of American men toward their women. On the surface, he wrote, the male citizen of the United States was chivalrous and courtly, but in actuality he paid only lip service to the ideals he professed. American men were totally lacking in manners: they rarely helped a lady from a carriage, elbowed

her out of their path on the streets, took the best seats for themselves in restaurants and even accepted the most comfortable accommodations at inns, forcing their wives and daughters to take
inferior quarters. In far too many ways, he wrote to Claire, the
women of the North were "semi-slaves," their position little better than that of the black slaves in the South of the United
States.

During the first months of his two-year stay in the United
States, Trelawny made New York his headquarters and visited
New Jersey, Pennsylvania, Delaware, Maryland and the New
England states. He stayed in New Haven for a week or two with
old friends from England who were then on the faculty at Yale,
and in Cambridge he was the house guest of President Quincy of
Harvard. Through William Emerson, a leader of the intellectual
community whom he had met in London, he struck up an acquaintance with the man's younger brother. Ralph Waldo Emerson had left the clergy the previous year and was establishing
himself as a writer and lecturer. He and Trelawny dined together on a number of occasions, but neither recorded the subjects of their conversations.

At some time in New York Trelawny met and became very
friendly with a fellow Englishman, Charles Kemble, the great
Covent Garden actor-manager who had brought a repertory
company to the United States. In Kemble's party was his daughter, Fanny, at twenty-four already one of the leading actresses on
the London stage. Her personality was remarkably similar to
Trelawny's, and they immediately became close friends.

Fanny Kemble was beautiful, a gifted actress, a devoted
feminist and a restlessly dynamic woman. Extraordinarily well
read, she could converse at length on any subject, and was one
of the few women in her profession who was accepted as more
or less an equal by English aristocrats. Endowed with unlimited
energy, she enjoyed nothing more than a long canter, a grueling
hike or a climb up a mountain.

Trelawny was seventeen years her senior and developed no romantic interest in her, but treated her more like a favorite niece.
Fanny had read *Younger Son* on the voyage across the Atlantic,
and the book had fascinated her, so she and Trelawny admired

each other inordinately. In her *Journal,* published two years later, she wrote of him:

*He's a curious being: a description of him would puzzle anyone who had never seen him. A man with the proportions of a giant for strength and agility: taller, straighter and broader than most men; yet with the most indolent carelessness of gait; and an uncertain, wandering way of dropping his feet to the ground, as if he didn't know where he was going, and didn't much wish to go anywhere. His face is as dark as a Moor's; with a wild, strange look about the eyes and forehead, and a mark like a scar upon his cheek; his whole appearance giving one an idea of toil, hardship, peril and wild adventure. The expression of his mouth is remarkably mild and sweet; and his voice is extremely low and gentle. His hands are as brown as a labourer's: he never profanes them with gloves, but wears two strange magical-looking rings: one of them, which he showed me, is made of elephant's hair.*

Charles Kemble invited Trelawny to join him, his daughter and Fanny's suitor, Pierce Butler, a wealthy young Philadelphian whom she subsequently married, on a visit to Niagara Falls. Trelawny was delighted to accept, and the group set out in a hired carriage. Fanny was familiar with the works of Shelley and Byron, and discussed the two poets at length with the man who had been their friend. Young Butler, perhaps annoyed because he was excluded from so much of the conversation, produced a volume by a contemporary, Alfred Lord Tennyson, and read at length from it. But Trelawny was not impressed and said Tennyson belonged to "the new, feeble race of ballad mongers."

The journey was marred by a carriage accident and Trelawny was knocked unconscious. But he recovered with astonishing rapidity, ate an enormous "invalid's meal" of honey, bread and milk, and then wandered out into the fields beyond the inn at which the party was staying to pick some wildflowers for Fanny. A half hour later, the pair went for a ride across the countryside, ending the afternoon with a wild gallop. The ever-gallant Trelawny permitted the girl to win the race.

Ultimately they reached Niagara, where they were awed by

the sight of the great falls, and there Trelawny, now in his forty-first year, had one of the most extraordinary experiences of his adventure-crowded life. He subsequently wrote a full account of the incident, perhaps intending to publish it as a magazine article. Fanny Kemble verified the accuracy of the details in her *Journal*, and Trelawny once again appeared on the front pages of newspapers around the world.

The story is best told in his own words, and therefore is reproduced here in full:

*Today I have been mortified, bitterly. The morning was hot and cloudless, I sauntered along the brink of the Rapids, descended the long tiresome spiral staircase which leads directly to the ferry on the river.*

*Instead of crossing over in the boat to Canada, I threaded my way along the rugged and rocky shore. I came to a solitary hollow by the river side, about a mile below the Falls. The agitated water mining the banks had broadened its bed and covered the shelving shore there with massy fragments of dark limestone rocks. The mural cliffs rose on each side two or three hundred feet almost perpendicularly, yet pine trees and cypress and yew managed to scale the steep ascent and hold their ground, boring into the hard rocks with their harder roots, till, undermined by the continual rising of the water, they had fallen. Even at this distance from the Falls the waters in the midchannel were still boiling and bubbling and covered with foam, raging along and spreading out in all directions.*

*Pieces of timber I threw in spun around in concentric circles. Then turning and twisting against the rocks like crushed serpents, it flowed on to the Rapids and formed dangerous whirlpools two miles lower down. Above the Falls this river is a mile broad, where I was now was less than half a mile, above and below me not more than a quarter; so that flowing through a deep ravine of rocks it was very deep even to its brink, and in the centre they say above 100 feet. The sun was now at its zenith, and its rays concentrated into the tunnel made my brains boil, the water was not agitated, was of that tempting emerald green which looks so voluptuously cool like molten jasper flaked with snow.*

*I never resist the syren pleasure when she is surrounded by her water nymphs in their sea green mantles, and my blood is boiling. I hastily cast aside my clothes, with nerves throbbing and panting breast, and clambered up to a ledge of rock jutting over a clear deep pool. I spring in head foremost. In an instant every nerve was restrung and set to the tune of vigorous boyhood. I spring up and gambol between wind and water.*

*To excel in swimming long and strong limbs and a pliant body are indispensable, the chest too should be broad, the greatest breadth of most fish is close to the head; the back must be bent inward (incavated), the head reined back like a swan's and the chest thrown forward; thus the body will float without exertion. The legs and arms after striking out should be drawn up and pressed close together, and five seconds between each stroke, as in running distances so in swimming distances it is indispensable. Your life depends on it, avoid being blown, the strongest swimmer like the strongest horse, is done when his respiration fails. Utterly regardless of these truths, notwithstanding it is the pure gold of personal experience, in the wanton pride of my strength and knowledge of the art, I gambolled and played all sorts of gymnastics; methought the water, all wild as it was, was too sluggish, so I wheeled into midchannel and dashing down the stream I was determined to try my strength in those places where the waters are wildest. I floated for some time over the eddying whirls without much difficulty and then struck through them right across the river.*

*This triumph steeled my confidence of the "ice-brook's temper," after gaining breath regardless that I had changed the field of action in having been borne a long way down the river, consequently that I was rapidly approaching the Rapids, which nor boat nor anything with life can live in.*

*Well, thinking alone of the grandeur and wildness of the scene, I swam on without difficulty yet I felt the chill that follows overexertion stealing up my extremities, cramping my toes and fingers with sudden twitches. I was again returned to the center of the vortical part of the river, I was out of sight of the Falls, the water was becoming rougher and rougher, I was tossed about and drifting fast down. I now remembered the terrible whirlpool below me, I could make no progress, the stream was mastering me. I thought I had no time to lose, so I incautiously put forth my strength, sprang in the water with energy to cross the arrowy stream transversely, conceiving that when I reached the smoother part, out of the vortex of midchannel, my work was done. I seemed to be held by the legs and sucked downwards, the scumming surf broke over and blinded me, I began to ship water.*

*In the part of the river I had now drifted to the water was frightfully agitated, it was broken and raging all around me; still my exertions augmented with the opposition, I breathed quicker and with increasing difficulty, I kept my eyes steadily on the dark-browed precipice before me, it seemed receding. I thought of returning, but the distance and difficulty was equally balanced; the rotary action of the water under its surface, when I relaxed my exertions, sucked my body, heels foremost, downwards. Whilst breathing hard I swallowed the spray, my strength suddenly declined, I was compelled to keep my mouth open panting and gasping, my lower extremities sank.*

*I looked around to see if there was any timber floating, or any boat or person on the shore. There was nothing and if there had been no one could have seen me enveloped in spray, and the distant voice of the Falls drowned all other sounds; the thought that my time was come at last flashed across my mind, I thought what a fool I was to blindly abuse my own gained knowledge and thus cast myself away; the lessons of experience like the inscriptions on tombs grow faint and illegible if not continually renewed. Why did I attempt to cross a part of the river that none had ever crossed before? There was not even the excitement of a fool on the shore to see or say he had seen me do it. Why had I not spoken to the man at the ferry, he would have followed me in his boat. I remembered too hearing the thing was not practicable; why what a wayward fool am I.*

*These things acted as a spur, these truths crossed my mind rapidly, and I thought of all the scenes of drowning I had seen; of my own repeated perils that way. I heard the voices of the dead calling to me. I actually thought, as my mind grew darker, that they were tugging at my feet. Aston's horrid death by drowning nearly paralyzed me. I endeavored in vain to shake off these thick-coming fancies, they glowed before me. Thus I lay* suspended between life and death. I had lost all power, I could barely keep my head above the surface, I waxed fainter and fainter, there was no possibility of help.

I occasionally turned on my back to rest and endeavor to recover my breath, but the agitation of the water and surf got into my mouth and nostrils, the water stuck in my throat, which was instantly followed by the agonizing sensation of strangulation. This I well knew was an unerring first symptom of a suffocating death. Instead of air I sucked in the flying spray it's impossible either to swallow or cast out again, and whilst struggling to do either I only drew in more. The torture of choking was terrible, my limbs were cold and almost lifeless, my stomach too was cramped. I saw the waters of the Rapids below me raging and all about hissing. I thought now how much I would have given for a spiked nail so fixed that I could have rested the ball of my toe on it for one instant and have drawn one gulp of air unimpeded, to have swallowed the water that was sticking into the midchannel of my windpipe; nay I would have been glad at any risk to have rested on the point of a lancet.

I had settled down till I was suspended in the water, the throbbing and heaving of my breast and heart and increasing swelling in my throat had now so completely paralyzed my limbs that [I thought(?)] of giving up a struggle which seemed hopeless. My uppermost thought was mortification at this infallible proof of my declining strength, well I knew there was a time in which I could have forced my way through ten times these impediments; the only palliation I could think of was the depth and icy chilliness of the water which came straight from the regions of the frigid zone.

This contracted all my muscles and sinews, my head grew dizzy from bending the spine backwards, the blow I had received from the upset I had not recovered; the ball, too, immediately over my jugular veins retards the circulation; my right arm has never recovered its strength and it was now benumbed. All this and much more I thought of, my body, said I, is like a leaky skiff no longer seaworthy, and my soul shall swim out of it and free myself. I thought the links that held me to life were so worn that the shock which broke them would be slight. It had always been my prayer to die in the pride of my strength—however it *approached, with wealth and power, or on crutches and in rags, was to me equally loathesome,—better to perish before he had touched me with his withering finger, in this wild place, on a foreign shore.*

*Niagara "chanting a thunder psalm" as a requiem was a fitting end to my wild meteor-like life. Thoughts like these absorbed me. I no longer in the bitterness of my heart struggled against the waters which whirled me along, and certainly this despair as if in mockery preserved me. For looking again towards the shore I saw that I had been carried nearer to it, and without any exertion on my part I floated lighter, the under-tow no longer drew me down, and presently the water became smooth, I had been cast out of the vortex and was drifting toward the rocks. I heard the boiling commotion of the tremendous Rapids, and saw the fume flying in the air a little below me, and then I lay stranded, sick and dizzy, everything still seemed whirling round and round and the waters singing in my ears.*

*The sun had descended behind the cliffs and my limbs shook so violently that I could not stand; I lay there for some time, and then, as the rocks were too rugged to admit of walking, I swam slowly up the shore. I was deeply mortified, the maxim which had so long borne toward my desires triumphantly—go on till you are stopped—fails me here. I have been stopped, there is no denying it, death would have pained me less than this conviction. I must change my vaunting crest.*

*My shadow trembling on the black rock as reflected by the last rays of the setting sun, shows me as in a glass, that my youth and strength have fled. . . . When I had recovered my breath I dressed myself and walked sullenly to the ferry boat. I took the two heavy oars and exerting my utmost strength I bent them like rattans as I forced the clumsy boat against the stream. The ferry man where I landed seemed impressed at my impetuosity, he said the sun's been so hot today he was dead beat. I said, "Why, how old are you?"*

*"Oh," he said, "that's nothing."—he was thirty eight.*

*"Thirty eight," I echoed, "then you are not worth a damn, you had better look out for the alms-house."*

*I started off running up the steep acclivity and heard him mut-*

*tering, "Why you aren't so very young yourself; what the devil does he mean?"*

*When I got to the summit I threw myself down on the ledge of rock, instead of over as I should have done, and fell asleep. Thus ended the day; I shall not however forget it.*

XXVI

*"People who are truly great have about them an
air of simplicity."*

In the newspaper interviews that followed Trelawny's near escape from death at Niagara Falls he stressed what he said
repeatedly in his own account of the adventure. He was mortified
because he had not been strong enough to master the elements.
Other men would have been relieved and gratified to find themselves still alive, but Trelawny was filled with self-disgust and
was saddened because the dramatic incident brought his youth
to an end. He continued to swim, hike and ride for the rest of
his long life, however, still believing that physical exercise combined with a Spartan diet were directly responsible for longevity
and good health.

Returning to New York from Niagara, Trelawny soon departed
again on a tour that took him to Washington City, then on into
Virginia, the Carolinas, Alabama, Tennessee and Kentucky. Ac-
quaintances in New York had given him letters of introduction to
Vice-President Martin Van Buren, President Andrew Jackson's
heir apparent, and the two men dined together in Washington.
Van Buren, who had returned from his post as United States
Minister to Great Britain to become Jackson's running mate in

the 1832 election, knew many of Trelawny's London friends, and the evening was so pleasant that the Vice-President proposed a call on the President later in the week.

Trelawny brought Andrew Jackson a signed copy of *Younger Son*, and was pleased to discover that Old Hickory had already read the book, which he had liked. Both men were surprised, Trelawny having expected to find an ignorant barbarian in the White House and the President having assumed the Englishman was a blustering adventurer. Each discovered that the other was a thoughtful man of depth and substance, and Trelawny was invited to remain for dinner.

He stayed until midnight, chatting with President Jackson and the man destined to become his successor, and in a half dozen letters to various friends he sang the praises of the old Indian fighter and hero of the battle of New Orleans, at the end of the War of 1812. Jackson, he said, was the most "simple yet complicated" man he had ever met, and he agreed with the majority of Americans, who believed their chief executive was a great man. "People who are truly great have about them an air of simplicity," he told Claire.

He also noted that the White House meal was delicious and sophisticated, and that both Jackson and Van Buren drank a little whiskey before they sat down at the table. No wine was served, and Trelawny drank only cold water, as was his custom. He took care to note that the President, contrary to rumor, wore a coat made of a rich material and highly polished boots.

Several owners of large Virginia farms and estates had invited Trelawny to visit them, and he spent two or three weeks moving from one house to another. He enjoyed daily rides on thoroughbred horses, and observed that life in Virginia was more like that of English country-house living than any he had ever known in England itself. In Virginia he first encountered the institution of slavery and was disgusted by it, even though the Virginians, he said, were ashamed of slavery and treated their chattels with great kindness and consideration.

His loathing became more intense as he moved through the Carolinas, and when he reached Charleston he became so upset that he felt he had to make a gesture to indicate his opinion of the system. He bought a black boy named John in a slave mart, spending one thousand dollars he could ill afford for the purpose, then set the boy free, gave him one hundred dollars for traveling expenses and sent him to New York to work for friends there.

Trelawny spent the autumn and early winter of 1833 exploring the American West, and there he felt completely at home. He and the frontiersmen spoke the same language, and he ventured as far as the Mexican province of Texas, where a number of adventurous American pioneers were settling and dreaming of winning their independence and joining the United States. In a rhapsodic letter to Claire, Trelawny expressed his opinion of the American frontier:

*These endless and eternal forests are my delight—so are the rivers. I go two thousand miles up the Mississippi, fifteen hundred up the Ohio, a thousand miles through the woods or along the mountains. In the wilderness, where the boundless horizon is unbroken by the trumpery works of man, I feel so elated that life is of itself a pleasure—when I enter a town it is a pain.*

*But the townsmen, like those who dwell in frontier clearings, are a wonderful, sturdy people—plain, unassuming, honest and hard-working, devoted to their form of government and the difficult way of life they have chosen for themselves. The wealthier classes attempt to imitate the English, but they are a small sect, with small means and little influence. Democratic institutions are using up their goose quills to the hilt.*

*The Sovereign people are working out this grand experiment—that all men are born free and equal! The only blot on their charter, slavery, will gradually disappear. It must be spunged out, or cut out—soon!*

By winter Trelawny was growing weary, writing to Augusta White Draper he was in perpetual motion, wanted rest but could not find it. He slowed his pace, spending longer periods in various towns in Illinois, Indiana and Ohio, and the spring and summer passed slowly. In the autumn he went across Pennsylvania to Philadelphia, where Fanny Kemble, now Mrs. Pierce Butler, had settled with her husband. He was delighted to renew his friendship with her, Fanny was equally pleased and he took lodgings near the Butler house.

Thereafter he and Fanny shocked proper Philadelphians by going for wild rides down bridle paths and across open country; on several evenings they danced what Trelawny called "an improvised Arab dance," and it must have been total improvisation, as Fanny knew no Arabs and had never visited an Arab country.

Bridegroom Butler must have breathed a sigh of relief when the peripatetic visitor departed for New York, after a hectic month. Trelawny spent the winter of 1834–35 in New York and New England, going from Boston to New Haven, then back to Boston and on to Maine because he wanted to camp in the deep woods there in the dead of winter. He built a cabin for himself, first felling the trees, bought flour, bacon and other supplies in a small general store, and learned to fish through a hole cut in the ice that glazed the surface of a nearby lake.

Trelawny spent four winter months alone in the cabin, reading, contemplating, cutting firewood, fishing and hiking. He saw no one during this time and apparently was at peace with himself. Once again he had fled from society, putting walls between himself and the people who wanted to lionize him. For reasons he explained to no one, he needed this interlude; it is impossible to determine whether he craved solitude for its own sake or whether he set a new test for himself, trying to emulate the frontiersman in an attempt to see if he could actually do it.

If that was his purpose, he was successful. He spoke to no one during his stay in the forest; he wrote no letters to any of his friends, and he thoroughly enjoyed himself. Early in the spring of 1835 he reappeared in Boston, lean, energetic and radiating good health. After a brief stay he went on to New York, and a letter to Mary indicated his thinking. He was tempted to settle permanently in the United States, he said, because he felt a greater admiration for the people and their experiment in government than for any other nation.

By late spring he had changed his mind and suddenly sailed for England. His correspondence indicates no reason for this abrupt change, and there is no way of knowing whether an untoward incident influenced him or whether his decision to remain in America had been no more than a passing fancy. In later years he frequently expressed his regret that he had not become an American, and said he would go without hesitation were he a decade or two younger.

Trelawny found England unchanged when he reached London, early in the summer of 1835. Society greeted him with the enthusiasm he had come to expect. He was more responsive now than he had been before his departure for America. He accepted invitations and even gave occasional small dinner parties in the lodgings he had lived in previously, near the Strand.

His elder daughter, Julia, was now married to John Burley, and Trelawny approved of the match, perhaps because Burley was an admirer of Shelley's poetry. But letters from Jane Boccella about Zella's conduct caused him anxiety. The child had an ungovernable temper, and her father wrote Claire he was afraid she had inherited one of his own worst traits. "The women of our family are all devils," he said.

Claire offered him a sensible suggestion: he should bring his daughter to England, where he could be near her and keep his eye on her. It was obvious she needed discipline, and Claire said a boarding school would cure her of her tantrums.

Trelawny hated all English schools, but he decided Claire was right and sent for his daughter. She was growing rapidly, had a quick, alert mind and was exceptionally pretty; Trelawny was proud to report to various friends that she resembled him.

Zella went off to school but hated the place so much she fell ill. Her unhappy father was forced to withdraw her, and at that juncture his elderly mother came to the rescue, suggesting the child be sent to her in Cornwall. Thereafter Zella lived alternately with Trelawny and his mother.

Claire made one of her periodic visits to England soon thereafter and went off to Cornwall to see Zella. More of an old maid than ever in her approach to life, the professional governess considered a dress and hat that Mary Shelley had sent Zella "frivolous." Trelawny had his complaints in return, having learned from Seymour Kirkup, who paid a visit to Zella and her grandmother, that old Mrs. Trelawny and Claire were urging the child to attend church regularly. This outraged the man who insisted he was a "pagan," and he told Claire he expected nothing more from an old lady "in her dotage" but that he was shocked to learn Claire agreed. "Are you alive," he demanded, "or transformed into a tree, girdled round by the axe—lifeless and leafless?" Not content with these insults, he became even more indignant in another letter, repeatedly calling her "Old Aunt" and sputtering:

*You are becoming so horribly prudish. I consider you very fishlike, bloodless and insensible—a counterpart of Werther's Charlotte, all bread, butter and worsted stockings.*

Then he himself went to Cornwall, and enjoyed himself so much he remained there for three months. The autumn of 1835 is memorable because it marks his complete reconciliation with his mother. Until this time he had barely tolerated her, paying her duty visits when the occasion demanded and otherwise ignoring her. Now, however, he was able to forgive the injustices to which he had been subjected in his childhood. In his forty-third year, he was finally growing more mature, and at last could see that his mother had been unable to stand up for him, correspond with him or otherwise maintain a close, loving relationship with him when she had been ordered by a stern husband to ignore her younger son.

At the Cornwall home of a neighbor, Sir William Molesworth, a member of Parliament known as a radical because he sought prison reforms and the abolition of the death penalty, Trelawny saw a great deal of two prominent politicians, Charles Buller and John Temple Leader. It is probable that he was already acquainted with Leader, as they had been in Florence at the same time.

John Leader was a prime mover in the campaign to force the Anglican bishops to resign their seats in the House of Lords, a movement that Trelawny enthusiastically approved. He also seconded another of Leader's proposals much closer to home, the ending of the ancient laws of primogeniture, which enabled the eldest son of a family to inherit the bulk of his father's estate. Neither Trelawny nor Leader realized they were tilting at windmills, and both seriously believed these tradition-flowing campaigns might succeed.

Posterity is in John Temple Leader's debt, because it was as a result of his specific request that Kirkup painted what has become the only authentic, full-scale portrait of Trelawny painted before he reached old age. It was Leader, too, who suggested he wear his Greek battle dress when posing. According to some sources the painting was done earlier in Florence, but most authorities agree that Kirkup painted it in Cornwall in the late autumn of 1835.

Trelawny seemed to be drifting again, and when Leader offered him a permanent suite in his magnificent London town house, Upper House, on Putney Hill, the offer was quickly accepted. Some of Trelawny's friends were worried about his lack of purpose in life, and Mary Shelley wrote him a stern letter:

*You have talents of a high order. You have powers: these, with industry and discretion, would advance you in any career. You ought not, indeed you ought not, to throw yourself away as you do.*

In her private *Journal,* which was not published in her own lifetime or Trelawny's, she was even more blunt, and wrote an appraisal of his character that even some of his more ardent admirers have been forced to admit is deserved:

He is a strange yet wonderful being—endued with genius— great force of character and power of feeling—but destroyed by *being nothing."*

In the winter of 1835–36 Trelawny moved into his Upper House suite and began a new period in his life; he was still the darling of London's salons, but he was much more. He formed a number of political friendships and at the same time came to know many other literary figures, as always establishing a close rapport with other writers. No social occasion was complete without his presence. His rudeness to poseurs became legendary, but he was putting on something of a front himself at these gatherings, his real interests lying in his associations with various authors.

One of the first with whom he established a new friendship was Benjamin Disraeli, at that time creating a name for himself as a novelist, and the ties remained unbroken, extending through the period when Disraeli became Prime Minister. Trelawny also grew close to Edward Bulwer, Lord Lytton, with whom he engaged in lighthearted verbal duels. He came to know Thomas Carlyle, who was too somber for his taste, but he was on amicable terms with William Makepeace Thackery in a relationship that lasted for many years.

Old friends were not forgotten, and in spite of his advancing years he still enjoyed a joke. When Fanny Kemble Butler came to England for a visit and went street-singing with her sister for a lark, Trelawny accompanied them, hovering nearby and ready to intervene if any passerby foolishly tried to molest them. Lord Byron's last mistress, Countess Guiccioli, came to London for a long visit, and it was Trelawny who first presented her to society and acted as her constant escort until she made other friendships. When one of the more prominent hostesses of the day, Caroline Norton, was sued for divorce by her husband, who named Lord Melbourne as co-respondent, Trelawny leaped to the lady's defense and was so vociferous on her behalf that he suddenly found himself named as another possible co-respondent.

Landor returned to England from Italy, and Trelawny not only saw him frequently but took him to see Mary Shelley, whom the older man had snubbed a decade and a half earlier. Gaining a new appreciation of her character, Landor profoundly regretted his misjudgment of Shelley and made amends to the best of his ability by introducing other colleagues to the works of the lyric genius.

In the main, this period in Trelawny's life was a time of lost opportunity, and no one knew it better than the friends who tried to encourage him to abandon the life of a dilettante and become more active. Mary Shelley, Disraeli, Bulwer-Lytton, Landor and a number of others urged him to write another book, but he seemed strangely reluctant to follow their advice.

He was eager to do a new book, as a matter of fact, but could not yet write it: a biography of Shelley was still very much on his mind, but Mary's continuing refusal to co-operate made it impossible for him to attack the project.

He did write a number of short pieces, however, most of them for the *Metropolitan Magazine*, the leading periodical of the day,

and his themes were always personal. His long visit to the
United States gave him much raw material and, in various articles, he wrote about frontier living, the success of the American
political system and the blight of slavery. In one article he said
that Ralph Waldo Emerson was the only literary figure of stature
on the far side of the Atlantic, a claim that caused several English and American authors to write furious rebuttals.

For a time Trelawny thought of entering politics, spurred by
his friendship with Leader and other Whigs who called themselves the Philosophic Radicals. But he discovered it was one
thing to believe in ideals, yet quite another to work for their realization. The art of compromise, essential to politics, was unknown to him, and he still lacked patience, so he lost interest in
the give-and-take of debates with the Tories.

During his years in London, Trelawny ended his friendship
with Landor. The exact date is unknown, and the details of their
rupture have never been learned. Each continued to speak
highly of the other, Trelawny always referring to Landor as "a
remarkable man," but he refused to discuss the reasons for the
break. Landor was equally closemouthed, and thereafter the two
men carefully avoided each other, even though both became
members of the Savage Club and traveled in the same circles.

In all, Trelawny drifted for about five years, from the time of
his return to England, in 1835, to 1840, when his life took another unexpected turn, perhaps surprising him as much as it did
his friends.

## XXVII

## "*Granite is harder than marble.*"

At some time after Trelawny's return to England from the United States he became acquainted with one of Mary Shelley's closest friends, Augusta Goring, a handsome, high-spirited feminist who had a strong personality and a mind of her own. He also met the lady's thoroughly unpleasant husband, Sir Harry Dent Goring, and the two men took such a dislike to each other that they found it impossible to spend any time together. Lady Goring found life boring on her husband's estate in Sussex, so she spent most of her time in London, and Trelawny, still at loose ends, happily acted as her escort.

By 1840 Trelawny found living at Upper House inconvenient. The mansion was too far from town to make commuting pleasant, and as Zella was growing up he needed a place of his own for the periods she spent with him. So he bought himself a small town house in St. James's, which was becoming the most fashionable neighborhood in London. This move enabled him to see a great deal more of Augusta Goring, and the ripening friendship became something else, the lady electing to spend the night with him on the frequent occasions when they dined together, attended the theater or visited mutual friends.

Sir Harry had his suspicions, hired detectives and then filed for divorce, naming Trelawny as co-respondent. The details were so spectacular that the London newspapers were forced to use asterisks when printing the charges in order not to offend the sensitivities of their readers. Society was duly shocked that Augusta and Trelawny had elected to live together openly, brazenly defying convention, but Sir Harry was so unpopular and had been known to have treated his wife with such disrespect that Trelawny and Augusta lost no friends. It was assumed by everyone concerned, including the two guilty principals, that they would be married in 1841, after Sir Harry won his uncontested divorce suit.

It is difficult to determine, more than one hundred thirty years later, why Trelawny and Augusta became serious in their attachment. As both were handsome, the physical attractions are obvious, but they were both so headstrong and opinionated, so determined to control, that it is equally obvious they were mismatched. A letter Augusta wrote to her good friend Mary Shelley, a short time before the marriage, indicates her approach to their future relationship:

*Edward behaved very well today. . . . He gives up his point entirely and wishes to do all things to please me. My first object will be to estrange him from my enemies in his own family— then to gain power—as I may—over self first—then him.*

At the same time, Trelawny was writing to Claire that "at the very sight of harness (particularly double)," he screamed with horror. But he and Augusta were married, and it is surprising the relationship lasted as long as it did. The road was rocky from the outset, in part because both were extravagant and inclined to be careless in the handling of money. But Augusta was far worse than her new husband, who had made it his lifelong practice never to owe money to anyone. The new Mrs. Trelawny did not abide by the same principle, however, and went on a wild buying spree, completely refurnishing the house in St. James's.

Trelawny remonstrated with her in vain. She refused to listen to him and continued to spend far more on the house than they could afford. So he felt compelled to take matters into his own hands, and as usual, his solution of the problem was drastic. One day when Augusta went out to keep a luncheon appointment with a friend, Trelawny, who had made careful preparations in advance, had every stick of furniture moved out and returned to the merchants from whom Augusta had made her purchases. She returned to find that even the rugs, the paintings on the walls and the curtains were gone.

By 1847, after six years of marriage, Trelawny came to the conclusion that city living was responsible for most of his marital difficulties, and notwithstanding the fact that Augusta actively disliked the country, he sold the house in St. James's and insisted on moving to a little village called Usk, in Monmouthshire. By this time the Trelawnys had two sons, Edgar and Frank, and their daughter, Letitia, was born in the local inn, where the family first lived.

Trelawny searched the area for a home, and first bought a small house, soon thereafter purchasing the largest estate in the parish, called Cefn Ila, where he made extensive repairs and improvements on the old manor house. There he and Augusta settled, far from the London social life they had loved, and somewhat to their own surprise they found contentment there.

Some of Trelawny's friends thought of him as a gentleman farmer, but they were mistaken. Cefn Ila was a working estate, and no one worked harder than the master. He ate his breakfast at dawn, spent his entire day in the fields with the hired hands, to whom he paid generous wages, and from the very first year he showed a substantial profit. For the rest of his life he boasted that farming was not a dying occupation and that a man who showed diligence could wrest a comfortable living from the soil.

He threw himself into his new vocation with his customary fervor. Augusta noted there were no fruit trees on the property, so he planted an apple orchard, a plum orchard and a pear orchard himself. He expanded the kitchen vegetable garden until it encompassed five acres, converted two acres around the main house into lawns, and put in flower gardens that he tended himself. His energy was unlimited, and he soon acquired a reputation for industry in Usk.

Everyone in the village knew and liked the new squire, who was known to be a famous man but who put on airs with no one. Augusta was equally well liked, even though neither she nor her husband attended church services. She was a kindly neighbor who always went out of her way to be helpful, and within a short time she established herself as the first lady of the area.

The Trelawnys enjoyed a very limited social life, but their Sunday-afternoon open house quickly became a local institution. The neighborhood physician attended regularly, as did the two attorneys who lived near Usk, and even the vicar was a frequent guest. Mrs. Trelawny served small cakes, taking pride in the fact that she had baked them herself. Her husband refused to offer guests alcoholic beverages, and instead brewed a very strong tea "in an Oriental manner" unknown in Usk, and he further flouted custom by serving it in huge tankards usually reserved for ale.

Zella lived with her father and stepmother, getting rid of her restless energy by going for long daily canters as well as teaching her little half brothers and half sister to ride. She and Augusta soon established a rapport, but she was inclined to quarrel with her father. Trelawny, always tolerant in his relationships with children, refused to argue with her but continued to write to Claire that her stubborn streak would cause her problems. He hired a tutor for the younger children, and at the end of his own day's work he read to the assembled family for an hour, insisting that only literature would prevent them from becoming barbarians.

Neighbors regarded Squire Trelawny as something of an eccentric, in part because he swam daily in the river that cut through his property, regardless of the weather or the season. In the summer months he erected a tent as a dressing room on the bank of the river, and the entire family went swimming. It was one of Trelawny's theories that a baby of a few months would swim naturally if thrown into the water, and he argued that this technique was used by the South Sea islanders, the world's best swimmers. He was hurt when no visitors would permit him to make the experiment with their small children.

His physical strength was prodigious. Everyone in the area knew he could crack three nuts by squeezing them with one hand, and it was said he could twist iron bars into corkscrews with little effort. He appears to have been completely happy, and said in a letter:

*Our outdoor simple sort of life keeps us all in health and strength—no doctor ever crosses our threshold professionally. I have all my land on hand—and do the best I can—but farming was never yet a very profitable business—at least for gentry, and free trade has not made it better. Nevertheless it works capitally for the country generally, so I am well content.*

Those of Trelawny's contemporaries who assumed he and Augusta had completely abandoned their sophisticated existence for exclusively bucolic pleasures were mistaken. Trelawny tried to give the world the impression that he had given up everything for farming, but he was assuming yet another pose that was far from reality. Two or three years after he and Augusta moved to Cefn Ila he bought a small but comfortable London town house at Number 7 Pelham Crescent, and they went into the city every few months for stays of two to three weeks at a time. On these visits they saw old friends, were entertained frequently and sometimes gave dinner parties of their own.

During the worst of the winter, when farmers usually hibernated, they made trips to Italy, usually taking all four of the children with them. They are known to have stayed at least twice in Florence, and one year they went to Leghorn, where Robert Browning, generally recognized as the leader of the younger romantic poets, called on them.

Browning was a great admirer of Shelley and his poetry, and consequently was eager to chat with the man who had been his idol's friend. But he and Trelawny struck discordant notes, an experience that was to be repeated on several occasions, and were unable to achieve a rapport. Browning wrote, however, that one day when visiting the rented Trelawny villa he found a physician probing for a bullet that had accidentally lodged in his host's leg during a hunting excursion the previous day. Trelawny conversed fluently, and did not show by word, gesture or expression that he was suffering pain.

The small dwelling at Cefn Ila where the Trelawnys lived when they had first moved to Usk was converted into a guest-

house and generally was occupied in the spring, summer and autumn by old friends and new. Augusta White Draper stayed
there when she came home from Canada to see relatives and
friends, and so did Claire Clairmont when she made one of her
periodic visits to England. No one was permitted to interfere
with Squire Trelawny's routines, however, and although guests
were invited to accompany him into the fields, he never gave up
any of his activities to spend time with them at the manor house.
Most guests learned his idea of a weekend's pleasures was to
plant trees, and he expected them to help, feeling miffed if they
begged to be excused.

Mary Shelley died in 1851, and Trelawny grieved for her, even
though they had moved apart in recent years. Her son, Sir Percy,
entrusted Hogg with the task of writing Shelley's biography, a
task undertaken in 1857 and halted by Lady Shelley after the
publication of the first two volumes of a four-volume series.
Early in 1857 the Shelleys invited Trelawny, now in his sixty-
fifth year to pay them a visit, saying that Hogg and Thomas
Love Peacock, another of the poet's old friends, would be there.
But Trelawny declined in a letter that demonstrated he had not
lost his bluntness:

> *To assemble together under your roof three of the Poet's old
> friends to tell their stories is a pleasant dream. It is something
> similar to the plot of Bocacio's Decameron, but the Italian takes
> care to have youth and summer weather.*
>
> *I told Percy when he was here that I was too old and selfish to
> leave my den. In my youth I railed at age as hard and crabbed,
> and so I find it.*
>
> *I don't believe that either of the men you have mentioned
> will do what you wish. Indolence and excessive sensitiveness to
> public opinion will prevent it—as it has already done.*

At about this same time Trelawny sent off a letter to an old
friend, Dan Roberts, who was now living on the small island of
Maddalena, a short distance from Sardinia. In it he discussed his
appearance and health:

> *I am becoming venerable—white beard, but, what is strange—
> I am perfectly sound and retain the flexibility of my joints and—*

*what is of less consequence—I won't say greater—all my facul-*
*ties—sight, hearing, memory, etc., are all as good as ever—no,*
*my eagle eyes are not so piercing certainly.*

Perhaps the thought that Hogg, for whom he still entertained
a cordial contempt, was to write the life of Shelley aroused the
creative urge that had been dormant for so long in Trelawny.
For, whatever the reason his muse stirred, and at the age of
sixty-five, thirty years after writing *Younger Son*, he sat down at
his desk and wrote a book about his friendship with Shelley and
Byron, as well as about his own experiences in the Greek War of
Independence. He called it *Recollections of the Last Days of
Shelley and Byron,* and it was published by Moxon the following
year.

Hogg attacked Trelawny bitterly in his correspondence, but
the latter turned the other cheek, a gesture that was new to him,
and was careful to praise Hogg and his book. He took issue with
only one point, contradicting Hogg's assertion that Shelley had
not been able to distinguish truth from falsehood. Many years
later, when asked in an interview what the bond had been that
had connected Shelley and his early biographers, Hogg and
Peacock, Trelawny replied:

*Why, they were both excellent scholars. Shelley was an enthu-
siastic student of the Greek poets and greatly influenced by
them, especially in his later years. No one who is ignorant of the
classics can thoroughly appreciate him. That is partly the reason
why Swinburne understands him so well: he has written better
things concerning him than anyone else. But he, too, has some of
the divine madness.*

It quickly became evident to startled contemporaries that
Trelawny possessed qualities of the divine madness himself. At
an age when many men were content to retire, he had resumed
his career as an author, and as the critics were quick to
emphasize, the book had considerable literary merit. It enjoyed a
great popularity, and immediately restored Trelawny to the
ranks of prominent authors. Indeed, a whole generation had
grown up since the publication of *Younger Son,* and there were
many readers who hailed him for the first time.

If Trelawny's professional standing was restored, his personal life was deteriorating. After twenty years of marriage his relations with Augusta were becoming strained, and a housekeeper, Mrs. M. B. Byrde, later wrote that Mrs. Trelawny avoided her husband's company, joined him only for necessary business discussions, and criticized him freely in the presence of members of the household, guests and the children.

Zella had moved to London and was leading her own life now; she was besieged by suitors, and her father was afraid she might marry the wrong man. Edgar worried Trelawny even more, and he wrote to Claire that his elder son was "worthless, a rogue and a vagabond." Eventually he sent Edgar to America in the hope the boy would make good there, but he took care to write to Augusta Draper and other friends not to permit his son to take advantage of them. They ignored his warnings, which infuriated him, and he took it upon himself to repay the substantial sums Edgar borrowed from them.

Frank was his father's favorite, a boy with "the heart of a poet." He was physically frail, in spite of his father's efforts to strengthen his constitution, and he died of consumption before reaching his majority.

Trelawny had a greater rapport with Letitia, his youngest daughter, than with any of his other children. Unlike Julia and Zella, from whom he had been separated for long periods, she enjoyed his constant companionship throughout her formative years, and she seems to have understood him better and sympathized with him more than did any of the others. She was the only one of his children who remained close to him until the end of his life. And in 1858, when put to the supreme test, she remained loyal to him, which was no mean feat.

## XXVIII

## "*This is not an age of poesy but of science.*"

In 1858, when Edward John Trelawny was a robust sixty-five years of age, a young woman known to posterity only as "Miss B." came into his life, and if her identity was known to any of his good friends they maintained a discreet silence. According to the verbose Mrs. Byrde she was tiny and not particularly attractive, but the housekeeper's judgment probably cannot be trusted. Trelawny never glanced a second time in the direction of any unattractive woman. Apparently he met Miss B. in London and, his marriage already falling apart, engaged in an affair with her.

He had lost none of the bravado that had long been his trademark, and certainly had not acquired tact through the years. He invited Miss B. to visit Cefn Ila, thereby directly challenging Augusta, who may have elected, until this critical juncture, to pretend she was unaware of the girl's existence.

Miss B. duly appeared in a carriage, and Trelawny went down to the front gate to greet her, gathered her in his arms and walked up the path to the house. This direct insult was too much for Augusta to tolerate, and she left that same day, taking her children with her and ending a marriage that had endured for two decades.

According to Mrs. Byrde, Trelawny promptly lost interest in Miss B. and in his farm. He sold Cefn Ila and disposed of most of his property in a three-day auction, selling almost all of his belongings except for his books and a few mementos. The auction resembled a huge party, because Trelawny threw open his larder and urged potential visitors to help themselves to food and drink. Only the wine and whiskey he had kept in small quantities for guests were excepted, and the visitors respected his rule, his dislike for alcoholic spirits being well known. When the auction ended, he left Monmouthshire and never returned.

He spent the summer of 1858 alone on the Channel coast, basking in the sun, swimming and sailing daily and keeping in physical trim. The new book, although less successful than *Younger Son*, was earning him enough so he could pay Augusta a substantial sum and still enjoy a holiday. He was so pleased with his physical condition and had such a good time that he bought a cottage and six acres of land outside the village of Sompting, near the town of Worthing, in Sussex. Thereafter he spent the better part of his time there, although he also kept the little house at 7 Pelham Crescent in London.

He needed little time to readjust to a bachelor state, and quickly resumed an active social life, still making new literary friendships. The death of his younger son, Frank, was a hard blow that caused him suffering, and Edgar also died young. Julia's husband had a substantial income, so she needed no help from her father; they were on friendly but not intimate terms, and the eldest of his children paid him several visits each year. He sometimes dined with her and her husband at their London home, and occasionally entertained them at his town house.

Zella married a man named Joseph Olguin, who had business interests in Argentina, and she went off with him to live in Buenos Aires for a number of years. Letitia, who eventually married Lieutenant Colonel Charles Call of the Royal Artillery, was the only one of Trelawny's children who saw him regularly. She defied her mother's order that she have nothing to do with him, and she accompanied him on several trips abroad. At Baden-Baden they saw Albert Edward, the Prince of Wales, later to be-

come Edward VII, and Trelawny embarrassed his daughter by
remarking in a loud voice that the prince was too fat and would
never live to an old age. Letitia also went with him on at least
two or three of his many visits to Florence, where he stayed at a
villa owned by the Leaders.

Among his new friends were William M. Rossetti and Alger-
non Charles Swinburne. The latter, fascinated by the life and poetry of Shelley, sought out the old man and soon became close to
him. John Leech, the political cartoonist whose work appeared
regularly in *Punch,* was a Trelawny admirer, as was Edgar
Boehm, the leading English sculptor of the period. Edward Lear
discussed Greece by the hour with Trelawny, often repeating his
anecdotes in hushed tones.

Through Rossetti and his younger brother, Dante Gabriel,
Trelawny became familiar with the poetry of William Blake, and
amazed them by memorizing long passages in a single reading. They were also responsible for introducing him to the work
of a contemporary American, Walt Whitman, and Trelawny
promptly revised his opinions of American literature, predicting
that Whitman's work would become immortal. The elder Rossetti
was editing the works of Shelley and frequently asked for Trelawny's advice but took care not to cross the old man when he
himself held a contrary opinion. Trelawny did not soften with
advancing age, and his temper was no less explosive than it had
ever been.

In England, on the Continent and in New World literary circles as well, Trelawny was already regarded as a living legend.
Swinburne, who dedicated his *Songs of the Springtides* to the
old man, revealed his reactions to their first meeting in a letter
he sent to a friend:

*I may say, I think, that I gained the friendship of a very fa-
mous old veteran of the sea in that and other capacities, the one
Englishman living I was really ambitious and anxious to know: I
need hardly name old Trelawny, who is certainly the most splen-
did old man I have seen since Landor and my own grandfather,
though, of course, a good deal younger than these.*

*He was most cordial and friendly in his reception of me,
whom he affirmed to be the last of the poets, having apparently*

*no faith in the capacity of this country to produce more of our breed; while I lament to add that he (metaphorically) spits and stamps on the bare suggestion that it did produce any between Shelley or Byron and myself.*

*I did think . . . I was a good atheist and a good republican; but in the company of this magnificent old rebel, a lifelong incarnation of the divine right of insurrection, I felt myself, by comparison, a Theist and a Royalist. . . . He was full of the atrocities (then just revealed, as you doubtless remember) of New California, and (of course) of passionate sympathy with the exiles of the Commune. Always energetic, whenever he speaks of Shelley the especial energy of his affection is really beautiful and admirable to see. There is some fresh air in England yet while such an Englishman is alive.*

So many stories have been told about the living legend that it is difficult to separate fact from fancy, and every literary man of the latter portion of the nineteenth century in England contributed to the fabric. William Rossetti liked to relate the tale that he had sent Trelawny a little gift of figs from a garden in the house in Sussex; Trelawny enjoyed them so much that he went down to Sompting to buy the tree, but finding he could not purchase it without the house, he immediately paid cash for the entire property.

In one phase of his life, fact was far stronger and more potent than fiction. In 1870 he took his last mistress, a Miss Taylor, and she lived with him for the last eleven years of his life. Victorian England frowned on open liaisons, so friends persuaded the old man to observe convention and call the girl his niece. Certainly Trelawny did not mean it when, on his eightieth birthday, he told William Rossetti he had decided to give up love affairs because they sapped his energy.

In 1874 the most prominent English painter of the day, John Everett Millais, wanted to paint a picture he intended to call the Northwest Passage, and decided that only Trelawny could depict the old sea captain he had in mind. Millais, a native of the Channel Isle of Jersey, had a strong feeling for the sea himself.

Trelawny refused, and it took all of Millais's powers of persuasion, aided by Miss Taylor, before the old man finally agreed. But Trelawny was just being his usual contrary self, a letter to Letitia indicating his secret pleasure:

*Mr. John Millais our best painter asked me to sit for a great picture he was compassing—of strength and meekness—he wanted a resolute man and a gentle girl—he had sought in vain over Town and could not find one—I was the only one that would do—it's a £2000-er and he has done it—the likeness is perfect—2 years ago you remember Mrs. Burley sent her daughter anticipating to find me bedridden &c. so you see the different views the interested and disinterested take—that's why I mention it. . . .*

According to conflicting rumors, the attractive young woman seated at the old man's feet in the painting is either Letitia or Miss Taylor. Her identity has never been established, but R. Glynn Grylls, the most authoritative of the modern Trelawny experts, is of the opinion that she was a professional model.

Trelawny did not see the painting until he attended its unveiling at a Royal Academy showing, and it is impossible to determine whether his anger was real or feigned when he fumed that Millais had insulted him, handing him down to posterity with a glass of rum and water in one hand and a lemon in the other. He relieved his feelings at dinner with some friends at the Savage Club, observing, "After all, I don't think it's Millais's fault. It's his wife's. She's a Scotchwoman, and the Scotch are a nation of sots." A roar of laughter was his reward, and he was satisfied.

In 1877, when Trelawny was in his eighty-fifth year, he finally responded to the pleas of the Rossettis, Swinburne and a number of others to enlarge his reminiscences of Shelley and Byron. He agreed, and wrote to Claire for her help. She was seventy-seven, a convert to Roman Catholicism and spending her last days in a convent in Florence. Her past had become distasteful to her, but for Trelawny's sake she tried to help—in spite of her apprehensions as to the sensationalism with which he might garb her youth. Trelawny continued to tease her, still called her "Auntie," and when she sent him some notes, he solemnly assured her, "I burn as I read."

His last book, which he called *Records of Shelley, Byron and the Author,* was published in 1878 by Basil Montagu Pickering. William Rossetti volunteered his services as a copy editor and corrected the author's always sloppy punctuation, spelling and grammar. He also proofread the work when Trelawny announced that the galley proofs bored him and that he had no intention of reading them.

*Records* is the least important of his works, repeating much that he had said previously, but it does contain some new material, including his candid observations of people long dead. He was freer now in revealing his dislike for Byron, and even indicated that he thought Mary Shelley unworthy of her husband. Scholars have given this book less credence than his previous efforts because of his advanced age, and his style certainly shows less vigor.

Most of the new material consisted of anecdotes about Shelley, and he continued to sing the poet's praises, saying in his preface that he had met men similar to Byron, but never to Shelley, and concluding that the latter was "the ideal of what a poet should be." It was astonishing that a man of Trelawny's age could write as coherently and as pungently as he did, and the critics treated the book with a respect tinged with awe. None dared to call *Records* insignificant, or even to suggest it might be a minor work. No writer dared to quibble with a legend whose life had already spanned the better part of a century.

Trelawny maintained many of his old friendships and resumed others. He corresponded with Claire until her death, in 1879, two years before his own, and he kept up his friendship with Kirkup until the artist died, in 1880. In 1872 he invited Jane Williams to dine with him in London for the purpose of meeting William Rossetti, and in 1874 Augusta White Draper paid a last visit to him, spending several days at his Sussex cottage and revealing that Letitia was spending some time there, unmindful of Miss Taylor's presence.

The old man remained in robust health and permitted no one to wait on him. He lighted his own fire every morning and always brewed his own coffee and tea, insisting that no one else knew how to make beverages to his taste. He continued to plant trees, and several acres of his property resembled a "cultivated jungle," as Dante Gabriel Rossetti called it. Every morning, regardless of the weather, he mounted his horse and rode two miles to the sea for his regular swim, and when visitors to the village were astonished, the natives merely shrugged.

No one was surprised, either, to see him cutting wood in the afternoons, and the local people took it for granted that he would work in his garden with spade and shovel, demonstrating the vigor and endurance of a man less than half his years.

He was still fearless, and when he learned, only two years before his death, that a local resident had pushed his wife into the village well, he marched to the rescue. With a score of slack-jawed people watching, among them the guilty husband, Trelawny hauled the woman out of the well, comforted her, and then wheeled on the astonished husband, picking him up bodily and hurling him into the depths of the well before brushing off his hands and returning to his work in his beloved garden.

His property became renowned as a bird sanctuary, and he acquired the patience that had never been one of his attributes by teaching birds to come to him for crumbs when he rang a little bell. According to a story he told Augusta Draper, he was feeding his birds one day when a pair of hunters came to him and asked permission to shoot a bird they had been stalking. It had flown into one of his trees, they said. Trelawny invited them into the property, then confronted them with his own loaded pistol. They looked into the open muzzle, saw the expression in the old man's eyes and promptly decided to take themselves elsewhere.

Although Trelawny spent most of his time at Sompting in his last years, he did not withdraw from the world. He continued to read almost everything of significance being published; he particularly admired the works of Victor Hugo. He admired the social aims of Charles Dickens, but was less enamored of the novelist's characterizations and style, and remarked that he had "been fed too much treacle as a child." Charles Darwin's *Origin of Species* excited him, and in the 1870s he arranged a meeting with his great contemporary, subsequently dining with him on a number of occasions and discussing his theories with him in detail.

With each passing year, Trelawny's personal asceticism became more pronounced. He gave up meat, then fish, and his diet became vegetarian except for his breakfast eggs; he subsisted principally on nuts, fruits and honey, and tried in vain to persuade others to adopt his regimen. He refused to wear either a hat or a greatcoat, regardless of the weather, and deciding his daily ride and swim, his wood-cutting and tree planting did not provide him with the necessary exercise, he went for a brisk walk of several miles before sundown each day.

These excursions took him through the village, and his progress resembled that of the Pied Piper. His jacket pockets were filled with Turkish Delight, his favorite candy, and he handed it out to the children who surrounded him and then trooped after him and his dogs on his constitutional.

One unpleasant incident marred the serenity of his final years. Zella and her husband returned to England, and one day Trelawny called on her to make her his annual gift of one hundred pounds, which he called "pin money." Father and daughter were so similar it is remarkable they had managed to maintain even a semblance of harmony for so long. In any event, Zella offered Trelawny a glass of wine, even though she well knew he no longer touched alcoholic spirits. Perhaps it was her way of taunting him.

The old man refused to accept the intended insult meekly. He took a token sip of the wine, made a wry face and announced that one could not expect better from the cellar of someone who had never been a gentleman. The outraged Zella summoned a servant and ordered him to show her father to the door.

Trelawny and Zella did not meet again, although he continued to send her one hundred pounds each year for the rest of his life. He did not write her out of his will; she inherited enough from him to help her rear her eight children in comfort. She lived until 1908, owned several homes and used her inheritance to provide the capital for a number of successful real estate ventures.

Two years before Trelawny's death, he decided to make all the necessary preparations for the event. First he wrote to the custodian of the Protestant Cemetery in Rome, sending the man a sum of money and asking that his grave be prepared for him. He wanted to be cremated, which could not be done in England, so he extracted a promise from William Rossetti and Miss Taylor that they would attend to all the necessary details for him. This took care of the future, and he continued to enjoy life.

He grew a variety of fruits in his garden, among them peaches, grapes, apples and pears. He was especially fond of his green figs, and one day confided to William Rossetti that they reminded him of his youth in the Indian Ocean and of Zela, "the one woman I truly loved."

A few years before his death, he wrote what was tantamount to his valedictory in a letter to Augusta White Draper:

*I am perfectly sound mind and body—old without the infirmities of age. Simple life and cold bathing and drinking are my practices winter and summer—especially light clothing—no woollen or worsted. I have made no change in my life or habits from age and my early convictions have hardened with my bones. I am a thorough Republican and free thinker—and see my opinions are spreading in Europe. The people are getting stronger everywhere—the free press and rapid communication is doing this.*

Late in July 1881, when he was in his 89th year, he felt tired and was forced to stay in bed. Miss Taylor wanted to summon a physician, but Trelawny refused, telling her his time had come and that he was able to face the end with equanimity. "I never clung to life, and would not live any part of it over again," he said, repeating words he had used many years earlier.

His decline was gradual; he suffered no pain, and three weeks later, early in the morning of August 13, 1881, he died peacefully in his sleep. Miss Taylor and Rossetti honored his request that no memorial service or other ceremony be held in England. His body was cremated in Germany, and his remains were escorted to Rome by Letitia, Miss Taylor and Rossetti.

Swinburne mourned his passing with lines that concluded, "*Shelley, Trelawny rejoins thee here.*"

But, as usual, Trelawny himself had the last word. A simple tombstone was erected over his grave, and on it, as per his own request, was inscribed a stanza of a poem by Shelley:

*These are two friends whose lives were undivided.
So let their memory be now they have glided*

*Under the grave: let not their bones be parted*
*For their two hearts in life were single-hearted.*

That marble slab has survived the ravages of time and the elements, and still stands.

# Select Bibliography

Agneli, Helen Rossetti. *Shelley and His Friends in Italy.* London, 1911.

Armstrong, Margaret. *Trelawny.* New York, 1941.

Blunden, Edmund. *Shelley.* London, 1946.

Brown, F. K. *Life of William Godwin.* London, 1926.

Church, Richard. *Mary Shelley.* London, 1928.

Dowden, Edward. *The Life of Percy Bysshe Shelley.* London, 1886, 2 vols.

Edgcumbe, Richard. *Talks with Trelawny.* London, 1890.

———. *Trelawny.* London, 1882.

Elwin, Malcolm. *Savage Landor.* London, 1941.

Grylls, R. Glynn. *Claire Clairmont.* London, 1939.

———. *Mary Shelley.* London, 1938.

———. *Trelawny.* London, 1950.

Hunt, Leigh. *Autobiography.* London, 1850.

———. *Lord Byron and Some of His Contemporaries.* London, 1828.

Kemble, Frances Ann. *Journal.* London, 1835.

———. *Records of a Girlhood.* London, 1878.

———. *Records of a Later Life.* London, 1882.

Marshall, Mrs. Julian. *The Life and Letters of Mary Wollstonecraft Shelley.* London, 1889.

Massingham, H. J. *The Friend of Shelley, a Memoir of Edward John Trelawny.* New York, 1930.

Maurois, André. *Ariel.* Paris, 1924.

———. *Byron.* Paris, 1930.

Mayne, Ethel Colburn. *Life of Byron.* London, 1928.

Morley, Christopher. *The Powder of Sympathy.* London, 1923.

Peck, Walter E. *Shelley: His Life and Work.* London, 1927.

Rossetti, Lucy Madox. *Mrs. Shelley.* London, 1890.

Rossetti, William Michael. *Some Reminiscences.* London, 1906.

Sanborn, F. B. *Odysseus and Trelawny.* New York, 1897.

Shelley, Mary. *Letters of Mary Wollstonecraft Shelley,* edited by Frederick L. Jones. Norman, Okla., 1944, 2 vols.

———. *Journal,* edited by Frederick L. Jones. Norman, Okla., 1947.

Trelawny, Edward John. *Adventures of a Younger Son.* London, 1831, 4 vols.

———. *Recollections of the Last Days of Shelley and Byron.* London, 1858.

———. *Records of Shelley, Byron and the Author.* London, 1878, 2 vols.

———. *The Letters of Edward John Trelawny,* edited by H. Buxton Forman. London, 1910.

White, Newman Ivey. *Shelley.* New York, 1940, 2 vols.

# DATE DUE

| | | | |
|---|---|---|---|
| | | | |
| | | | |
| | | | |
| | | | |
| | | | |
| | | | |
| | | | |
| | | | |
| | | | |
| | | | |
| | | | |
| | | | |
| | | | |
| | | | |
| | | | |
| | | | |
| | | | |

#47-0108 Peel Off Pressure Sensitive